Video Cultures

Video Cultures

Media Technology and Everyday Creativity

Edited by

David Buckingham
Director, Centre for the Study of Children, Youth and the Media, Institute of Education, University of London, UK

and

Rebekah Willett
Lecturer in Education, Institute of Education, University of London, UK

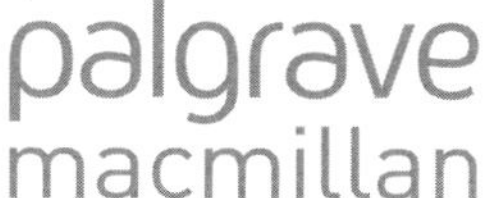

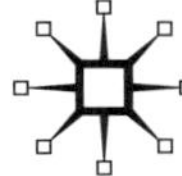

First published 2009 by
PALGRAVE MACMILLAN

Palgrave Macmillan in the UK is an imprint of Macmillan Publishers Limited, registered in England, company number 785998, of Houndmills, Basingstoke, Hampshire RG21 6XS.

Palgrave Macmillan in the US is a division of St Martin's Press LLC, 175 Fifth Avenue, New York, NY 10010.

Palgrave Macmillan is the global academic imprint of the above companies and has companies and representatives throughout the world.

Palgrave® and Macmillan® are registered trademarks in the United States, the United Kingdom, Europe and other countries

ISBN: 978-0-230-22186-4   hardback

This book is printed on paper suitable for recycling and made from fully managed and sustained forest sources. Logging, pulping and manufacturing processes are expected to conform to the environmental regulations of the country of origin.

A catalogue record for this book is available from the British Library.

A catalog record for this book is available from the Library of Congress.

10   9   8   7   6   5   4   3   2   1
18   17   16   15   14   13   12   11   10   09

Printed and bound in Great Britain by
CPI Antony Rowe, Chippenham and Eastbourne

Content

Figures and Table

Acknowledgements

The research reported in this book was conducted as part of a three-year project titled 'Camcorder Cultures: Media Technology and Everyday Creativity' (2005–8), based at the Institute of Education, London University. We are very grateful to the Arts and Humanities Research Council for their support.

The authors all worked on the project over this period. David Buckingham is Director of the Centre for the Study of Children, Youth and Media at the Institute of Education. Rebekah Willett is a Lecturer in Education, specialising in Media and ICTs in education, and is also based at the Centre. Maria Pini was a researcher on the project. Jo Henderson and Daniel Cuzner were both PhD students attached to the project and are currently completing their doctoral theses.

We would like to express our thanks to many people who have assisted us in different ways: our colleagues – Liesbeth de Block, Andrew Burn, Shakuntala Banaji, Diane Carr, Sue Cranmer and John Potter for their input on the project; Tim Neumann for supporting us on the survey; Jerome Monahan for help with publicising the project; Ryan Martinez, our student intern, for the hours he spent at the computer; Monica Chan for helping to finalise the chapters; and finally all our participants – many of whom are named as requested in individual chapters and others for whom we have used pseudonyms – for allowing us to view their videos and gain an understanding of their cultures.

1
In the Frame: Mapping Camcorder Cultures

Rebekah Willett

Over the past decade, the video camcorder has become a commonplace household technology. In the US, over 45% of households now own camcorders (Consumer Electronics Association, 2006), while in the UK, the figure is around one-third. A further proportion uses older analogue models, while growing numbers of people are able to record video on still cameras or mobile phones: for example, 15% of UK adults and 33% of 12- to 15-year-olds report using video on camera phones (Ofcom, 2008a, 2008b). Basic video-editing software is now routinely 'bundled' with standard computer purchases. Meanwhile, the rise of YouTube and other video-sharing sites has made it significantly easier to distribute amateur video productions; and national broadcasters are also increasingly interested in 'user-generated content' and the work of so-called citizen journalists. With falling prices of compact and easy-to-use camcorders and other video recording devices, the means of producing video is increasingly coming within reach of the everyday consumer.

As we shall see, this growth in access to video production is seen by some as part of a wider democratisation of media, and the emergence of a much more participatory media culture. The boundaries between the mass of ordinary consumers and the elite of cultural producers are becoming increasingly blurred, or so it is alleged. Some have seen this phenomenon as part of a broader 'pro-am revolution', which will have significant implications for culture and the economy; while others have argued that it is providing creative alternatives to mainstream entertainment that will eventually revolutionise dominant media. However, others argue that such practices amount to little more than a trivial domestic pastime, that does little, if anything, to challenge the power of the established mass media; while some fear that the ubiquity of video recording technology may create a new culture of narcissism, in which the image has come to substitute for real, direct experience.

To date, there has been very little academic research – and virtually none in the UK – exploring this popular use of video production technology. This book is based on an extensive three-year project, funded by the UK Arts and Humanities Research Council, which explored the diversity of 'camcorder cultures' in contemporary Britain. In other studies arising from the project, we have looked in more detail at everyday home video production and its place in domestic life (Buckingham et al., 2010). While some chapters here do consider relatively 'casual' or occasional users, this book focuses primarily on more dedicated or specialised forms of amateur video-making: our case studies range from citizen journalists to amateur pornographers, and from teenage pranksters to elderly members of video-making clubs. Through our discussion of these specific video-making practices, we address a range of key themes in contemporary cultural studies, including creativity, social capital, identity and the social uses of technology.

In this introductory chapter, we give a fairly descriptive account of the contemporary proliferation of amateur video-making. The chapter starts with a brief history of the evolution of the domestic camcorder from its inception through to the current rise of mobile phone video-making and video-sharing websites. Following this, we relate the findings from a national UK survey, providing a broad overview of current video-making practices among what we term 'serious amateurs'. The chapter concludes with brief summaries of the remaining chapters of the book.

A short history of amateur video-making[1]

Although our research focuses on video-making and related technologies at the beginning of the twenty-first century, amateur movie-making has a long history dating back to the early 1900s. Indeed, many of the key landmarks of early cinema – like those in the early history of photography – were produced by 'gentlemen amateurs', mostly wealthy middle-class men with sufficient time and resources to dedicate to what was essentially a hobby. 'Home movies' became more widely available with the development of the 16 mm Cine Kodak and Kodascope Projector in 1923. The camera weighed about seven pounds, and had to be hand cranked at two turns per second during filming. It cost $335 (by comparison a new Ford car could be bought for $550). The first major period of home movie-making began after 1932, when Kodak developed the Cine Kodak Eight which used 16 mm film but only exposed half the film at a time, enabling double use. Other manufacturers emulated Kodak, with Bell and Howell developing the Filmo Straight Eight camera which carried 8 mm film only. In 1936 Kodachrome colour film was developed to meet the ongoing boom in home cinematography, even though the equipment and film costs were still prohibitively expensive for most. World War II halted major technical advancements for the domestic film market, and it was not until the 1960s that technological changes created significant opportunities for those interested in home movie-making.

With the launch in 1965 of Kodak's Super 8, an easy-load cartridge system which ran through the camera once, filming was made easier, and at the same time cheap plastic cameras were reducing the cost of home movie production. The 1960s also saw the advent of video, which allowed the film-maker to watch a production back immediately, without having to send it away for expensive developing. In 1963, the Neiman Marcus Christmas Catalog included the Ampex 'home video' system, which included a large camera (weighing 100 pounds), a TV monitor and a video recorder, all costing about $30,000 (including home installation). The first affordable portable video recording system was released by Sony in 1965 – although its affordability and portability are certainly arguable. Aimed partly at recording programmes from television, Sony's CV-2000 'videocorder' weighed 66 pounds, videoed in black and white and cost $695 plus $40 for each one-hour reel of tape (see Figure 1.1). The camera kit, which weighed 20 pounds, could be purchased for an additional $350, for a total of $1085 including one tape. (Calculations based on the consumer price index indicate that with inflation this would equate to over $7000 in 2008.)

In 1967, the Sony DV-2400 Video Rover emerged as the first truly portable video recording system. According to the Sony product literature, 'The Battery Operated Videocorder, in a comfortable, compact shoulder-pack weighs a mere 11 pounds!' (SMECC, 2008). The Rover, or portapak, required separate playback equipment, had a maximum recording time of 20 minutes and cost $1250 (equivalent to over $8000 in 2008, with inflation). Panasonic and JVC followed soon after with their own portable models, eventually reducing the weight of the entire pack to 30 pounds (see Figure 1.2).

In the 1970s portapaks were widely used by news agencies as well as countercultural movements (producing 'guerrilla video') and avant-garde artists such as Nam June Paik. Although portapaks were designed for use by a single person, generally one person used the camera while another operated the separate video tape recorder component. The year

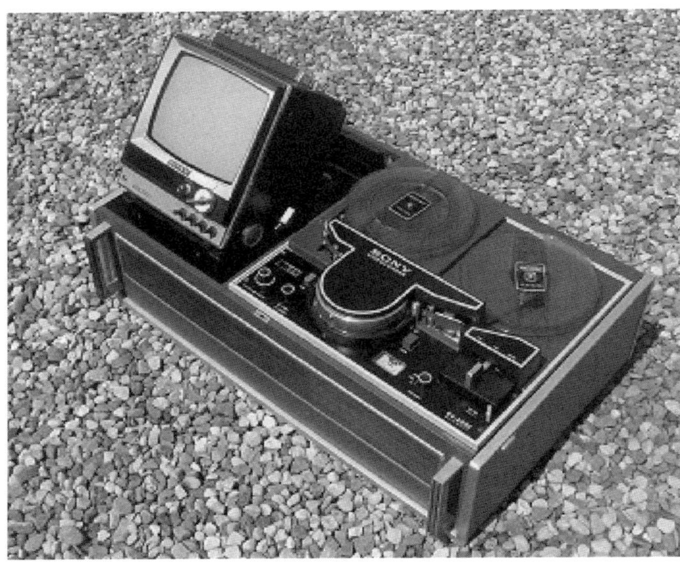

Figure 1.1   Sony CV-2000, the first domestic 'videocorder', 1965. Printed with permission from www.rewindmuseum.com

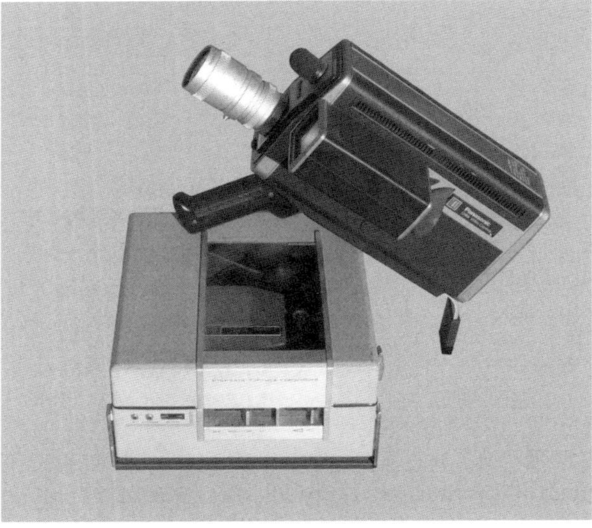

Figure 1.2   Sony AV-3420 and camera, 1975 (Sony portable). Printed with permission from www.totalrewind.org

1971 also saw the invention of the video cassette (the U-Matic which ran a three-quarter-inch video tape), which meant that users no longer had to thread the videotape through the recording machine. Video also made editing easier, via the possibility of recording from deck to deck, particularly in the early 1970s when time coding was introduced and every frame was numbered. Although the image quality was reduced during editing of the video (because the analogue image was being copied), this was far easier than cutting and taping film.

By the mid-1970s home video-making was becoming more economically viable, partly due to the introduction of domestic videocassette recorders (VCRs) and the development of inexpensive half-inch videotape cassettes (with two main formats emerging, namely Sony's Betamax in 1975 and JVC's video home system (VHS) in 1976). Sales in film cameras dropped dramatically with the introduction of cameras which could be attached to VCRs, although until the early 1980s video-making required separate camera and VCR devices. In 1982, Sony introduced a professional camera, the Betacam, which was both a *came*ra and a re*corder* (or camcorder). This first camcorder was used primarily by news agencies, as the Betacam videotape recorder cost up to 100 times the price of a consumer VHS machine. In 1983, Sony released the first camcorder for domestic consumers, the Betamovie BMC-100, costing $1500 and weighing just 2.5 kg (equivalent to $3250 in 2008) (see Figure 1.3). In reference to the Betamovie camcorder, Sony's advertisements claimed:

> Simply pop in a standard Beta cassette and you're ready to shoot continuously for up to 3 hours and 35 minutes. Without carrying an awkward separate recorder. Without getting tangled in wires and cables. And without being weighted down by heavy equipment … Betamovie takes all the trouble out of making home movies and gives you all the fun.
>
> (Totalrewind, 2008)

In just two years, from 1981 to 1983, home movie production shot up, with 6% of US households reporting owning a video camcorder in 1981 and 28% in 1983 (Chalfen, 1987). During this time, JVC had developed the compact VHS format (VHS-C) which was designed for more portable VHS players, and was eventually used in the first JVC camcorder in 1984, the GR-C1. In 1985, Amstrad developed the first low-budget camcorder, the VMC100, which cost $400 (equivalent to $800 in 2008) and weighed just under one kilogram. Cheap and simple camcorders

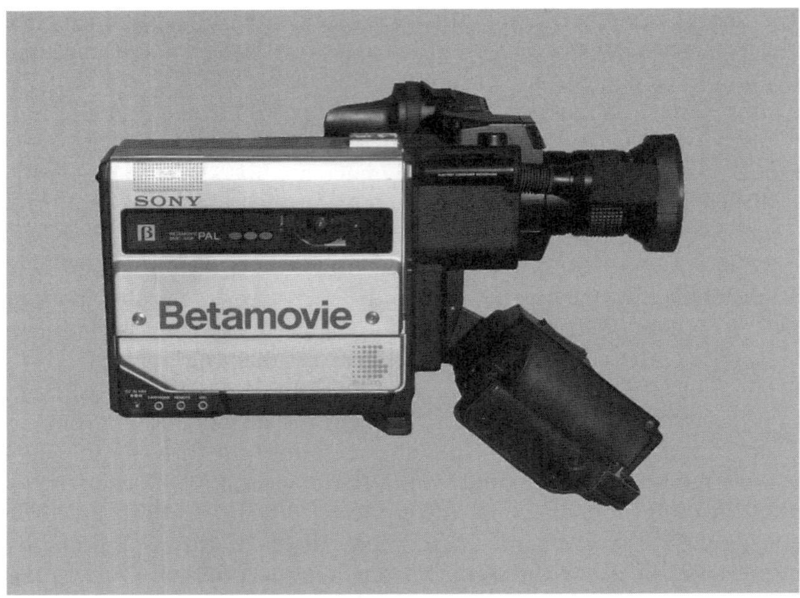

Figure 1.3   The first domestic camcorder, the Sony Betamovie BMC-100, 1983. Printed with permission from www.totalrewind.org

were even developed for children as early as 1987, with the Fisher-Price PXL-2000, priced at $99 ($188 in 2008) (LabGuy's World, 2008) (see Figure 1.4).

The size of the video in Betamax and VHS camcorders (recording onto 12.7 mm video) meant that these camcorders were far from the hand-held models we know today, with tripods or strong shoulders required to hold the equipment. In 1984, Kodak developed its first 8 mm camcorder, the KodaVision 2000, followed in 1985 by Sony's Handycam (using Video8) which allowed manufacturers to produce smaller and lighter domestic camcorders and also improve the sound quality. However, these formats were not compatible with standard home video players (VCRs), and required the user to play the video through the camcorder into the VCR to make VHS copies. JVC's models which used the VHS-C allowed consumers to play videos in a standard VCR with a simple adaptor (see Figure 1.5). The running time of Video8 was two to three times that of VHS-C, although the battery life on camcorders was limited.

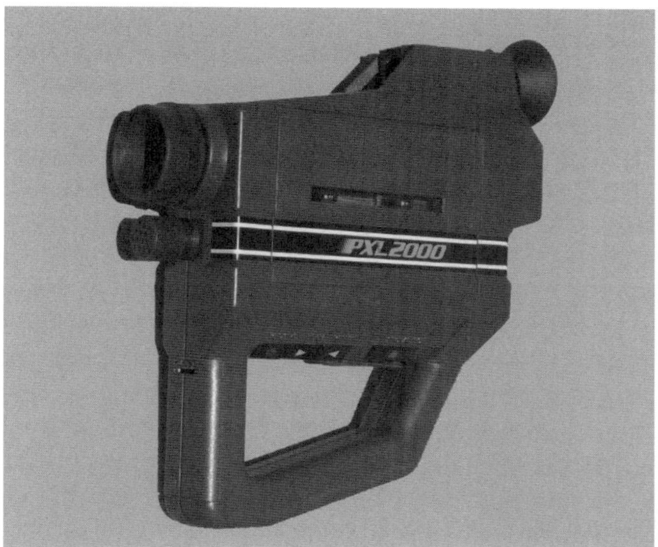

Figure 1.4   The first children's camcorder, Fisher Price PXL-2000, 1987. Printed with permission from www.totalrewind.org

The market was split between these two formats, and both formats developed higher quality versions in 1989 (S-VHS-C and Hi8). In spite of these developments, camcorders were still significant financial investments for the average household. Issue 1 of the UK's *Camcorder User* magazine (Spring 1988) listed the average selling prices of a camcorder as around £1100 ($2035 in 1988 equivalent to about $3700 in 2008). Numerous advertisements in this issue offered 0% finance deals for camcorder purchases, and one article discussed negotiating with sellers to have a 2- to 4-day trial period, describing the purchase of a camcorder as 'an awesome task' which 'can be a very frustrating experience … and a very costly one if you make a mistake!' (Hi-Spek Electronics, 1988). Clearly, camcorders were not yet for the average consumer.

In the following years, a series of high profile news events drew attention to some of the less expected aspects of home video-making. In 1991, plumbing company manager George Holliday filmed four Los Angeles policemen beating an African-American suspect, Rodney King, following a car chase. The footage appeared on news networks around the world

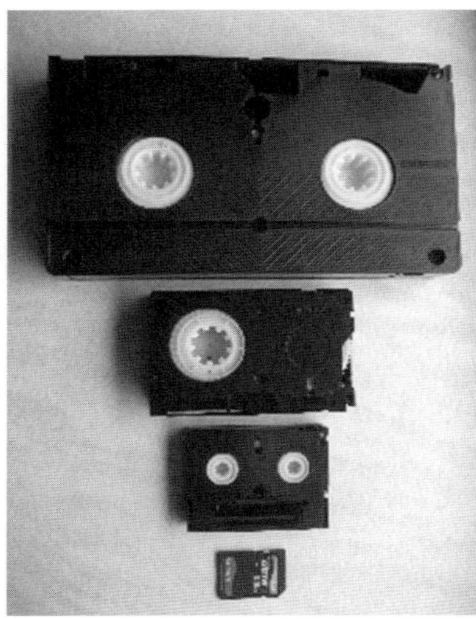

Figure 1.5   Changing recording formats: VHS Cassette, VHS-C, miniDV, flash disk. Photograph by author

and contributed both to the dismissal of all charges against King and the arrest of the policemen involved. Thanks in part to Holliday's film, the policemen subsequently faced federal charges and two were jailed, while King received $3.8 million in compensation from the city of Los Angeles. In 1995, home movies made by ex-*Baywatch* star Pamela Anderson and her then husband Tommy Lee Jones were featured in celebrity news stories when widespread distribution of the tapes (supposedly stolen by workmen) showed them having sex while on a sailing holiday. The incident hinted both at the role video could play in recording people's most intimate moments and at the power of the Internet as a distribution tool.

The next significant technological breakthrough was in 1995 when the first digital camcorders were introduced. More than 50 companies had agreed on a digital video (DV) tape format the previous year, and these first camcorders released in 1995 were aimed at professionals. In 1996, the digital camcorder hit the amateur market with miniDV tapes which allowed transfer to computer hard drives via Firewire or USB. This would lead to various digital formats, including Digital8, DVD, micromv, hard drive and solid-state (flash) semiconductor memory (see Figure 1.5).

Firewire technology combined with digital editing software on home computers (which came 'bundled as standard') brought sophisticated and good quality film-making and editing within the reach of ordinary people. At the same time, hand-held camcorders were starting to be used more widely by professional film-makers: in 1999, *The Blair Witch Project* which featured footage from low-budget camcorders generated enormous box office business with the $30,000 movie taking $48 million in its first week and grossing over $150 million in all.

The role of the Internet in the distribution of camcorder footage continued to grow; and in 2000, arguably the first-ever videoblog entry was posted online by Adrian Miles, a lecturer in new media at RMIT University in Australia. Also in 2000, MTV launched the first of three series of *Jackass* TV programmes in which 'presenters' videoed themselves performing dangerous stunts often designed to cause them injury. The show attracted controversy from the beginning with several deaths in the US being attributed to young people attempting to perform and videotape stunts they had seen on the show.

In 2000, video-related sales in the US grew by 15%, with total sales of $3.3 billion. Prices continued to drop: between 2001 and 2005, the average unit price fell from $423 to $319 (Consumer Electronics Association, 2006). In 2005, disposable camcorders were available for just $30 (plus $12 processing fee). In the UK, industry reports suggested that sales of video cameras continued to show dramatic growth, with an 80% increase from 2000 to 2005 (Mintel, 2006). By 2004, digital formats contributed to over 90% of sales, with analogue models down to 7% (compared with nearly one-third in 2002) (Mintel, 2006). Parents with young children were particularly keen purchasers, with almost half owning a video camera in 2005. Meanwhile, in the US camcorder sales rose 11% to 5.9 million units in 2007 and were forecast to rise another 4% to 6.16 million in 2008 (Consumer Electronics Association, 2008).

The turn of the twenty-first century also brought video to other platforms such as mobile (cell) phones and still cameras. In 2000, the first mobile phones with built-in cameras were launched, followed shortly by the development of phones with built-in video recording facilities and large memory cards. By 2004, camera and video came as standard on mobile phones; and in 2007, 87% of camera phone owners reported using the camera function on their phone (PMA Foresight, 2008). Camera phones have become ubiquitous in many parts of the world leading to enthusiastic reports of the potential for 'citizen journalism'. In 2004, amateur video footage of the Asian tsunami that cost over 200,000 lives became a mainstay of news coverage and subsequent documentaries. The mass media's reliance on such personal camcorder coverage set the scene for a trend that continues today, with broadcasters calling for images and film sequences from the general public after major news events (see Chapter 5).

At the same time as citizen journalism was emerging, darker uses of camera phones and camcorders came into the public spotlight. 'Happy slapping' (whereby an unsuspecting victim is physically assaulted, with an accomplice videoing and later distributing images of the assault) became a widely reported phenomenon, having supposedly originated in the London garage music scene and then evolved into a form of playground bullying. In six months, from October 2004 to March 2005, the London Transport police investigated over 200 incidents of happy slapping. More covert videoing appeared in classrooms, where disgruntled pupils were reported distributing illicit videos of teachers' classroom activities. Although some were benign, teachers' unions expressed worries about videos that appear more vindictive in purpose: some recordings reportedly showed teachers being sworn at, mocked and imitated, and in one instance a teacher was shown having his trousers pulled down while standing with his back to his class. In response to covert videoing, the Video Voyeurism Prevention Act was passed in the US in 2004. The Act prohibits videotaping 'a private area of an individual without their consent' (House of Representatives, 2004), and was apparently spurred by the increase in 'up-skirting' – using a camera phone to photograph or videotape up women's skirts as they stand on crowded trains or escalators. Meanwhile, that same year, there was considerable discussion of the role of amateur video-making in the war in Iraq, including soldiers' video diaries showing evidence of a lack of basic equipment, as well as the infamous 'trophy footage' taken by US guards at Iraq's Abu Ghraib prison showing systematic abuse of prisoners.

The distribution of video footage was radically transformed with the emergence of free video-sharing sites, particularly YouTube which was launched in December 2005. YouTube was an instant success: during their public preview the month before the official launch, co-founder Chad Hurley claimed YouTube was moving '8 terabytes of data per day through the YouTube community – the equivalent of moving one Blockbuster store a day over the Internet' (Market Wire, 2005) – although clearly much of this material was not produced by amateurs. Numerous video-sharing sites followed, some of which promised to distribute advertising revenue to contributors. Video-sharing site users reported watching less broadcast television as a result of spending more time watching videos online. Very quickly, YouTube captured the attention of journalists who wrote about 'clip culture' and the 'YouTube effect', and companies brokered deals with YouTube to set up channels and release copyrights on their videos. Google ultimately bought YouTube for $1.65 billion in October 2006, less than a year from its original launch (Geist, 2006).

A number of amateur videos became overnight hits on YouTube, earning the makers considerable publicity in conventional media: James Provan's film showing the making of pancakes accompanied by a song he composed received nearly 3 million hits in one year and was broadcast in the US on ABC's Good Morning America, Fox News and Sky News, Five News in Britain and on the Australian Broadcasting Company (ABC). Peter Oakley, known as 'Geriatric1927', posted short autobiographical videos on YouTube and was an instant success, becoming the most subscribed user within a week. He maintained his popularity, staying within the top 20 most subscribed users over the next two years, and appearing on mainstream news programmes. Current news articles suggest that in 2007 'YouTube consumed as much capacity as the entire internet took up in 2000' (Carter, 2008); and in January 2008 alone 'nearly 79 million viewers, or a third of all online viewers in the U.S., watched more than three billion user-posted videos on YouTube' (Yen, 2008). Other figures suggest that between 150,000 and 200,000 videos are published each day on YouTube, with 80% of those being 'unambiguously user-generated (amateur)', and calculations indicate that it would take 412.3 years to watch everything on YouTube (Wesch, 2008).

These technological developments have undoubtedly made video production available to more people. At present, video comes standard with mobile (cell) phones, costing as little as $50, as well as with many digital still cameras. Camcorders (with miniDV) cost as little as $180 and weigh 13 grams (compared with the very first $1500 camcorder, equivalent to $3250 in 2008, which weighed 250 grams), while the 'Flip' camcorder which plugs directly into a computer (without a wire) is the size and weight of a small digital still camera and costs around $100. Yet with the availability of video facilities on so many different platforms, it is difficult to assess current levels of video-making. While the technology is undoubtedly available to more and more people, questions remain about whether more videos actually are being made, who is making them and for what purpose, and whether different kinds of things are being videotaped, edited and distributed than was the case in earlier decades. Video appears to be ubiquitous, to the point where it has become a taken-for-granted aspect of everyday life for many people;

and yet there has been relatively little systematic analysis of what this entails, or indeed of its consequences.

Understanding amateur video-makers

How are we to understand the social and cultural dimensions of this apparent proliferation of amateur video-making? In setting out to research this area, we wanted to gain a broad picture of the range of amateur video-making practices, the technologies that are being used, people's motivations for making videos, and the role of clubs and online communities in supporting them. To examine some of these issues, we conducted a detailed online survey aimed at UK amateur video-makers. The survey ran for 18 months, from January 2006 to July 2007, and we received just under 400 responses.

By advertising in a range of places (schools, film and video clubs, different websites and magazines), we aimed to reach a broad range of users, from enthusiasts taking part in online discussions to more occasional users, such as parents and grandparents videotaping family holidays and celebrations, as well as young people taping nights out on their mobile phones. In practice, however, our sample was rather narrower than this. Monitoring the responses, we noted increases when the advertisements went to places that were dedicated to film- and video-making, such as online forums, clubs and magazines. The survey results confirm that the sample is skewed towards those who are dedicated video-makers – or what might be called 'serious amateurs'. We asked respondents to indicate how well different labels such as 'expert' or 'amateur' described them. The terms 'novice' and 'casual user' were rejected by 63% and 40% of the sample, respectively, who indicated that these terms did not describe them at all. However, a vast majority of the sample also refused the labels 'professional' or 'prosumer' (79% and 71%, respectively, indicated these terms did not apply to them at all), and even the term 'semi-professional' was rejected by 68% of the respondents. Rather, they chose to associate themselves with more descriptive, less profession orientated and, in some ways, more ambiguous terms such as 'hobbyist', 'amateur' or 'serious' (75%, 79% and 63%, respectively, indicated that these terms described them extremely or somewhat well). From these figures, we can say that a majority of the respondents are serious camcorder users or enthusiasts – not semi-professionals, yet not casual users who get the camcorder out only for family holidays and celebrations and then leave the videos unedited on the original tapes. Filtering out those who indicated that the term 'professional' described them extremely well (7.4%) and those who associated themselves most strongly with the terms 'novice' and 'casual user' (5.4%), we can make more definitive statements about what we will call *serious amateur* video-makers (we have left in those who label themselves 'semi-professional').

These committed respondents were distributed across the British Isles. There were more men responding than women, with a 64 to 36% split. The sample represents a range of educational experiences, but is skewed towards those with higher education, with 42% having completed a bachelor's or postgraduate degree. The sample included respondents from ages 14 to 82, but was skewed towards the older age range, with 30% aged under 30 and 45% over 60. Given the image of technology as being part of the young 'digital generation', one might have expected more respondents under the age of 30, although this may reflect the methods we used to gather our sample.

These serious amateurs invest considerable amounts of time and money in their video-making. Over half the respondents have been using camcorders for more than five years, and almost one-third used Super 8 movie cameras before their current model (indicating a long-standing interest in film- and video-making). Only 3% of the respondents were using their first camcorder, and two-thirds had owned two or more camcorders before purchasing their most recent one. Nearly 95% of the respondents were using camcorders that were five years old or less, and a majority were using digital video. These figures indicate that a majority of the respondents have a long-standing interest in film- and video-making – they invested in technology over several years and continue to upgrade their equipment. The accessories that users owned also show this. Tripods were owned by 78% of the respondents and used frequently by over one-third of the sample. External microphones were owned by over half the respondents, and lens converters, filters and external lights were owned by nearly 40%. A further 35 or so items were also listed in open-ended responses, including green screen, waterproof cover, clapperboard and a small theatre for animation.

Their investment in terms of time is further indicated by their frequency of use and commitment to editing: one-third of the sample reported using their camcorder once a week or more, and 71% indicated using it once a month or more. Nearly 90% of the sample reported editing their footage, with around 60% indicating that they edit frequently and 44% indicating that they use advanced editing software (Final Cut Pro, Avid Xpress, Media Composer, Adobe Premiere). Their investment may be connected with their sense of audience: over half of the respondents reported exhibiting their videos publicly at festivals or in film and video clubs, though most (over 75%) do not distribute their videos online, either publicly or privately. Further, family and friends make up the viewing audience 'frequently' or 'occasionally' for around three-quarters of the respondents, with well over one-third of respondents indicating sending videos to friends and family frequently or occasionally. These figures are very different from the stereotype of the home camcorder user as someone who has boxes of unedited and unwatched videos. Although the respondents are committed to using camcorders, accessories and editing equipment on a regular basis, they are not semi-professionals who are hoping to become professional some day. As described below, the committed amateur video-maker is a complex mix of family videographer, creative producer and technician.

This kind of serious amateur video-making fits into the dynamics of the household in rather more predictable ways. Our survey suggested that in households with more than one person, the large majority of frequent users are men (79%). Overall, the serious users living with others indicated that the decision to buy a camcorder was mainly one person's, with nearly 80% indicating it was either their decision or their partner's decision, and 15% indicating a joint decision with partner, spouse or children. Together these figures indicate that in households with more than one person, there is generally one committed camcorder user, frequently a man, who makes decisions about purchases and who operates the camcorder most of the time. These findings correlate with the stereotype of the camcorder as 'daddy's toy', which is portrayed in magazines and instruction books, as we shall see in Chapter 3. A closer look at female users follows later in this section.

The marketing of both camcorders and editing programmes typically represents them as simple and easy-to-use. It is not unreasonable to expect that most users will learn about video-making primarily through trial and error, and only occasionally use resources such as manuals, books or classes. However, our sample of committed users was interested in more than simple 'point-and-shoot' techniques, and therefore required more than trial and error. Eighty-three per cent of the sample said they used trial and error frequently or occasionally; however, three-quarters also indicated using the manual frequently or occasionally. Other learning sources (books, magazines, online sources, friends/relatives and clubs) were fairly equally distributed with around half of the respondents indicating that they used these frequently or occasionally. Classes were attended by fewer respondents, with 28% indicating they had learnt from classes at some point (and our sample includes respondents who were recruited through classes).

Beyond these questions about technology, household dynamics and learning, the survey gave us a fair idea of the different ways in which video was used. By far the most frequently reported use of the camcorder was for recording holidays (vacations), with just over 90% of respondents indicating use of the camcorder for this purpose (over half of the sample said they did so frequently). A majority of the respondents (80 to 90%) also reported recording everyday occurrences, family events and other special events (sports, school plays, performances, etc.), although respondents indicated that they recorded these less frequently than holidays. Overall, these figures indicate that the primary use of the camcorder is for 'home mode' content,[2] even for these serious amateur video-makers. However, committed camcorder users also tend to go beyond the home mode. Nearly two-thirds of the sample reported recording either *wildlife* or *documentary* at some point, with 20% of the sample reporting frequent videotaping of documentary. One-third of the sample reported using more specialised genres, including *video diary, spoof, music video* and some other form of *fiction*. (These figures include those who reported working in these forms frequently, occasionally and rarely.) The only genre that respondents claimed not to use to any significant degree was 'erotica', which 92% reported never making – in spite of the rhetoric surrounding camcorders as bedroom toys (see Chapter 9). Further evidence about the variety of uses for the camcorder came from write-in responses, in which various genres were listed such as animation, instructional videos, railway films and 'story films (with written scripts)', as well as different purposes such as records of progress, medical records, teaching aids, university work and analysis of golf swings. Two-thirds of the sample agreed or strongly agreed with the statement, 'My camcorder is used primarily for creative uses,' and nearly half indicated agreement with the statement, 'I carefully plan what I'm going to film before I pick up the camcorder.' Over 70% of the respondents claimed to be interested in watching other people's videos and aimed to have a video shown on mainstream TV. These figures point to the considerable diversity of amateur video-making, and to the serious intentions at least of this relatively dedicated sample.

As discussed above, there is some indication that the camcorder is 'daddy's toy'. Further responses also indicated that a slightly higher proportion of men were interested in the technological aspects of video-making than women, although many of the women who responded to the survey also expressed an interest in technology. Half of the female respondents agreed or strongly agreed with the statement, 'I am very interested in the technological aspects of video making' (compared with

83% of the men); and 60% of the female respondents reported editing frequently or occasionally (compared with 89% of the men). A majority of women (59%) reported using the camcorder once a month or more (compared with 77% of the men reporting the same usage). Compared with men, proportionally, women described themselves more often as casual or novice camcorder users, rather than experts or serious users. In terms of content, the survey showed little difference between men and women's recordings in popular areas such as holidays, everyday occurrences, family events and other special occasions.

Our survey was clearly not representative, but it does provide some indication of the range and diversity of contemporary amateur video-making. Undoubtedly, a good deal of amateur video-making would conform to the common stereotype of 'home movies' as rarely viewed, repetitive, poorly shot, unedited footage of birthday parties and family vacations videotaped by fathers using simple point-and-shoot techniques. As we have noted, elements of this stereotype can be found even in our sample of committed and experienced amateur camcorder users. Nevertheless the range of amateur video-making is broader than this – perhaps increasingly so. In the course of our research, we have sampled a wide range of videos on different online video-sharing sites, which display a degree of diversity that is often bewildering and sometimes bizarre. In addition to videos of self, family and friends, we find forms of video art, documentary, pornography, spoofs or parodies, video diaries and instructional videos, as well as material that seems almost impossible to categorise or classify. People are making videos not merely for recording everyday life, or simply for fun, but also as a means of learning, as research and for a wide range of social, political and artistic purposes. Our further research, both with families (Buckingham et al., 2010) and with the more specialised groups represented in this book, also suggests that a wide range of social and age groups are involved in video-making, from young children acting out narratives with toys, to retired media professionals who are interested in developing their skills in different areas.

However, there are certainly some dominant motivations and genres here. A random sample of YouTube videos, taken by Michael Wesch and researchers in March 2008, for example, indicates that music, entertainment and comedy represent over half (52.2%) of the video content, with people and blogs representing another significant portion (14.2%), and smaller proportions of video dedicated to sports, education and autos (around 6% each) (Wesch, 2008). Unlike the stereotype of home video as synonymous with family and holiday video, only 1.3% of YouTube videos were classified as travel. While YouTube and similar sites may appear to include an almost infinite diversity of content, this too may ultimately fall into rather more predictable patterns.

Studying 'the means of media production' in the twenty-first century

Technical and economic changes have meant that the 'means of media production' (and distribution) are now coming within reach of more and more people. But how are people using moving image technologies to represent themselves, to communicate with others and to produce meaning? How do these practices function as part of people's everyday lived experiences? How does the experience of media production impact back on their ways of seeing and experiencing the world? And to what extent is this growing popular participation in media production likely to create a more democratic media environment, or indeed a more democratic society? The remaining chapters in this book address these questions in different ways.

The research in this book is drawn from a wider project on the everyday uses of video camcorders in the UK. The project began with the online survey analysed in this chapter, which provided us with a broad view of amateur video practices taking place in the UK. Another part of the project involved more longitudinal in-depth fieldwork with a relatively small group of participants, with the aim of examining how video camcorders are integrated (or not) into households. For this study, we gave 12 households a camcorder each, and tracked what they did with it over a period of around 15 months (see Buckingham et al., 2010). To provide us with an understanding of more specific uses and practices surrounding camcorders, the chapters in this book focus on particular 'video cultures'. Sometimes these practices were quite casual, involving little or no specialised equipment, although for the most part our focus here is on 'serious amateurs', for whom video-making was a sustained leisure-time pursuit involving considerable investments of time and, in some cases, money.

The chapters utilise a range of methods to examine these cultures, from broad-ranging surveys of video-sharing sites to more in-depth ethnographic studies of video-making communities (Chapter 10). We draw on a variety of methods in each case. All of the chapters rely on in-depth interviews with video-makers, which involved discussing their practices and specific issues related to their videos. Viewing videos was an essential part of many of the chapters, and in several cases involved analysing large numbers of videos found on both generic and specialised video-sharing sites. Finally, as discussed in Chapters 2 and 3, the wider public discourses surrounding specific practices are considered in relation to the interview and video data. By triangulating what people say with what we see in the videos and examining these within the context of the broader discursive field, we aim to provide a rigorous interpretation of the diversity of meanings and practices that constitute contemporary video-making.

Chapter 2 introduces and discusses some of the broader issues raised by the phenomenon of amateur video-making, and their relationship to more general themes in contemporary social theory. It begins with a brief review of previous research on domestic photography and film-making, and related debates about 'first-person media' and 'reality television', before moving on to address some of the broader theoretical issues at stake. These include questions about the domestic uses of technology, the nature of creativity, the relationship between self-representation and identity formation, the changing relations between professional and amateur producers and the nature of informal learning.

Chapter 3 focuses on the discursive construction of amateur film- and video-making within popular books, manuals, magazines and guides, dating from 1921 to the present day. It begins by exploring the broad rhetoric of 'democratisation' that characterises popular discussions of the potential of amateur film- and video-making. This leads on to a discussion of how the technology itself is framed and defined, how the identity of the amateur film-maker and the social uses of amateur film-making are constructed and how the aesthetic dimensions of this practice are identified. Despite the excitement that commonly surrounds new visual representational technology and despite the accelerating pace of technological change, the analysis suggests that there is a considerable historical continuity in terms of how amateur film-making is framed and defined.

Chapter 4 focuses on *domestic* amateur video production, which is read by many as constituting one of the least creative, ambitious and meaningful of all amateur genres. Drawing upon data collected from a number of video-makers who use their cameras primarily for recording family life, this chapter complicates common images of home mode production as meaningless, uncreative or inevitably conservative. In concentrating upon the more subjective aspects of its production, the chapter explores some of the fantasies, fears and desires seemingly invested in the production of home mode video. The analysis illustrates how such footage can function in the ordering of memory, history and place, and by extension, in the construction and consolidation of a narrative of family identity.

Chapter 5 addresses the emerging phenomenon of 'citizen journalism'. It begins by exploring some of the rhetoric that currently surrounds the use of video (and other digital media forms, such as blogging) as a means of democratising the mainstream media industries. It locates this work within a longer tradition of alternative or independent media, and looks at how mainstream broadcasters are attempting to accommodate – and indeed recuperate – such 'user-generated content'. This leads on to detailed case studies of three 'citizen journalists' (although not all would describe themselves as such) highlighting the diversity of motivations that lie behind such practices, and the forms of 'journalism' that they entail. Overall, the chapter cautions against any inflated optimism about the imminent demise of mainstream journalism, and points to the need for a more cautious, contextualised analysis.

Chapter 6 focuses on spoof productions found on video-sharing sites. It includes an analysis of a survey of over 120 spoofs and a more in-depth look at the text, audience and producers of selected examples. The productions and practices are analysed with reference to literary theory (around the notion of parody), play theory and research on new and emerging digital cultures. The young men who are largely responsible for such spoof productions are described as working alongside the mainstream media industry, concentrating on their immediate friendship group, rather than challenging the industry or forming new ways of knowledge sharing. This raises questions about the common claim that young people are undermining the power of dominant media, offering social critiques or creating new global networks through their involvement in media production.

Chapter 7 explores an area of youth culture in which visual representation – in the form of photography and now video – has been a significant, long-running concern: namely, skateboarding. The chapter looks at the status of skateboarding as a form of youth 'subculture': the particular functions and purposes of video-making within it, the ways in which young video-makers learn their craft and the typical content and form of skateboarding videos. The research here is based on extensive viewing of the videos themselves, immersion in specialist websites and personal interviews with a range of skateboarding video-makers. The chapter looks at the role of 'subcultural capital' within this community of video-makers, and draws attention to some of the tensions and ambiguities that arise from the relation between amateur producers and the professional (and semi-professional) industry.

Chapter 8 examines amateur video productions made for the BBC's Video Nation, a web-based participatory project within a mediated, online community archive (as opposed to a more open video-sharing site). It explores the history of the BBC's work in the field of access television, arguing that it embodies institutionalised definitions of citizenship and community that inevitably influence the ways in which particular views or experiences of the ordinary and the everyday can be represented. The chapter outlines the range of practices and productions contained within the Video Nation project, and raises questions about the extent to which individual contributions are mediated and presented in this context. In-depth case studies of two Video Nation contributors are chosen to illustrate the contrasting relationships between the individual participants and the institutional context and aims of the BBC.

Chapter 9 explores the link between sexual practice and visual representational technologies. Here, the use of camcorders for recording sex is investigated through, firstly, a survey of contemporary discourses surrounding the production of do-it-yourself (DIY) pornography; and, secondly, an analysis of in-depth interviews conducted with amateur video-makers who have used their camcorders for producing pornographic or erotic footage. The chapter raises a number of questions about the 'hype' which has often surrounded this practice. Far from signalling any major disruption to professional/amateur distinctions, and by extension to the porn industry, this analysis indicates that the visual recording of sex is a far more mundane, private, playful and even 'conservative' activity carried out by couples with little or no interest in publicly exhibiting their footage.

Chapter 10 looks at the culture of amateur film-making clubs. At a time when more people than ever before are making use of camcorder technologies, the organised amateur film world exists almost in parallel with wider trends in camcorder use: technological developments are taken on board, but otherwise club life changes little, and in contrast to 'youth' trends in film-making, membership of clubs is largely the preserve of people of retirement age, many of whom have links to other organisations in their local area. This chapter, which is based on a long-term ethnographic case study, discusses the social organisation of the film club and the social identities of its members: the films that individuals and small groups produce and the position of the club within a network of other clubs, film and non-film, as a source of 'social capital'. Contrary to claims that film clubs are 'dying out', this chapter argues that organised amateur film-making has an important role even in the age of the Internet.

Chapter 11 analyses new and emerging practices connected with camera phones. With changes in technology, video-making using phones is now commonplace, with higher quality images and larger files being saved, viewed and distributed. Through interviews with ten camera phone users, this chapter examines the particular affordances (properties and possibilities) of camera phone videos in comparison with camcorders and still cameras. The chapter also examines some of the camera phone videos produced by the ten participants and categorises them in relation to other domestic video-making practices. Further, mobile phone video-making is analysed as a way of defining, performing and constructing individual and group identities.

The brief concluding chapter summarises some of the key themes of the book, and looks to the future of amateur video production. While recognising the apparently revolutionary potential of such practices, it argues that there is a great deal of continuity here with earlier forms of amateur cultural production, and that claims for a wholesale democratisation of media are at least premature.

Notes

1. The information in this section about different film and video technologies came largely from virtual museums and individual email correspondence. I would like to thank Jerome Monahan for his help with this section as well as Richard Diehl, Andy Hain and Colin McCormick, the webmasters of the following sites: www.labguysworld.com, www.totalrewind.org and www. colin99.co.uk.
2. The term 'home mode' derives from the work of Richard Chalfen (1987), and will be discussed in more detail in Chapter 4.

References

Buckingham, D., Willett, R. and Pini, M. (2010) *Home Truths? Video Production and Domestic Life*. Ann Arbor, MI: University of Michigan Press.
Carter, L. (2008) Web could collapse as video demand soars. *Daily Telegraph*. 9 April 2008. Retrieved from http://www.telegraph.co.uk/news/uknews/1584230/ Web-could-collapse-as-video-demand-soars.html on 8 May 2008.
Chalfen, R. (1987) *Snapshot Versions of Life*. Bowling Green, Ohio: Bowling Green State University Popular Press.
Consumer Electronics Association (2006) Digital Camcorders Dominate Analog. Retrieved from http://www.ce.org/Press/CEA_Pubs/2089.asp on 1 May 2008.
Consumer Electronics Association (2008) Digital America 2008. Retrieved from http://www.ce.org/Press/CEA_Pubs/1964.asp on 8 May 2008.
Geist, M. (2006) The rise of clip culture online. *BBC News*. 20 March 2006. Online. Retrieved from http://news.bbc.co.uk/1/hi/technology/4825140.stm on 17 July 2007.

Hi-Spek Electronics (1988) Advertisement. In *Camcorder User* magazine, Issue 1 (Spring 1988). p. 34

House of Representatives (2004) Video Voyeurism Prevention Act. Retrieved from http://bulk.resource.org/gpo.gov/reports/108/hr504.108.txt on 8 May 2008.

LabGuy's World (2008) Museum of Extinct Video Cameras. Retrieved from http://www.labguysworld.com/VTR-Museum_002.htm on 8 May 2008.

Market Wire (2005) YouTube receives $3.5M in funding from Sequoia Capital: Internet commerce pioneers from PayPal reunite to make videos fast, fun and easy for consumers to create their own personal video network. Retrieved from http://www.marketwire.com/mw/release.do?id=736129&sourceType=1 on 8 May 2008.

Mintel (2006) Britain develops into a nation of budding Spielbergs. Retrieved from http://www.mintel.com/press_releases/204553.htm?id=204553 on 8 May 2008.

Ofcom (2008a) *Media Literacy Audit: Report on UK adults' media literacy.* Retrieved from http://www.ofcom.org.uk/advice/media_literacy/medlitpub/medlitpubrss/ ml_adult08/_on 10 June 2008.

Ofcom (2008b) *Media Literacy Audit: Report on UK children's media literacy.* Retrieved from http://www.ofcom.org.uk/advice/media_literacy/medlitpub/ medlitpubrss/ml_childrens08/ml_childrens08.pdf on 10 June 2008.

PMA Foresight (2008) Data Watch: Differences in usage and printing by resolution of camera phones. Retrieved from http://pmaforesight.com/2008/04/28/ data-watch-differences-in-usage-and-printing-by-resolution-of-camera-phones. aspx on 8 May 2008.

SMECC (Southwest Museum of Engineering, Communications and Computation) (2008) DVK-2400 product literature. Retrieved from http://www.smecc.org/ sony_cv_series_video.htm on 8 May 2008.

Totalrewind (2008) Sony BMC-100. Retrieved from http://www.totalrewind.org/ cameras/C_BMC1.htm on 8 May 2008.

Wesch, M. (2008) YouTube statistics. 18 March 2008. Retrieved from http:// mediatedcultures.net/ksudigg/?p=163 on 8 May 2008.

Yen, Y.-W. (2008) YouTube looks for the money clip. 25 March 2008. CNNmoney. com. Retrieved from http://techland.blogs.fortune.cnn.com/2008/03/25/you-tube-looks-for-the-money-clip/ on 8 May 2008.

2
A Commonplace Art?
Understanding Amateur
Media Production

David Buckingham

Despite the growing popularity of amateur video-making, documented in Chapter 1, it has been generally neglected by academic researchers. While the widespread availability of video cameras is a relatively recent development, popular photography and amateur film-making have a much longer history; yet these too have largely fallen below the academic radar. This chapter considers previous work on these topics, and seeks to identify some of the broader questions at stake in understanding such popular representational practices. In the process, it looks beyond these visual media to other forms of artistic endeavour, as well as considering more general issues to do with amateurism, leisure, creativity and learning.

Media in the home: From consumption to production

Recent research on the everyday use of media in the home has focused almost exclusively on people's activities as 'consumers' rather than producers. There is quite a long history of research on families' uses of television (e.g. Morley, 1986; Lull, 1990), although in recent years much of this work has concentrated on Information and Communication Technologies (e.g. Berker et al., 2006; Haddon, 2004; Silverstone and Hirsch, 1992). This research focuses on the 'domestication' of technology: that is, on the ways in which it is appropriated and incorporated into the fabric of domestic life. It considers how the use of technology changes over time, how it relates to the dynamics and power-relationships within the household and how it varies according to the values or 'moral economy' of the family. More recent research has pointed to the flexibility of these processes, and to the fact that the boundaries between the home and the wider world may be fluid and porous (e.g. Bakardjieva, 2006).

This research usefully cautions against deterministic ideas about the 'effects' of technology on family life, and linear notions of how technological innovations are diffused within society. However, it remains strangely focused on *equipment*. While there is some discussion of what people do with equipment, or the content that they access through it, these things often appear only as examples: the focus is typically on the television, the computer or the mobile phone as a medium in its own right.

Furthermore, these studies rarely refer to people's creative or productive uses of media, even in the case of home computers; and studies of domestic photography, film- or video-making are few and far between. There is only one book-length study of home video production, James Moran's *There's No Place Like Home Video* (2002) – although, as we shall see below, it remains curiously evasive when it comes to discussing what people actually do with video cameras in the home.

One of the most useful starting points remains Richard Chalfen's account of domestic photography and film-making, *Snapshot Versions of Life* (1987), which is based on material gathered from middle-class US families during the 1960s and 1970s. Chalfen's analysis of what he calls the 'home mode' – that is, the use of media to represent the private world of domestic life – is essentially anthropological: he is interested in domestic media-making as an everyday symbolic practice, and is concerned to uncover the implicit social norms on which it is based. He provides a useful analytical method that focuses, for example, on the different roles that people take up when making home movies; what, when and how they choose to film; what counts as a 'good' shot or sequence and how the resulting footage is edited, manipulated and exhibited. The focus here, then, is on the rules and conventions that govern the social practice of media-making, rather than its psychological significance for the individual.

Chalfen finds that there is a complete contrast between the prescriptions offered in 'How To Do It' manuals about photography and home movie-making and what people actually do in practice – an issue that we shall return to in the following chapter. Thus, people rarely plan or edit their films; they pan and zoom wildly in their efforts to capture events; and they show people posing or 'acting up' rather than behaving naturally. Home movies typically focus on a very narrow spectrum of the available subjects: they avoid banal or potentially taboo areas in favour of predictable footage of vacations, special family events or shots of people posing, waving or simply staring at the camera. Likewise, snapshot photographs tend to feature carefully chosen moments in the life course, which show progress or development – the child's first steps, the award of a school diploma, rites of passage and family vacations: there are no disasters, illnesses or problems and very few mundane everyday events.

Chalfen sees this kind of amateur media-making as a means for individuals to construct their own visual history, and thereby also to feel that their lives are coherent and meaningful (a theme which is addressed in Chapter 11 in relation to camera phones). These represented histories are clearly partial and selective, even if people tend to regard them as truthful documentary 'records': they follow socially expected parameters, and thereby reaffirm particular values or forms of cultural membership. This cultural or ideological dimension is emphasised more strongly in Patricia Zimmerman's history of amateur film-making in the United States, *Reel Families* (1995). Essentially, Zimmerman argues that the focus on the 'home mode' that steadily increased during the early decades of the twentieth century effectively reduced amateur film-making to a trivial, privatised leisure pursuit. This 'domestication' of amateur production defused its radical democratic potential, and its ability to address social or political issues: it became 'an atrophied, impotent plaything, a toy to endlessly replay repressive ideologies' (142).

Even so, Zimmerman's history suggests that this was a gradual and uneven process. In the early part of the century, the boundary between amateurs and professionals was somewhat blurred (just as many of the famous early photographers were wealthy 'gentlemen amateurs' – although some were women). The amateur was seen to enjoy a degree of freedom from commercial imperatives, and hence a degree of creativity, that was less available to the professional, although this was typically manifested in a specific amateur aesthetic of 'pictorialism' that was carried over from still photography and painting. Publications for dedicated amateurs occasionally traded on the aspiration of 'making it in Hollywood', although amateur production was persistently defined as a pale imitation of the real thing. However, from the 1910s to the 1950s, the innovative potential of amateur film-making was steadily channelled into a narrow focus on the nuclear family. Instructional books and popular magazines persistently 'directed amateurs toward creating a narrative spectacle of idealized family life' (46). By the 1950s, Zimmerman suggests, the 'familial' ideology was effectively triumphant: film-making was defined as an affirmation – even a celebration – of the blissful domain of the (nuclear) family home.

Zimmerman argues that this ideological construction of amateur film in publications and marketing was reinforced by industry practices. She traces the ways in which the industry maintained barriers to entry for amateurs, for example by standardising distinctions between amateur and professional gauges of film (16 mm versus 35 mm, and subsequently 8 mm versus 16 mm). In the 1950s, the market became more differentiated, as further distinctions emerged between amateurs and more serious hobbyists, although the key boundary between amateurs and professionals was strongly sustained. Similar arguments have been made about the 'amateurisation' of still photography (Burgess, 2007; Slater, 1991). On the one hand, Kodak's mechanised system of photographic processing – 'you press the button, we do the rest' – made possible the mass popular use of the medium; but it also constrained the possibilities for innovation, both technically and aesthetically. As Slater (1991) argues, the representations of the family in Kodak's marketing materials also tie in with the emergence of mass consumer culture: family photography is steered towards idealised images of children and holidays that have much in common with those in mainstream advertising. As I shall argue in more detail below, such apparent 'democratisation' of access to media production does not necessarily result in significant changes in existing structures of power and authority.

Zimmerman's history focuses primarily on the public discourses and commercial practices that sought to define the proper place of the amateur film-maker, rather than on actual films themselves. (We consider a range of such material in relation to video – such as advice manuals and consumer magazines – in Chapter 3.) The few specific examples of amateur film she describes are not so much 'family films' as travelogues drawn from museum archives and produced by dedicated amateur anthropologists (several of whom, interestingly, are women). Indeed, one of the problems of this kind of historical work is that it is almost bound to rely on material deposited in archives, which is by definition rather untypical.

Heather Norris Nicholson has produced several studies of such amateur films drawn from public and academic archives in the North of England. Her interest is partly in the use of such films as a source of data or visual evidence for historical or geographical enquiry (Norris Nicholson, 1997): thus, the films are analysed for what they reveal about the social circumstances of children (2001) or about the changing nature of Mediterranean or Balkan locations in the years before the advent of mass tourism (2004, 2006). However, Nicholson also reads this material for what it tells us about the social position of the film-makers, who were generally male and middle-class, and the ideological values or biases that were implicit in their selection of material – for example, to do with colonialism, nation-building or domesticity. She also draws attention to the social organisation of amateur production, notably in regional cineclubs (Norris Nicholson, 2004), and more broadly to the emergence of movie-making as a popular leisure activity that was strongly associated both with family life and with tourism. Nevertheless, these are far from typical 'family films'. (Some parallel work on the US history may be found in Stone and Streible, 2003, while Daniel Cuzner's account in Chapter 10 provides an analysis of contemporary video-making clubs.)

The histories provided by such authors generally end before the advent of video, although both Chalfen and Zimmerman do discuss the possible implications of this new technology in their closing pages. As James Moran (2002) suggests, there have been significant shifts in the intervening period, not just in technology but also in the nature of family life. Although he is keen to avoid overgeneralising about the specific nature of the medium, Moran argues that the affordability of video as compared with film, and its facility for instant recording, replay and erasing of footage, may well result in greater quantities of material being produced – and thus perhaps in less selective representations of family life than those identified by Chalfen. Meanwhile, changing family structures have undermined many of the assumptions of the 'familialism' Zimmerman describes, and potentially led to greater diversity in representations of the domestic sphere. Jose van Dijck (2005) goes further, arguing that home video has fundamentally subverted the idealised images of the family contained in home movies and on mainstream television: the realism of video, he suggests, is 'a weapon in the struggle for emancipation'. According to van Dijck, digital technologies accentuate this further: the possibilities of better quality, easier editing and distribution of material 'appear to give the individual amateur more autonomy and power over a more complex, (multi) mediated portrayal', that is more attuned to 'contemporary, fractured notions of family and individuality' (33). While such claims may seem overstated, they do suggest that the 'home mode' has continued to evolve historically in the light of changes both in technology and in family life.

Moran (2002) makes a strong case for the 'home mode', arguing that (unlike high culture) it 'affirms a sense of continuity between life and art' (xix). He is strongly critical of Zimmerman's argument about the ideological recuperation of amateur production, suggesting that it is based on a kind of political elitism; and he also challenges, on similar grounds, those who have celebrated the 'radical' use of home mode footage in the work of avant-garde film-makers such as Maya Deren and Stan Brakhage. Like

Chalfen, Moran asserts the positive functions of 'home mode' production: it is 'an authentic, active mode of media production for representing everyday life'; 'a liminal space in which practitioners may explore and negotiate the conflicting demands of their public, communal, and private, personal identities'; it helps to articulate generational continuities, communicate family legends and stories, and establish the role of the home as a 'cognitive and affective foundation situating our place in the world' (59–61). Nevertheless, Moran seems strangely reluctant to discuss any actual examples of home mode video, or of the people who make it. The focus of his empirical work is not on home video, but on semi-professional 'event videography' (in the form of wedding and memorial videos), which he accuses of somehow colonising authentic home mode production; and, at even greater length, he discusses the use of home video-style material in commercial movies and television shows (from sitcoms like *The Wonder Years* and *Ozzie and Harriet* through to independent or art movies such as *Sex, Lies and Videotape* and *Family Viewing*). By default, this approach defines home video in terms of what it is not: it represents an imagined authenticity – as compared with the variously inauthentic ways in which it is used or misused – but it is not explored in its own right.

Photography as private and public practice

There are some parallels between these discussions of amateur film- and video-making and research on amateur photography – although here again, there have been relatively few substantial academic studies. In particular, the ideological significance of the home mode – or, in this instance, the 'family album' – has been equally contested.

Susan Sontag's (1977) well-known critique pauses briefly on the relationship between photography and the family, although her targets are more wide ranging. Photography in general is indicted here for condoning moral superficiality, regressive nostalgia, predatory voyeurism and other forms of 'mental pollution'; and while Sontag's most scathing observations are reserved for 'concerned' photo-journalism, she also notes how the use of photography within the family functions as a 'social rite, a defense against anxiety, and a tool of power' (8). Like Zimmerman, Sontag regards the popularisation of photography not as a means of democratisation but as a way of shoring up the 'claustrophobic unit' of the nuclear family in a social climate of growing insecurity.

Critical accounts of photography typically dismiss family photography as little more than an endless repetition of the same story: the happy, unified, stable family narrative. Pierre Bourdieu (1990), for example, argues that 'ordinary practice seems determined to strip photography of its power to disconcert' (76). As Gillian Rose (2003) puts it, there is general agreement within studies of family photography that 'family photos are stifling in the limited possibilities they offer for self-representation' (6). Families are shown as happy, at leisure, integrated and safe. 'Otherness', conflict, tension and difference are all erased in favour of images of sameness and cohesiveness. In Don Slater's (1995) words, family photographs are 'generally regarded as a great wasteland of trite and banal self-representation(s)' (134).

This argument has been taken up to some degree, but also challenged, in the tradition of critical feminist work on family photography that dates back to the 1970s and 1980s. On one level, the family album is seen here as a source of sanitised images of happiness and together-ness that gloss over and repress the conflicts and inequalities of power that are actually central to family life. As Holland (1991) argues, family photography attempts to reassure us of the solidity and cohesion of the family at precisely the point where it is becoming fragmented and atomised. These images of 'immaculately happy families' are seen to support a form of 'romantic social fantasy': this 'warm, exclusive, per-fected family' belies the contemporary reality of more complex family structures and networks, and erases the other institutional settings in which people live their lives. However, the critical analysis of family photographs can allow us to read 'against the grain', allowing the telling of hitherto suppressed stories and linking personal memory to broader public myths and political narratives. In the photographic work of Jo Spence (1986), this critique informs a kind of 'counter-photography', that seeks to disrupt and deconstruct such conventional images, for example by representing taboo or previously excluded aspects of family life, by problematising the relation between photographer and subject, or by directly challenging or subverting traditional stereotypes.

In the case of Spence and her colleagues, this led to the development of a form of feminist 'photo-therapy', which can involve participants re-enacting images or scenes from their own family history in order to bring out and confront previously hidden contradictions and tensions (see Martin, 1991; Spence, 1991). Likewise, Annette Kuhn (1995) uses her own family photographs as the basis for a form of 'memory work', which seeks to connect personal memory with collective or cultural memory. Delving behind photographs from her childhood, she reveals some of the hidden hostility and repression of her early family life, while linking this with national memories expressed in both documentary photographs and fictional films. Such work often focuses on the experience of upward class mobility, and the feelings of inadequacy that can accompany it. It also draws to some extent on the inspiration of Roland Barthes (1984), whose reflections on a photograph of his own mother as a child form the basis of a broader meditation on grief and remembrance. Here, Barthes argues against the notion that photographs are 'mere' representations: on the contrary, he suggests, they have an 'evidential force' – they provide a 'certificate of presence', which may be particularly powerful in the case of amateur rather than professional photographs. Marianne Hirsch (1997) makes similar use of photographs in exploring cultural memories of the Holocaust, while Michelle Citron (1998) uses home movies in an avant-garde feminist memoir of her early family life, which notably blurs settled distinctions between fact and fiction. These latter approaches all move beyond ideological critique towards a form of therapeutic practice, that seeks in various ways to address the psychic and emotional dimensions of such images; although, in line with some feminist autobiography (e.g. Steedman, 1986), individual subjective experiences are understood here in their relationship to the broader social and historical context. (Some of these issues are taken further by Maria Pini in her account of 'home mode' video production in Chapter 4.)

A very different account of photography is provided by Pierre Bourdieu and his colleagues (1990). Like Chalfen (1987), Bourdieu's concern is with photography as a social practice: he directly opposes psychological explanations (for example, about the 'needs' photography is seen to address, or the 'satisfactions' it offers) in favour of a sociological analysis of how the uses of this medium are socially organised and distributed. As with Chalfen, this means identifying the rules and conventions that define what is deemed to be 'photographable', or appropriate subject matter for a photograph, and the social contexts in which photographs are produced and displayed. Bourdieu argues that the 'family function' of photography is crucial, particularly for lower social classes: photography is used to mark formal occasions, to 'solemnize' and 'immortalize' the high points of family life, and to reinforce the integration of the family – although there are some 'deviants', such as dedicated members of camera clubs, who reject such 'ordinary' functions and aspire to a different set of aesthetic norms. Meanwhile, in some instances – for example in the case of professionally produced wedding photographs or studio portraits of children, as distinct from 'snapshots' – the photograph also faces outwards to the wider world, enabling the family to assert its social position and influence relative to others. It is notable in this context,

Bourdieu suggests, that 'the arrival of the domestic practice of photography coincides with a more precise differentiation between what belongs to the public and what to the private sphere' (29).

More broadly, Bourdieu is also concerned to define the social position of photography as a 'middle-brow' cultural practice or a 'minor art'. He argues that it is not regarded as entirely legitimate in comparison with established elite art forms, partly because it appears easy to do, and partly because it is indelibly associated with 'vulgar' everyday uses. Like jazz and cinema, it occupies an intermediate position in the cultural hierarchy, and is constantly seeking to establish itself; and it is partly for this reason that serious amateur photographers are most likely to be individuals who themselves occupy an intermediate or ambivalent social position. Bourdieu's co-authors go on to analyse a range of photographic practices that can be situated on a continuum between the amateur and the professional, and which clearly illustrate this ambivalent status. Camera-club members are divided into middle-class aesthetes and working-class technicians; 'art' photographers are seen as insecure about their own cultural status, and as perpetually seeking to assert their legitimacy, for example, by disclaiming the more technical aspects of their work; while the eventual status of professional 'trade' photographers is seen to depend on their mode of entry into the profession, which in turn depends largely on social class. Here again, different social rules and conventions apply in these different settings, and are subject to a kind of collective 'policing' that establishes what counts as legitimate practice.

As is the case with Bourdieu's work more broadly, his account of photography displays a somewhat deterministic view of social class. *Photography* was originally published in French in 1965, and describes a world in which the distinctions between 'peasants', 'petit bourgeoisie' and 'haute bourgeoisie' seem starkly defined. As with the work of Chalfen, or the historical account of Zimmerman, one could argue that increased social mobility has at least complicated some of these assertions: distinctions between high art and popular art (and hence the meaning of a category such as 'middle-brow') are no longer so secure, and practices of representation (both elite and popular) have arguably become much more diverse. Gender is almost entirely absent as a dimension of analysis, which seems quite paradoxical when compared with the work of Kuhn, Spence and others, described above. Furthermore, while Bourdieu does provide some interesting reflections on the role of the family album in sustaining 'social memory' (30–31), the psychic dimensions that are addressed in feminist work on photography are clearly marginalised here.

Even so, Bourdieu's work raises interesting questions about the practice of domestic photography and about the place of the 'amateur' that cut across many of the studies considered thus far. While Chalfen (1987) is more narrowly concerned with the home mode, he raises similar questions about the social norms and conventions that govern different types of representational practice: questions about what it is appropriate or legitimate to photograph (and when and how) will clearly be answered in different ways in the home mode, as compared with the work of various categories of amateurs (or indeed artists or 'trade' photographers). As Zimmerman's (1995) account suggests, the boundaries between the amateur and the professional are not fixed or necessarily clear: they evolve historically, and may need to be redefined as technologies and social circumstances change. Likewise, Moran's (2002) analysis of semi-professional 'event videographers' suggests that the space of the amateur can be invaded or colonised by (actual or aspiring) professionals, giving rise to hybrid categories and practices. In order to explore these issues further, we need to look beyond visual media to broader analyses of leisure, creativity and social learning.

The space of the amateur

The term 'amateur' is itself a somewhat ambivalent one (as can be seen in several chapters in this volume, particularly in relation to 'amateur pornography' – Chapter 9). On one level, the distinction between the amateur and the professional is quite straightforward: an amateur receives no financial payment for their participation in an activity, while a professional does – although the existence of categories such as 'semi-professional' would suggest that in many cases this boundary is somewhat blurred. The term 'amateur' is often used pejoratively – to categorise a person as a 'complete amateur' is to cast aspersions on their ability; yet an 'amateur' is also a lover, a person who engages in something for the pleasure it affords, and not because of sordid commercial motives. As Zimmerman (1995) explains, this double valency was apparent in early discussions of amateur film-making: amateurs were seen as incompetent in comparison with the Hollywood professionals, but they were also seen to enjoy a freedom from the constraints and imperatives of alienated wage labour. Historically, amateurism was identified with middle- and upper-class leisure: it was 'a cultural reservoir for the liberal pluralist ideals of freedom, competition, fluidity among classes, upward mobility, and inalienable and creative labor' (1995: 5).

These different constructions of amateurism are also apparent in contemporary debates. Charles Leadbeater and Paul Miller's short book *The Pro-Am Revolution* (2004), published by the UK's New Labour think tank, Demos, offers a powerful validation of the 'serious' amateur. Leadbeater and Miller are concerned specifically with those whom they define as dedicated amateurs 'working to professional standards'; and their examples include garden designers, tennis players, house builders and astronomers. These Pro-Ams are described as a 'new breed' of amateurs: they are 'knowledgable, educated, committed and networked by new technology', and are creating 'new, distributed organisational models that will be innovative, adaptive and low-cost' – and in this respect, they represent a manifestation of Leadbeater's wider analysis of the 'flexible', post-Fordist economy (Leadbeater, 2000). Pro-Am leisure is a very serious activity: it entails a long-term 'career', involving training, competition and grading, and it affords opportunities for intense creativity and self-expression. Pro-Ams appear to cross the boundary between traditional categories of work and leisure, or professional and amateur: they are a 'new social hybrid', and they will (the authors predict) play a crucial role in generating economic innovation, and in ensuring the future of democracy.

What Leadbeater and Miller see as a productive blurring of boundaries is regarded by Andrew Keen (2007) as the cause of an urgent social crisis. Keen provides a damning indictment of the new forms of amateur activity that are arising in the context of 'Web 2.0'. He argues that the proliferation of participatory media – in the form of blogs, wikis and user-generated content sites – is leading to 'the death of culture'. Inanity, trivia and self-advertisement are taking the place of genuine argument and scholarship. Far from bringing about a democratisation of public debate, the removal of intermediaries (such as editors) and the general challenge to established expertise is leading to a situation in which nothing can be trusted, while the undermining of copyright is rapidly destroying the basis for serious journalism, authorship and creative work. Rather than empowering the 'noble amateur', the Internet has become a forum for shrill opinion, distortions of truth and superficial observation – an 'endless digital forest of mediocrity'. Keen's argument has predictably generated widespread outrage among the 'digerati'; and it is somewhat vitiated by his tendency to attribute such a broad range of social evils to the influence of the Internet. (Some of the broader issues at stake in relation to 'participatory media' will be considered in a later section of this chapter.)

One of the underlying confusions in this debate, however, surrounds the status and extent of 'serious' amateur activity. Leadbeater and Miller focus primarily on amateurs who are 'working to professional standards'; and some of the individuals in their case studies are paid for what they do, and are seeking to move into full-time employment in their chosen field. By contrast, Keen's target seems to be the 'rank amateurs', the people who occasionally post a blog or a video on YouTube, but who are not especially concerned about observing 'professional' standards, let alone following any kind of amateur 'career'. (This debate applies particularly well to 'citizen journalists', discussed in Chapter 5 of this book.) Leadbeater and Miller make surprisingly high estimates of the extent of people's participation in 'Pro-Am' activity, but the inclusion of activities like gardening and do-it-yourself (DIY) (or home improvement) seems to rather inflate the figures. On the other hand, Keen fails to acknowledge any distinctions between different categories of amateurs: he operates a very fixed distinction between amateurs and professionals, and appears to see no value whatsoever in committed but unpaid participation.

An academic account of amateurism can be found in the work of Robert Stebbins, who has generated numerous analyses of what he terms 'serious leisure' (e.g. Stebbins, 1992, 2004, 2007). Stebbins (2007) makes a useful distinction here between serious, casual and project-based leisure. Serious leisure – which would include the activities of Leadbeater and Miller's Pro-Ams – has six distinguishing characteristics: it involves perseverance in the face of possible frustration or disappointment; the managing of a leisure career, with its own stages of development and achievement; the expenditure of personal effort on acquiring knowledge and skills; durable personal benefits, for example, in the form of self-actualisation or self-esteem; the unique 'ethos' or values shared among a community of participants; and the tendency of participants to identify strongly with their chosen activity (and hence to see it as a key element of their identity).

Stebbins makes some key distinctions among the range of serious leisure activities, and develops detailed taxonomies in each case. *Amateurs* are found in fields such as sports, science, entertainment and the arts, and can be defined as people who engage in activities for little or no remuneration, for which others (professionals) are paid. The world of such amateurs is also connected in complex ways with the worlds of their professional counterparts: professionals may support the work of amateurs (for example, by teaching or by acting as 'commodity agents' who make, sell or advertise commodities related to the activity). By contrast, *hobbyists* do not have such professional alter egos: they include collectors, 'tinkerers', arts 'buffs' and participants in non-competitive pursuits such as fishing or barbershop singing, or sports for which there are no (or very few) professional counterparts such as long-distance running or swimming. Finally, *volunteers* work for the benefit of others in the non-profit sector (for example, in education, civic affairs or religious organisations), specifically without payment.

While Stebbins does discuss the personal rewards of serious leisure – for example, like Leadbeater and Miller (2004), he refers to the psychological experience of 'flow' as a key characteristic of involvement in such activities – his primary interest lies in the social worlds of serious leisure enthusiasts. He considers how serious leisure is socially organised, both through formal associations and less clearly structured networks; how it relates to family, work and lifestyle; and how leisure careers evolve over time, typically towards greater specialisation. (Daniel Cuzner's analysis of film- and video-making clubs in Chapter 10 has clear parallels with this aspect of Stebbins' work.) Stebbins concedes that serious leisure is a minority preoccupation, involving perhaps 15–25% of the population (2007: 76). He notes that it may be skewed towards men (2004: 58), and towards 'more moneyed and educated groups' (2007: 62), while at one point he implies that it may be a particularly Western concept (ibid: 124). Stebbins' approach is quite a long way from the more elaborate theoretical analysis of Bourdieu (1990): he describes and categorises, but rarely explores broader conceptual issues in any depth. However, there are some connections between his account of the 'cultures' of serious leisure groupings, with their patterns of mutual obligation and shared values, and Bourdieu's analysis of how the practice of amateur photography is regulated according to accepted social norms, for example, in the work of camera clubs. Ultimately, however, Stebbins' approach is a normative one: for him, as for Leadbeater and Miller (2004), serious leisure is clearly a Good Thing, a key part of an 'optimal leisure lifestyle' (2007: 134), and indeed something for which individuals should be specifically trained.

Stebbins' examples of serious leisure are deliberately eclectic and wide ranging; and there is no mention of amateur media production specifically. However, when it comes to arts activities, a useful parallel can be found in Ruth Finnegan's (1989) work on amateur musicians in the English 'new town' of Milton Keynes. Finnegan's research uncovers a rich and diverse world of amateur music-making, including symphony orchestras, choirs, brass bands and jazz and rock groups. Here again, the particular focus is on how these activities are socially organised, and the socially accepted conventions that make them possible. The different groupings Finnegan discusses have their own more or less formal structures and systems for decision-making; they maintain connections with other such groups, with the local community and with national associations; and they observe collectively agreed, and quite rule-governed, methods for devising, evaluating and publicly performing work. These processes offer encouragement, support, models to emulate and rewards for successful achievement, and thereby help participants to define for themselves the value and significance of the activity.

Finnegan draws particularly on the sociologist Howard Becker's (1982) influential study of 'art worlds'. Becker shows that the production of art is a social process, which involves a whole range of shared activities: it is not simply about the execution or physical creation of the work, but also entails forms of support, distribution and response. The work of professional visual artists, for example, depends upon the availability of physical resources and tools; access to training; various kinds of technical and personal support; the activities of dealers, patrons or state funders; the maintenance of spaces for exhibition; the existence of a critical apparatus (such as the work of reviewers and specialist journals); and so on. Some of these things are material, in the sense that they involve physical resources and commercial transactions; but others depend upon forms of cultural capital – that is, a shared knowledge of conventions, rules or traditions. When taken together, these effectively serve to define what *counts* as art, and to sustain distinctions between art and non-art, or high art and other categories such as craft or folk art. These definitions and conventions clearly vary in different settings, and change over time; and they can be challenged, for example by avant-garde artists. Yet however flexible such social norms may be, the production of art would be impossible without them. (These arguments have much in common with those of Bourdieu; and I will return to some of them in a discussion of creativity in the following section.)

Finnegan's (1989) work on the musicians of Milton Keynes clearly shows how these processes also apply to the work of amateurs. Their diverse musical worlds entail different conventions and social expectations, for example, about the importance of notation or improvisation, or about the 'rules' of public performance, that vary significantly between the different musical genres; and (as we shall see in more detail below), they also reflect different sources and styles of learning, and different ways of evaluating achievement. As Finnegan (1997: 127) describes, 'these conventions encompassed musical training, composition, performance and audience behaviour, even concepts about what "music" really was.'

It is through such processes that participants come to develop a sense of their own identity, both on an individual level through the investment of time and personal commitment and also on a social level through their involvement in particular social groups. As both Finnegan and Stebbins (2004) imply, this may be particularly important in a context of increasing social mobility and change.

Creativity and learning

These sociological studies of leisure and amateurism raise broader questions about the nature of both creativity and learning. Creativity is a highly contested term, which is defined in very different ways in different contexts (Banaji et al., 2006). Traditional views tend to rest on the Romantic notion of individual creative genius; although, paradoxically, there may also be an insistence here on the need to adhere to established rules and traditions. From this perspective, modernity and popular culture are typically dismissed as vulgar, while true cultural value is seen to reside only in a narrowly defined literary or artistic canon. Cultural Studies has generally rejected such views, arguing for a much more inclusive, 'democratic' notion of creativity. Raymond Williams (1961) famously asserted that culture was 'ordinary' – and that creativity was to be found not only in the production of elite art works, but in the everyday activities of ordinary people. More recently, Paul Willis (1990) has asserted the need to recognise the forms of 'symbolic creativity' that characterise young people's appropriation of popular cultural forms, not only as cultural producers but also as 'active consumers'. Willis takes a combative stance towards elite art forms, and enthusiastically celebrates the creativity that he detects in everyday cultural practices such as watching television, listening to music and even hanging out in pubs. In a direct affront to what he calls 'old-fashioned Marxist rectitudes', Willis argues that it is through 'the commercial provision of cultural commodities' rather than through the official institutions of 'high art' that 'the main seeds for everyday cultural development' are to be found. In the field of education, this approach has parallels in the notion of 'ubiquitous creativity' – the idea that creativity is a very general quality that infuses all human activity, and is an essential dimension of learning (Craft, 2000).

More recently, the development of participatory media has been discussed in terms of the notion of 'vernacular creativity'. The word 'vernacular' derives from the notion of vernacular speech, which is typically applied to the 'native' speech of a population, as opposed to the official language of the social elite (for example, English as opposed to Latin in medieval Britain); and it has been applied to the academic study of subcultures by Thomas McLaughlin (1996). Jean Burgess (2006, 2007), for example, uses this term in her study of digital storytelling and image-sharing sites to refer to 'creative practices that emerge from … non-elite social contexts and communicative conventions' (2006: 206). As Burgess acknowledges, however, there is a risk of a kind of celebratory populism here, in which the boundaries between creativity and everyday life are entirely blurred. As I have argued elsewhere (Buckingham, 1993), Willis's account of young people's creativity collapses the distinction between 'consumption' and 'production', and leads to a rather empty celebration of young people's autonomy that neglects the material and economic constraints on cultural activity and expression.

Working within a broad Cultural Studies perspective, Keith Negus and Michael Pickering (2004) recognise the appeal of this anti-elitist stance, and the connections between creativity and everyday life. Ultimately, however, they argue that creativity needs to be distinguished from everyday life – and indeed that moments of 'heightened creativity' can involve stepping outside the realm of ordinary habitual experience. They argue that creativity is simultaneously 'ordinary' (in Williams' sense) and 'exceptional', and that it can entail a form of 'genius' or special talent. At the same time, and in line with Becker (1982), they suggest that creativity depends upon 'existing rules, devices, codes and procedures' (ibid: 68): it may involve the innovative reworking or recombination of familiar elements, but it needs to rely on socially shared conventions and norms if it is to be recognisable and meaningful. This approach thus effectively moves beyond the polarisation between 'elitist' and 'democratic' approaches, and points towards a more social, collaborative theory of creativity.

If we accept that creativity is not merely spontaneous, or a quality with which particular individuals are mystically endowed, it becomes important to understand how people *learn* to be creative. Lucy Green's (2002) work on popular musicians (whom she sometimes calls 'vernacular musicians') is particularly important in this respect. Like Finnegan (1989), Green is concerned to recover the culture of amateur music-making – a culture that she argues has historically been denigrated, and partially destroyed, by formal (that is, classical) music education. For the popular musicians whom Green studies, learning is not primarily about formal training in technique and notation, but occurs through 'purposive listening', observation and imitation – particularly of recordings. Technical knowledge and skill are important, although they are rarely acquired in a self-conscious or formal way. While this learning is generally not externally assessed, it nevertheless involves forms of (self-)discipline and systematisation. It is partly solitary, although it is also likely to entail collaboration with peers or groups of people in the context of a particular 'art world', and in some cases, collaborative composition through 'jamming' or improvisation. (There are some striking similarities between the comments of Green's respondents and those in Paul Berliner's (1994) monumental study of jazz musicians, although the latter are mostly professionals.)

Here again, creativity is seen not as a matter of the spontaneous outpouring of creative genius, but as an incremental process that involves the use of 'historically constructed norms', which apply both to the music itself (the forms and qualities of particular genres) and to the ways in which it is produced, distributed and received (Green, 2002: 75). Even so, this is not simply a matter of reproduction. Individual musicians need to be able to innovate; and in popular music, in particular, 'feel' is perceived as more important than correct or precise technique. Listening to and copying existing recordings enables musicians to develop 'good ears', which is crucial if they want to engage in creative improvisation. Green argues that formal music education has a great deal to learn from these different priorities and methods of learning, not least because they relate to the kinds of music that most young people are likely to enjoy.

Green's approach has much in common with the notion of 'situated learning' developed by Jean Lave and Etienne Wenger (1991). From this perspective, learning is seen not primarily as an inner, cognitive process, but a matter of participation in social practice. Lave and Wenger focus on 'apprenticeship' situations, in which people learn through observing, imitating and, subsequently, working alongside established experts. Learning, they argue, occurs through participation in a 'community of practice': newcomers start on the periphery, but gradually occupy a more central role as they become 'old-timers'. In a subsequent work, Wenger (1998) has significantly extended this approach, looking at learning as a process of identity formation which involves a dialectical relationship between the learner and the social world. James Gee (2004) adopts a similar approach in his account of learning in the area of computer games, where individuals are seen to come together in 'affinity spaces' in which knowledge is shared and developed collaboratively – although there is clearly a danger here of romanticising such communities or spaces, and ignoring the ways in which forms of power and exclusion can operate within them.

As Green notes (2002: 16), there are some differences between the situated learning approach and the work of the popular musicians in her study. Young musicians are not typically surrounded by an adult community of practising popular musicians, but rather a community of peers; and much of their learning involves solitary goal-directed activity. It is also worth noting here that most of Green's respondents play what she calls 'guitar-based' rock music; and it would be interesting to speculate about how such processes might be different for rap artists, DJs or those working primarily with digital (sampled or synthesised) music genres. There are also some general differences between music-making and media production in these respects. Some forms of media production (for example, making a fictional drama) may require collaboration with a group, while others (such as animation) are more likely to be undertaken by individuals working alone. Films or videos may be publicly exhibited, just as music is often publicly performed, but they can be distributed in other ways that do not involve the physical presence of the producer. Most forms of music could be seen to follow more clearly defined generic or formal 'rules' than most forms of media production: it is possible to make 'mistakes', for example, in editing a film sequence, but for the most part, these do not have the same status as playing a 'wrong' note in music.

Even so, there are as many significant differences *within* these different media as there are between them. Just as different musical genres rely on different social conventions, and involve different styles of learning, so too do different forms of media production. As our research in this book will show, there are multiple 'video cultures' with distinctive conventions, which govern not only the formal or aesthetic dimensions of the productions themselves but also the ways in which they are produced, circulated and exhibited. The 'home mode' is one of these, but it is by no means the only one. In some instances, for example, the capturing of content is much more significant than formal technique. Some practices prioritise planning and editing, while others privilege spontaneity; in some cases, public exhibition and dialogue with audiences is important, while in others it is entirely irrelevant.

These general ideas about learning and creativity might therefore offer some ways of understanding the social dimensions of amateur (or, for that matter, professional) media production. Rather than simply celebrating popular creativity, they enable us to address the social conventions on which it depends, and the social contexts and processes that make it possible. Yet they also allow a space for individual agency – for innovation and rule-breaking, or simply personal talent or 'feel'.

Changing media power

As I have noted, one of the recurring claims about amateur media production is the idea that it can permit a form of democratisation of media. Successive generations of political and academic commentators have asserted that gaining access to the 'means of production' would empower individuals to give voice to marginalised experiences, to address social and political issues and to create alternatives to dominant forms of representation. As we shall see in the following chapter, these claims about the potential for 'empowering' ordinary people have also been a recurring feature of popular discourse about amateur film- and video-making, for example in consumer magazines and advice manuals.

Yet, until fairly recently, there has been little evidence that any such democratisation has transpired. As we have seen, Zimmerman (1995) argues that in respect of home movie production, this potential for radical change was systematically defused by the growing dominance of the 'home mode'. Similarly, Laurie Ouellette (1995) argues that amateur video has failed, or, more precisely, not been allowed to live up to its radical potential. Looking at the debut in the US of television shows such as *I Witness Video* and *America's Funniest Home Movies*, Ouellette argues that the selection of amateur video footage that gets shown remains firmly within the 'home mode'. As she suggests, the actual practice falls radically short of the hype which surrounded the debut of these shows, which typically presented video as a revolutionary tool that would bring 'power to the people'. Contrary to such claims, she argues, 'the people' are anything but free to create their own programming. On the other hand, as Moran (2002: 51) suggests, there is a danger here of implying that people are simply passive dupes of ideology – that if they had not been brainwashed by Kodak commercials and their ilk, the masses would be spontaneously volunteering as grassroots video activists.

Even so, such claims about the empowering potential of amateur media production have significantly resurfaced with the advent of the Internet. Henry Jenkins (2006) focuses particularly on the ways in which fans are now becoming active and productive participants in media culture. Jenkins' notion of *convergence culture* refers partly to the technological convergence between different media that has been made possible by digitisation, and the new trans-media franchises that have emerged in its wake (his most sustained example of this is *The Matrix*). However, it also refers to the convergence between producers and consumers that has accompanied this. Jenkins argues that technological change has enabled consumers to actively seek out new information and make connections across a wide range of cultural content. In this changing environment, we are seeing the emergence of a new *participatory culture*, in which consumers – and particularly fans – are becoming producers of media, by appropriating, annotating and reworking mainstream media content. According to Jenkins, this new 'DIY' , vernacular culture is a key source of innovation that is pushing mainstream media in new directions. It is also a networked culture, which is creating new forms of *collective intelligence* that are more attuned to the mobility and fluidity of contemporary life: media audiences are organising themselves into democratic 'knowledge communities', which allow them to exercise greater collective power in relation to media producers.

Jenkins' examples range from fans of the TV show *Survivor* circulating online 'spoilers' about future developments in the series, to writers of *Harry Potter* fan fiction or creators of *Star Wars* fan movies, to 'modding' and 'machinima' using material from computer games, through to the use of participatory media in the 2004 US presidential election campaign. His primary focus is on the interactions between fans and mainstream commercial media culture, and in this respect, there is a clear continuity with his earlier work on media fandom (Jenkins, 1992): the difference now is that fan culture has become significantly more visible, more productive and perhaps more powerful. Nevertheless, Jenkins also considers the potential of these new media in the more overtly political sphere: he argues that 'culture jamming', blogging and alternative media – for example, in the form of re-edited 'mashups' or digital photomontages based on existing material – have the potential to extend civic participation, and to create new forms of 'deliberative democracy'.

According to Jenkins, these developments do have something in common with earlier forms of productive 'folk culture', for example, in the focus on 'grassroots creativity' and an economy based partly on barter rather than commercial transactions. However, he argues that digital technology has overcome many of the obstacles that led to the marginalisation of previous amateur film-making, partly because of the accessibility and quality of digital editing and also because of the ease with which such material can be distributed online. The fan productions he describes are no longer 'home movies' but 'public movies', both in the sense that they can be circulated to wider audiences and in that they rework popular mythologies and engage in a public dialogue with mainstream commercial cinema (Jenkins, 2006: 143).

The crucial question here, however, is the extent to which any of this amounts to a form of 'empowerment' – and indeed, what that might mean. As Jenkins shows, the media industries are very keen to exploit the possibilities of these new participatory media in their efforts to extend and deepen consumers' emotional identifications with their brands. They may occasionally find the productive activity of fans disruptive, challenging and hard to handle; and this can result in struggles, particularly over copyright. However, there is a distinct danger here of overestimating, and indeed merely celebrating, the power of media fans. As I have argued elsewhere (Buckingham and Sefton-Green, 2003), contemporary media often depend upon 'activity' on the part of consumers, but that does not necessarily mean that consumers are more powerful: *activity* should not be confused with *agency*. In many ways, fans are consumers *par excellence*: from the point of view of the media industries, their consumption practices may sometimes prove excessive – particularly where they involve copyright theft – but their intense commitment and loyalty also make them exceptionally lucrative. Furthermore, since such activities are commercially driven, there are likely to be significant inequalities in the extent to which people are able to participate in them – inequalities which, as Jenkins acknowledges, are not simply to do with access to equipment, but also to do with cultural capital and expertise (see also Jenkins, 2007).

Ultimately, Jenkins' focus is almost exclusively on the ways in which consumers rework existing, commercially produced media content – particularly through the activity of editing. Yet there is a significant difference between such fan productions and original productions in which people create their own content. This is not to imply that fan productions are somehow lacking in creativity or indeed that 'original' productions do not also depend on existing cultural forms and conventions. The boundaries between production and consumption may indeed be blurred: consumption can be an active process, and this activity may well find expression in creative production. Even so, there is a difference between blurring boundaries and erasing them altogether.

Jean Burgess (2007) draws critically on some of Jenkins' ideas in her research on online photo sharing and 'digital storytelling'. Unlike most of Jenkins' examples, however, these forms involve the original production of images rather than the reworking of existing media content. Burgess argues that there is a danger of elitism if Cultural Studies academics focus primarily on the more spectacular or 'cool' manifestations of this DIY culture, such as machinima, fan films or video 'mashups': such an emphasis can validate quasi-artistic (or perhaps merely 'arty') practices at the expense of more 'ordinary', less obviously innovative ones. Digital storytelling, in which people create short autobiographical films or multimedia presentations, is one example of the more mainstream 'vernacular creativity' that Burgess explores – although, as she makes clear, it is a workshop-based process that tends to occur in quite specific institutional settings (in the UK, for example, it has largely been pioneered by the BBC). Such digital stories tend not to display the irony or witty reflexivity of many fan productions: on the contrary, they are typically sincere, poignant, gently humorous – and even somewhat 'uncool'. While they are heavily dependent on the collaborative social setting of the workshop, they also draw on everyday communicative practices, such as the telling of personal stories and the sharing of family photographs. In Burgess's terms, digital storytelling provides a powerful means of narrating personal experiences, and (through distribution on the Internet) of making them visible and audible in the wider public culture. This is particularly important for the less technologically and culturally privileged individuals at whom such workshops are most frequently targeted.

Even so, the political implications of these developments remain to be seen. On one level, it is undoubtedly the case that 'Web 2.0' technologies have offered significant new opportunities for communication among already-established radical groups (Clark, 2007) – although one would have to acknowledge that they have also served this function for extreme right-wing groups, and indeed conspiracy theorists and lunatics of all kinds. The case that remains to be made here is whether such technologies are genuinely 'empowering', and in what ways. The extent of active participation, for example in user-generated sites, is vastly less than is often assumed: one recent study suggested that only 0.16% of visitors to YouTube from the US actually contribute videos, while only 0.2% of users upload images to Flickr (Auchard, 2007). It is likely that those who make the most use of such facilities are also well provided with other such opportunities in other areas of their lives; and so these technologies might in fact serve to widen the gaps between participants and non-participants rather than to reduce them. Furthermore, it is entirely possible that the apparent enthusiasm for 'user-generated content' in the contemporary media industries is little more than tokenistic and superficial. I will return to some of these issues in my discussion of 'citizen journalism' in Chapter 5.

Other commentators have pointed to a rather less sanguine account of these developments. Jon Dovey (2000) locates the use of portable video within a wider analysis of 'first person media', which ranges from the overtly subjective documentaries of Nick Broomfield and Michael Moore to reality TV, talk shows, video diaries and 'docu-soaps'. Such material is, of course, relatively cheap to produce, and it is partly for this reason that it has become significantly more prevalent on broadcast television in the years since Dovey's book was written. Dovey argues that these new forms represent a 'foregrounding of individual subjective experience at the expense of more general truth claims' (ibid: 26), which is symptomatic of broader cultural and social changes. This focus on personal identity can be seen as suitable fodder for the reflexive 'project of the self' that theorists such as Anthony Giddens (1991) regard as characteristic of late modernity: such practices promise a degree of personal control and authentic individuality in a world that is increasingly experienced as unstable and chaotic. On the other hand, this proliferation of first-person forms might equally be seen as evidence of a new form of self-regulation and surveillance – a means of producing new norms of socially acceptable individuality and self-hood.

Dovey's analysis usefully challenges totalising accounts of such phenomena, and emphasises their ambivalence. On the one hand, there is a kind of empowerment being offered here; but on the other, it could be argued that television, and public discourse more broadly, is steadily retreating into a focus on the private and the personal that is easily aligned with neo-liberal ideology. For example, the extreme personal 'revelations' of the contemporary talk show (such as *Jerry Springer*) could be seen as an eruption into the public sphere of hitherto repressed forms of 'deviance'; but they could equally be seen as the modern form of the confessional, as discussed by Foucault (1979), whereby the individual is charged with the need to discipline their own desires in line with dominant social norms (Buckingham and Bragg, 2004; Gamson, 1999). Likewise, the genre of the video diary could be seen to permit new forms of self-disclosure and self-expression; but it could also be seen merely to promote socially sanctioned forms of narcissism and self-promotion. Indeed, as Peter Humm (1998) points out, the forms of authenticity apparently offered by the broadcast video diary format are heavily constrained by institutional imperatives and expectations; and as Jo Henderson describes in Chapter 8, the scope for self-expression is also circumscribed by the broadcasters' own definitions of acceptably 'eccentric' individuality.

It is perhaps only a short step from here to the all-encompassing gloom of authors such as Frederic Jameson (1991) – or indeed to the more popular account of the 'death of culture' proffered by Keen (2007). From this perspective, the ubiquity of video, and its seemingly irresistible permeation into all areas of public and private life, is typically seen as symptomatic of a wider retreat into the 'society of the spectacle' – a world of superficial images with only a tenuous relationship to what we once used to call reality. Ultimately, such totalising rhetoric is no more convincing – and rather less seductive – than the optimistic claims about democratisation with which we began.

Conclusion

In this chapter, I have reviewed a very disparate range of literature. This has been necessary partly because of the comparative academic neglect of amateur media production. Finding theories and concepts with which to explore the area has meant casting the net fairly widely. Even so, there have been some shared themes and questions in this material, which it is possible to sum up in conclusion.

Firstly, it is clear that we cannot regard technology as a determining force in its own right. The social impact and consequences of media depend very much on the ways in which they are used. Technologies do have inherent possibilities and constraints (or 'affordances'): video offers different opportunities for creative production as compared with film, while digital video is different again from analogue. However, the social contexts in which these media are used, and the social purposes of users, shape the technologies themselves, and the cultural or ideological meanings they carry. As we have seen, these meanings change historically, and they vary across different social settings.

Secondly, amateur media production is a diverse and constantly evolving cultural field. While the 'home mode' may have been the dominant form of amateur production in the age of home movies – and may indeed remain so – there is an increasingly wide range of amateur practices that go well beyond the focus on domestic life. Indeed, the home mode may itself be evolving, as both technology and the forms of family life have changed. These different practices have their own rules and traditions, and their own modes of social organisation, and they cannot be simply collapsed together.

Thirdly, and following from this, I have argued for a social analysis of both creativity and learning. In some instances, media production is essentially a private practice; and the personal and psychic investments people make here cannot be ignored. In most cases, however, it is distinctly public and collective, and it depends upon a shared knowledge of social norms and cultural conventions. Ideas like 'art worlds', 'communities of practice' and 'affinity spaces' all represent attempts to define the social, collaborative nature of cultural learning, production and expression.

Finally, there is the perennial question of power. Historically, amateur production has been positioned as marginal and subsidiary to the work of the professional media industries. The apparent proliferation of amateur production in the contemporary world is still largely confined to enthusiasts, hobbyists and media fans; and we should not fall prey to an easy celebration of the apparently 'empowering' or democratising possibilities afforded by new technologies. Even so, amateur media production is likely to play an increasingly significant role in the future cultural landscape. Studying this phenomenon as it evolves will raise significant new questions about creativity, identity and culture; and as such, it should become a much more significant focus of investigation in the future than it has been in the past.

References

Auchard, E. (2007) 'Participation on Web 2.0 sites remains weak'. *Reuters*. 17 April 2007. http://www.reuters.com/article/internetNews/idUSN1743638820070418 accessed 3 December 2007.

Bakardjieva, M. (2006) 'Domestication running wild: from the moral economy of a household to the mores of a culture'. In T. Berker, M. Hartmann, Y. Punie and K. Ward (eds) *Domestication of Media and Technology*. pp. 62–79. Maidenhead: Open University Press.

Banaji, S., Burn, A. with Buckingham, D (2006) *The Rhetorics of Creativity: A Review of the Literature*. London: Arts Council of England.

Barthes, R. (1984) *Camera Lucida*. London: Fontana.

Becker, H. (1982) *Art Worlds*. Berkeley, CA: University of California Press.

Berker, T., Hartmann, M., Punie, Y. and Ward, K. (eds) (2006) *Domestication of Media and Technology*. Maidenhead: Open University Press.

Berliner, P. (1994) *Thinking in Jazz: The Infinite Art of Improvisation*. Chicago: University of Chicago Press.

Bourdieu, P., Boltanski, L., Castel, R., Chamboredon, J.-C. and Schnapper, D. (1990) *Photography: A Middle-Brow Art*. Stanford, CA: Stanford University Press.

Buckingham, D. (1993) 'Re-reading audiences'. In D. Buckingham (ed.) *Reading Audiences: Young People and the Media*. pp. 202–18. Manchester: Manchester University Press.

Buckingham, D. and Bragg, S. (2004) *Young People, Sex and the Media: The Facts of Life?* London: Palgrave Macmillan.

Buckingham, D. and Sefton-Green, J. (2003) 'Gotta catch 'em all: structure, agency and pedagogy in children's media culture'. *Media, Culture and Society*. 25(3): 379–99.

Burgess, J. (2006) 'Hearing ordinary voices: Cultural Studies, vernacular creativity and digital storytelling'. *Continuum: Journal of Media and Culture Studies*. 20(2): 201–14.

Burgess, J. (2007) Vernacular Creativity and New Media. PhD Thesis. Queensland University of Technology.

Chalfen, R. (1987) *Snapshot Versions of Life*. Bowling Green, OH: Bowling Green State University Press.

Citron, M. (1998) *Home Movies and Other Necessary Fictions*. Minneapolis: University of Minnesota Press.

Clark, J. (2007) *Big Dreams, Small Screens: Online Video for Public Knowledge and Action*. Washington, D.C.: Center for Social Media, American University.

Craft, A. (2000) *Teaching Creativity: Philosophy and Practice*. London: Routledge.

Dovey, J. (2000) *Freakshow: First Person Media and Factual Television*. London: Pluto.

Finnegan, R. (1989) *The Hidden Musicians: Music-Making in an English Town*. Cambridge: Cambridge University Press.

Finnegan, R. (1997) 'Music, performance and enactment'. In H. Mackay (ed.) *Consumption and Everyday Life*. pp. 113–58. London: Sage.

Foucault, M. (1979) *The History of Sexuality, Volume 1*. Harmondsworth: Penguin.

Gamson, J. (1999) *Freaks Talk Back: Tabloid Talk Shows and Sexual Nonconformity*. Chicago: University of Chicago Press.

Gee, J. P. (2004) *Situated Learning and Literacy: A Critique of Traditional Schooling*. London: Routledge.

Giddens, A. (1991) *Modernity and Self-Identity*. Cambridge: Polity.

Green, L. (2002) *How Popular Musicians Learn*. Aldershot: Ashgate.

Haddon, L. (2004) *Information and Communication Technologies in Everyday Life*. Oxford: Berg.

Hirsch, M. (1997) *Family Frames: Photography, Narrative and Postmemory*. Cambridge, MA: Harvard University Press.

Holland, P. (1991) 'History, memory and the family album'. In J. Spence and P. Holland (eds) *Family Snaps: The Meanings of Domestic Photography*. pp. 1–14. London: Virago.

Humm, P. (1998) 'Real TV: camcorders, access and authenticity'. In C. Geraghty and D. Lusted (eds) *The Television Studies Book*. pp. 228–37. London: Edward Arnold.

Jameson, F. (1991) 'Video: surrealism without the unconscious'. In *Postmodernism, or the Cultural Logic of Late Capitalism*. pp. 67–96. Durham, NC: Duke University Press.

Jenkins, H. (1992) *Textual Poachers: Television Fans and Participatory Culture*. London: Routledge.

Jenkins, H. (2006) *Convergence Culture: Where Old and New Media Collide*. New York: New York University Press.

Jenkins, H., Clinton, K., Purushotma, R., Robison, A. J. and Weigel, M. (2007) *Confronting the Challenges of Participatory Culture: Media Education for the 21st Century*. MacArthur Foundation, http://www.digitallearning.macfound.org accessed 27 November 2007.

Keen, A. (2007) *The Cult of the Amateur*. London: Nicholas Brealey.

Kuhn, A. (1995) *Family Secrets: Acts of Memory and Imagination*. London: Verso.

Lave, J. and Wenger, E. (1991) *Situated Learning: Legitimate Peripheral Participation.* Cambridge: Cambridge University Press.

Leadbeater, C. (2000) *Living on Thin Air: The New Economy.* London: Penguin.

Leadbeater, C. and Miller, P. (2004) *The Pro-Am Revolution.* London: Demos.

Lull, J. (1990) *Inside Family Viewing.* London: Sage.

Martin, R. (1991) 'Unwind the ties that bind'. In J. Spence and P. Holland (eds) *Family Snaps: The Meanings of Domestic Photography.* pp. 209–21. London: Virago.

McLaughlin, T. (1996) *Street Smarts and Critical Theory: Listening to the Vernacular.* Madison, WI: University of Wisconsin Press.

Moran, J. (2002) *There's No Place Like Home Video.* Minneapolis: University of Minnesota Press.

Morley, D. (1986) *Family Television.* London: Comedia.

Negus, K. and Pickering, M. (2004) *Creativity, Communication and Cultural Value.* London: Sage.

Norris Nicholson, H. (1997) 'In amateur hands: framing time and space in home-movies'. *History Workshop Journal.* 43: 198–213.

Norris Nicholson, H. (2001) 'Seeing how it was? Childhood geographies and memories in home movies'. *Area.* 33(2): 123–40.

Norris Nicholson, H. (2004) 'At home and abroad with cine-enthusiasts: regional amateur film-making and visualizing the Mediterranean ca. 1928-1962'. *GeoJournal.* 49(4): 323–33.

Norris Nicholson, H. (2006) 'Through the Balkan States: Home movies as travel texts and tourism histories in the Mediterranean, c. 1923-39'. *Tourist Studies.* 6(1): 13–36.

Ouellette, L. (1995) 'Camcorder dos and don'ts: popular discourses on amateur video and participatory television'. *The Velvet Light Trap.* 36: 33–44.

Rose, G. (2003) Family photographs and domestic spacings: a case study. *Transactions of the Institute of British Geographers.* 28(1): 5–18.

Silverstone, R. and Hirsch, E. (eds) (1992) *Consuming Technologies: Media and Information in Domestic Spaces.* London: Routledge.

Slater, D. (1991) 'Consuming Kodak'. In J. Spence and P. Holland (eds) *Family Snaps: The Meanings of Domestic Photography.* pp. 49–59. London: Virago.

Slater, D. (1995) Domestic photography and digital culture. In M. Lister (ed.) *The Photographic Image in Digital Culture.* pp. 129–46. London: Routledge.

Sontag, S. (1977) *On Photography.* New York: Farrar, Strauss and Giroux.

Spence, J. (1986) *Putting Myself in the Picture.* London: Camden Press.

Spence, J. (1991) 'Shame-work: thoughts on family snaps and fractured identities'. In J. Spence and P. Holland (eds) *Family Snaps: The Meanings of Domestic Photography.* pp. 226–36. London: Virago.

Stebbins, R. (1992) *Amateurs, Professionals and Serious Leisure.* Montreal: McGill-Queens University Press.

Stebbins, R. (2004) *Between Work and Leisure.* New Brunswick, NJ: Transaction.

Stebbins, R. (2007) *Serious Leisure.* New Brunswick, NJ: Transaction.

Steedman, C. (1986) *Landscape for a Good Woman.* London: Virago.

Stone, M. and Streible, D. (eds) (2003) *Small-Gauge and Amateur Film.* Special Issue of *Film History: An International Journal.* 15(2).

van Dijck, J. (2005) 'Capturing the family: home video in the age of digital reproduction'. In P. Pisters and W. Straat (eds) *Shooting the Family: Transnational*

Media and Intercultural Values. pp. 25–40. Amsterdam: Amsterdam University Press.

Wenger, E. (1998) *Communities of Practice: Learning, Meaning and Identity.* Cambridge: Cambridge University Press.

Williams, R. (1961) *The Long Revolution.* London: Chatto and Windus.

Willis, P. (1990) *Common Culture: Symbolic Work at Play in the Everyday Cultures of the Young* Milton Keynes: Open University Press.

Zimmerman, P. (1995) *Reel Families: A Social History of Amateur Film.* Indianapolis: Indiana University Press.

3
'Take back the tube!': The Discursive Construction of Amateur Film- and Video-Making

David Buckingham, Maria Pini and Rebekah Willett

Anyone who uses – or even considers purchasing – a video camera is bound to encounter a large amount of advice of different kinds. Family members, friends and salespeople are likely to offer more or less helpful suggestions; but beyond personal contact, there is a whole world of advice literature in the form of manufacturers' publicity materials, handbooks, consumer and hobby magazines, television programmes and websites aimed both at novices and at more experienced users. Such material typically offers quite prescriptive ideas about what to film, where to film, who to film and how to film. While it is certainly diverse, it all serves to define and construct the *meaning* of amateur video-making in particular ways. It specifies what counts as proper or desirable forms of practice, identifying what is to be emulated and what should be avoided at all costs; and in the process, it also helps to define what it means to be an amateur video-maker.

The activity of amateur video-making is thus by no means simply a matter of individual self-expression. On the contrary, the video-maker enters into and participates in a practice that is already socially constructed and defined in specific ways. In line with Pierre Bourdieu's (1990) analysis of the 'middle-brow art' of photography (discussed in Chapter 2), this chapter explores how the *cultural field* of amateur video-making is discursively constructed. According to Bourdieu, any given cultural field is regulated by discourses that attempt to legitimate and accord social status to particular practices, and to delegitimate or marginalise others. In the case of photography, he suggests, only quite specific events, practices and people are considered 'appropriate' subject matter for filming.

In this chapter, we analyse the discursive construction of amateur film- and video-making within books, manuals, magazines and other material, dating from 1921 to the present day.[1] The literature we discuss here defines the practice and purpose of amateur moving image production in quite specific ways: it addresses the user as a particular type of person, with particular aims and needs, and thereby seeks to regulate their practice in particular ways. As we shall see, the policing of boundaries between the 'amateur' and the 'professional' is one key dimension of this broader process whereby social and cultural identities and hierarchies are established and sustained.

We begin by exploring the broad rhetoric of 'democratisation' that characterises popular discussions of the potential of amateur film- and video-making. To what extent is this practice seen as an alternative, even a challenge, to dominant modes of audio-visual expression – or is it merely recuperated as a harmless, trivial family pastime? This leads on to a discussion of how the technology itself is framed and defined, how the identity of the amateur video-maker is constructed and how the aesthetic dimensions of this practice are characterised. Despite the excitement which commonly surrounds new visual representational technology, and despite the accelerating pace of technological change, we argue that there is a considerable historical continuity in terms of how amateur film- and video-making have been framed and defined.

A rhetoric of empowerment

As we saw in Chapter 2, increasing levels of access to media production technologies have been seen to promise considerable democratic potential. Video and digital media in particular are believed to reconfigure the relationships of power between 'producers' and 'consumers', or 'professionals' and 'amateurs'. Such arguments are by no means confined to academic discussions: they are also quite strongly apparent in some of the advice literature produced for amateurs themselves. For Matt York, who started publishing *Video Maker Magazine* in 1986, camcorders are all about empowerment:

> Camcorders today are more like what paper and ink were ten years ago when anybody who was literate could express their spiritual or political feelings on paper. Now people use videos to get on television. There are more and more outlets that provide more power to the individual.
>
> (*Video Maker Magazine* 1986, quoted in Baum, 1991 n.p.)

The political potential of these developments is most apparent in popular discussions of 'citizen journalism', an area that will be addressed in more detail in Chapter 5. As early as 1988, the first edition of *Camcorder*

User was informing readers about how to make money by becoming 'video newshounds': when filming local sports events or weddings, there was always the chance that they could stumble upon something newsworthy, which could then be sold to television news departments (whose telephone numbers the magazine helpfully provided).

However, such claims about the democratisation of the media are not limited to news. Amateur film-making is seen by many to provide potential alternatives to mainstream entertainment. Within the material we have analysed, the pleasures and the value of amateur film-making are often articulated in terms of its otherness to, or independence from, a 'mainstream'. *The Complete Idiot's Guide to Making Home Videos*, for example, explains the challenge camcorder users are supposedly able to make to mainstream media:

> Most people turn to television these days as a major source of information and entertainment. Modern camcorders are perfectly capable of delivering broadcast-quality images, and with a little creativity and a basic knowledge of shooting and editing, you're perfectly capable of keeping your friends and family entertained for years to come. You hold the power of TV in the palm of your hand … It's time to take back the tube!
>
> (Beal, 2000: xix)

Echoes of such ideas about creativity, access and expression recur throughout camcorder magazines, buyers' guides and manufacturers' publicity material. While apparently aimed primarily at the amateur market, such publications do to some extent appear to blur the distinctions between amateur and professional practice. In May 2003's edition of *Camcorder and DVD Moviemaker* magazine, for example, one article proclaims the emergence of 'a new breed of ambitious film-makers who want to get their work on the big screen and no longer see technology as a barrier' (17). In *What Digital Camcorder* (November 2005) the reader is reminded that 'with securing a distribution deal becoming more difficult, directors are resorting to do-it-yourself (DIY) solutions' (82). Many such magazines include tips on how to break into the film market, information about film-making courses and film competitions, and advice on applying for film project funding. Even the mobile phone is now commonly sold on its ability to 'unleash your movie maker potential' (product comparison test in *Which Digital Camera*, November 2005: 48).

At the same time, the amateur is also seen to enjoy some advantages over the professional, and to embody an alternative, perhaps more satisfying, mode of production. Writing in 1962, Michael Bordwell explains this in symptomatically masculine terms:

> In the big film industry, the numerous workers keep strictly to their own jobs. The director cannot touch a camera, the cameraman never thinks of moving a light, and the lighting assistant would feel very out of place in the cutting-room or projection-box. The amateur, however, is his own master. He can, in turn, write the script, direct, act, shoot, edit and project. And he need not worry about critics or box-office receipts.
>
> (13)

One dominant strain in this literature, therefore, is the construction of the amateur film- and video-maker as a free agent, able to record, edit and exhibit what they like. In the process, it is claimed, they are able to use technology in more creative and potentially challenging ways, that might ultimately revolutionise 'big' media.

Recuperation and the home mode

Yet to what extent is this technologically induced revolution actually taking place? As we saw in Chapter 2, critics like Laurie Ouellette (1995) remain unconvinced by what they regard as the empty rhetoric of empowerment through video production. For a number of reasons, Ouellette argues, amateur video has failed, or more precisely not been allowed, to live up to its radical potential. Looking at US amateur television shows such as *America's Funniest Home Movies,* Ouellette argues that the material that is shown generally remains confined within what Richard Chalfen (1987) calls the 'home mode' (see Chapters 2 and 4): it mostly comprises 'funny' moments depicting the socially sanctioned rituals of the heterosexual nuclear family – weddings, family barbeques, the arrival of the first born child, pets and toddlers, and so forth. Similar arguments could certainly be made for *You've Been Framed,* the longest-running camcorder footage show on British television.

As Ouellette suggests, the actual practice falls radically short of the kind of hype which surrounded the debut of these shows, and which is illustrated in the following voice-over introduction to the first episode of *I Witness Video* (Spring 1992):

> Any revolution puts power in the hands of the people, and the video revolution is no different. With camcorders in hand, we the people don't just watch TV, we create programming that we can all watch on television.
>
> (quoted in Ouellette, 1995: 40)

Contrary to such claims, argues Ouellette, 'the people' are anything but free to create their own programming. As she puts it, 'A powerful matrix of media discourses has worked quickly to construct and contain camcorder practices within a variety of boundaries' (ibid: 42).

Ouellette is here addressing footage which is actually broadcast; but to what extent can such arguments be applied to amateur film-making more broadly? In fact, the advice literature we have analysed here makes mention of a wide range of genres. Lescaboura (1921) focuses on 'photoplays', while Lovell-Burgess (1932) suggests producing religious dramas, romances and educational films, and the Amateur Cinema League (1940) discusses theatrical movies, 'personal' movies and 'special purpose' movies (including business and ethnological films). Contemporary magazines also typically include references to an enormous variety of genres, including horror, spoofs, documentary, citizen journalism and music videos. Growing levels of access to video technology – including, we must assume, among individuals who do not form part of a nuclear family – might lead one to expect greater diversity in its social uses. Even so, most of the publications we have analysed continue to assume that 'personal', family-oriented films are likely to dominate.

Thus, in his introduction to *Amateur Cinematography*, published in 1962, Bordwell writes of amateur films:

> These films are a faithful record of our lives. Big events and small have been telescoped into a few vivid moments, which we can experience again as often as we wish. Intimate family reunions or crowded public meetings; the back garden or a panorama of woods and mountains; scenes from childhood, from holidays at home and abroad – it's all there, only needing the projector to bring it to life.
>
> (13)

Likewise, in Kodak's *How to Make Good Movies*, written in 1966, the authors assert, 'Most [film-camera] owners are not at all interested in using their cameras for subjects other than purely personal films of family and friends' (Kodak, 1966: 5). Throughout the 1970s and 1980s, the home mode continues to be identified as the central function of amateur film-making. Cleave (1988), for example, provides a typical list of subjects for filming, including weddings, family vacations, sports events and children's birthday parties; and the same categories routinely recur in subsequent handbooks and manuals.

This emphasis on the home mode is also strongly apparent in contemporary marketing pitches. The dominance of the *family* in the older advertising material surveyed by Zimmerman (1995) has perhaps been replaced by a more individualistic emphasis, but the notion of the technology as residing in the personal sphere is nevertheless sustained. A Sony advertisement from 1991, for example, attempts to entice younger consumers to buy smaller camcorders for their vacations as follows:

> Something happens between the milestones. Between the weddings and the birthday parties. It's called the rest of your life.
>
> (quoted in Baum, 1991)

A similar emphasis is apparent in a more recent example from 2007:

> Your trip to Paris. Your child's first steps. College graduation. Life is full of moments that are well worth remembering. There's no better way to capture those moments than with a Sony Handycam® camcorder.
>
> (Sony Electronics, 2007)

In such material, the primary function of the amateur film is the registration of particular aspects of 'personal' life. For critics such as Ouellette and Zimmerman, this continuing dominance of the home mode represents a kind of betrayal of the revolutionary potential of the technology – although, as we shall argue in Chapter 4, it is important to question the assumption that the home mode is inevitably conservative, and merely acts to reinforce traditional 'family values'. The advent of the camcorder may not have revolutionised mainstream media, but its role in the sphere of personal life is unlikely to have straightforward or predictable consequences.

The power of technology?

One of the evident dangers in such debates is that of technological determinism – the notion that technology will single-handedly precipitate social change, whether for good or ill. Discourses about the impact of technology, and about the rapid pace of technological change, are perennially rehearsed throughout the historical material we have surveyed. In 1929, we find Wheeler claiming: 'Amateur cinematography is advancing so rapidly that for some time to come it will not be easy to keep pace with it in the matter of instructions' (v). More than 75 years later, in the editor's introduction to the magazine *What Digital Camcorder* (October 2005), the reader is told 'it's fair to say that the digital video marketplace is virtually unrecognisable to what it was just 18 months ago and consumers are all the better for it' (3).

Part of this rapid evolution is seen to involve an ongoing *simplifi-cation* of technology. In 1928, Cameron celebrated the advent of the 16 mm film, stressing how this enabled the 'normal man' to make a motion picture film. As he put it, 'a motion picture record of baby from the day of his birth up through the years may be made by anyone capable of operating an ordinary Kodak, at a cost well within his means' (6). In 1938, Sewell likewise stressed the growing ease of amateur film: 'As time goes on more cameras will be evolved which will be utterly simple to load and to use and which will embody within themselves every possible foolproof gadget, so that taking movies will be as nearly trouble-free as is humanly possible' (113). This simplification is somehow seen to permit a more direct registration of the complexity and richness of personal identity and personal life: thus, in April 2005, a camcorder is advertised in *What Digital Camcorder* magazine as the 'simple camera for more than simple people' (6).

Related to this theme of simplification is the idea that technology is blurring the boundaries between professional and amateur film-making. In 1940, The Amateur Cinema League produced *A Guide to Making Better Movies,* which refers repeatedly to the 'small and determined faction of film camera owners whose goal it is to make theatrical films with all the professionalism at their command' (Katelle, 2000: 252). More than 65 years later, *Digital Video Magazine* enthusiastically supported the challenge that amateurs pose to professionals as a result of new technology: 'Inexpensive moviemaking kit in the hands of people who want to prove their film-making talent by making great films is a hundred times more appealing than expensive kit in the hands of people who are deliberately churning out tosh simply to pander to the trendily ironic' (December 2006: 27).

'Format wars', in which film-makers debate the merits of different formats in terms of quality of sound and image and ease of use, have been raging since the first camcorders emerged (and previously with different gauges of film). Nevertheless, advances in technology are generally seen to improve the quality of film-making. The argument here is that new technologies aid creativity – instead of getting bogged down with technology, film-makers can focus on the creative aspects of making a film. As Squires (1992) describes, '[camcorders'] capacity to "think for you" means that you can spend less time worrying about technology and more concentrating on good video-making' (5).

Even so, these arguments about the benefits and the democratic potential of technology sit awkwardly alongside a continuing emphasis on the need for *learning*. For example, Squires (1992) goes on to warn that automatic functions inhibit the experimentation and creative solutions which are required with manually operated equipment (10); and in this respect, the user is seen to need specialised knowledge of the technology in order to put it to best use. In all the literature discussed here, the camera is presented as a piece of technology which requires a careful and ongoing process of familiarisation, while film-making itself also requires education, aided by manuals, guides, handbooks and even instructional films. In a 2005 issue of *What Digital Camera*, the reader is told: 'To get the most out of it, a camcorder should be like a new best friend. So it's worth taking the time to get to know the ins and outs of its technology before deciding which one you want to make part of the family' (October 2005: 18). Accordingly, current magazines are filled with technology-demystifying tips, 'jargon busters' and advice.

The discourse around technology within these publications is thus somewhat double-edged. On the one hand, readers are told about new cameras which are 'completely idiot proof', 'suitable even for complete techno-duffers' (*What Digital Camcorder*, November 2005: 63). Yet on the other hand, there is a recurring emphasis on the need for extra learning and the effort that is required to keep abreast of technological developments. As we shall see, this suggests that distinctions between 'amateurs' and 'professionals' are not so much being abolished as reformulated: technological expertise comes to serve as a marker of distinction, not just between the professional and the 'complete techno-duffer' but also between different grades or categories of amateurs.

Defining the amateur

As we have seen, the distinction between the professional and the amateur can be defined in various ways. On the one hand, the amateur can be regarded as an individual with simple needs, restricted skills and limited ambitions. Yet on the other hand, amateurs can also be seen to enjoy a degree of creative freedom that is denied to the majority of professionals. Rather than a binary distinction, the material we have surveyed constructs a continuum, with true professionals at one end and users who simply 'point and shoot' at the other. In between these poles, the amateur is variously addressed and defined – as the 'ordinary user' or 'man in the street', in contrast with 'the out-and-out enthusiast with his peculiar needs and peculiar standards' (Sewell, 1938: 11); as someone who is 'his own master', in contrast with someone who has to worry about critics and box-office receipts (Bordwell, 1962); as someone who has to cover all the aspects of the film-making process, in contrast with those who have specialised professional skills (*Digital Video Magazine*, November 2005); as someone who takes time to plan, instead of filming whatever catches his or her fancy (Cleave, 1988); as someone who is ambitious and sees post-production as challenging and creative, rather than someone who always films the same subjects and has no desire to produce a finished product (Squires, 1992); and as someone who is interested in learning about and applying their knowledge of technology, film grammar and editing, rather than being content with faults such as poor lighting, too much zooming and a lack of advance planning (*What Digital Camcorder*, November 2005: 71).

These different positions on the continuum are to some extent reflected in the range of technological devices that are available on the market. As Zimmerman (1995) explains, the production of different film gauges (8 mm, 16 mm or 35 mm) was partly a matter of defining particular kinds of users – and indeed, for the industry, of sustaining and policing the distinction between amateurs and professionals. Contemporary discussions of current models of camcorders make similar distinctions, for example, between camcorders designed for 'the beginner', 'for those users looking to take more control over their moviemaking', 'for enthusiasts that offer a real taste of pro performance on a budget' and those that are 'broadcast-quality' (*Digital Video Magazine*, March 2007). Likewise, CNET's review website (reviews.cnet.com) identifies cameras that are appropriate for several distinct categories of amateur video-makers, including the 'home and vacation video-maker', the 'budget buyer', the 'trendsetter' (who wants 'the coolest, most cutting-edge features available'), the 'independent film-maker' (who wants to 'shoot like a pro') and the non-professional 'business videographer' wanting to please their boss.

However, the key distinction in the material we have analysed is between the *serious amateur*, the enthusiast who invests in technology and creates artistic finished products and the *everyday user*, who owns relatively inexpensive technology (with no accessories) and does not plan or edit his or her films. Everyday users are typically identified with the home mode in its crudest and most unreconstructed form: their video cameras are used primarily for keeping records of family life. These polarised positions are thus distinguished in terms of their *purpose* for using the technology, their *identity* as users of technology and the *time and money* they devote to their pastime. By definition, most of the books and magazines we have analysed are addressed to readers who are aspiring to move (or in the process of moving) from being everyday users to becoming more committed amateurs, and hence have an interest in improving their practice (and in investing in more expensive equipment). It is through the process of 'othering' the everyday users that this key distinction is created and sustained: it is always *others* who are uncreative, who do not plan their filming and who bore their audiences with poorly shot, unedited family movies.

Even so, there are some interesting historical variations in how these distinctions are defined and maintained. In fact, the earliest example of such material we could obtain addresses the amateur cinematographer as someone who wanted to make a finished movie. Lescaboura's *Cinema Handbook* (1921), which is generally seen as the first manual for the non-professional film-maker (Katelle, 2000), instructs the reader in how to produce a 'photoplay', complete with script, cast, makeup and director. Here the amateur is very clearly constructed as wanting to emulate the professionals. As we shall see, the emphasis on 'learning from the professionals' is a continuing strain in this literature, although in general the home mode is much more prevalent than in this first handbook by Lescaboura. Indeed, from 1928 onwards, the key handbooks invariably make great play of the filming of babies and children growing up. Magazines aimed specifically at 'home movie making' existed from the 1950s onwards (*Home Movies*, 1951); and current magazines (with subtitles such as 'The practical guide to making better home movies') continue to feature clips of family vacations and special events in their features on editing.

Yet even if readers are defined primarily in relation to the home mode, they are nevertheless seen to be interested in improving their film-making. From the earliest books, the reader is constructed as ambitious, as wanting to know about the rules of film and needing practical knowledge before starting to film. The reader is defined not just as a recorder of family life, but also as an entertainer, as someone interested in technology, as someone who wants to construct 'a film which shows his particular handwriting' (Strausser, 1937: 7). By the 1960s, it was common to psychologise (or characterise the 'mental' properties of) the 'good' film-maker. The notion of the amateur film-maker as an 'artist', as opposed to a mere technician, was firmly established. In 1964, Broderick writes of the good amateur film-maker as follows:

> Firstly he must have imagination. Good films don't just happen. He is going to have to think up the ideas for his films, interpret the mood of the scene he is shooting in terms of angle etc ... Secondly, he must have a degree of technical know-how. Thirdly, he must have a calm and patient personality ... Finally, the cine film enthusiast should be a man of understanding and compassion.
>
> (12)

As implied in these (again, symptomatically masculine) constructions of the amateur, it takes *time* to become more than a 'point and shoot' user. Planning and editing obviously involve an investment of time on the part of the serious amateur, as does learning about the technology, film grammar and techniques.

The *exhibition* of films is also an important concern for the committed amateur. As early as the 1930s, writers were encouraging amateurs to form film clubs to share finished projects as well as to offer advice and assistance (Hobbs, 1930; Lovell-Burgess, 1932). The emphasis on showing a finished product runs throughout the literature, with extensive advice on how to create a home cinema for sharing films (including notes on installing dimmer switches and pelmet lights) continuing through the 1980s. Alder (1951) suggests running film evenings which include showing rented films alongside home movies, while magazines from the 1980s contain numerous ads for feature films to rent interspersed with articles about home mode filming. In contemporary publications, the same emphasis is given to sharing films online, with reviews and feature articles on video-sharing sites, advice on formatting for online sharing and competitions featuring videos posted online. Furthermore, magazines have their own forums for readers to exchange advice and get assistance; URLs of wider amateur camcorder communities are commonly listed; and magazines include features on monthly film festivals, as well as information on courses for amateurs. A common organisational structure for recent books and magazines is to have three sections – create, edit and share. As this implies, one characteristic that distinguishes the serious amateur from the everyday user is the desire to create finished products that can be shown to an audience beyond one's friends and family.

Money is an issue here, albeit an ambivalent one. On the one hand, as we saw in Chapter 1, changes in technology have steadily reduced the cost of making and distributing films – and this has contributed to the belief in the democratic potential of moving image technology. Yet this is by no means a new idea. As early as 1928, Cameron claimed that the 'advent of the 16mm film, with its low cost for finished prints, has been greatly accountable for the steadily increasing army of "take-your-own-movie" fans' (5). In 1929, Wheeler argued that film-making was available to 'workers in various walks of life and variously situated as regards ways and means' (v). Yet although costs have fallen, this has not meant that creating an amateur film (at least as constructed by the literature) has been within the means of everybody. In the earliest magazines through to magazines from the 1980s, we see mention of investing 'life savings' on equipment, advice on renting a camera for a few days before making a serious investment and advertisements for used equipment, rentals and 0% loans for purchases. These elements no longer feature in contemporary magazines, which obviously reflects the fact that (once a camcorder is purchased) the cost of filming, viewing and distributing are less significant compared with previous costs of buying and processing film and purchasing a projector. Even so, contemporary magazines generally assume that readers possess up-to-date computers and have fast Internet access (for editing, distributing and viewing, and for finding information). The economic status of the contemporary 'amateur' is clearly reflected in the media packs for such magazines, which state that their target audience is ABC1 males, aged 18–40 years, and also by books such as *Shooting Digital Video* (Fauer, 2001), which directly addresses readers as 'skilled professionals' in other walks of life.

As is apparent from the media packs, and from some of our earlier quotations, gender is another component of the construction of the amateur film-maker. In 2000, Beal noted that 'national sales figures suggest that men are responsible for 75% of all camcorder sales' (219). Yet although men might be the main purchasers, the magazines are careful not to portray the market as male dominated. In contemporary magazines, photographs of both male and female camera operators are included throughout, and featured 'experts' are both male and female. Zimmerman (1995) discusses the early role of women as amateur film-makers, and the gendered definition of skills and technology. She points out that certain ads made during the 1920s actively promoted women as film-makers, in an attempt to stress the ease, lightness and simplicity of their cameras. Furthermore, women were seen to have the right temperament, namely patience and attention to detail, to make good film-makers. This contrasts with the majority of the early literature which we reviewed (e.g. Hobbs, 1930; Reyner, 1939; Bomback, 1953), in which the amateur film-maker was presented as almost certainly male. In writing about amateur film in the home for example, Hobbs (1930) refers to 'daddy's new camera', and his book consistently addresses the one who films, exhibits and achieves 'professional effects' as male. This may reflect the male dominance of the market at that time: for example, in discussing family film-making from the 1950s, East Anglian film archivist, David Cleveland, states that 'it was always dad who worked the camera, very seldom were women allowed to film with the family movie camera' (Cleveland, 2007: n.p.) – although Zimmerman's US study quotes several examples of women amateur film-makers (Zimmerman, 1995). Even so, within the material we are considering here, it would appear that women are only explicitly referred to when 'feminine' qualities are being emphasised.

Constructing the home mode

As we have indicated, the emphasis on the home mode has been a continuing theme throughout the history of amateur film- and video-making. As Beal's *Complete Idiot's Guide to Making Home Videos* puts it:

> Many people buy camcorders for one reason: to document their children's lives as they grow up ... Never before in human history have we been able to record and document with such accuracy the most important events in our lives.
>
> (Beal, 2000: 203)

As in this quotation, films of the family are frequently referred to as 'records' of the nearest and the dearest (e.g. Sewell, 1938; Bordwell, 1962): the key emphasis is on capturing children growing up, producing 'a complete record that parents will treasure in years to come' (Davies, 1951: 204).

Nevertheless, for the serious amateur, the making of such home mode films is more than simply a matter of neutral record keeping. In order to create this 'accurate' picture, according to the literature, the film-maker must plan carefully so as to capture 'typical' actions rather than random events. This developed form of the home mode is seen to entail a wide range of technical, creative and formal choices. Considerations of taste and aesthetics – for example to do with issues such as film grammar, lighting, sound and the 'feel' of a film – are an abiding preoccupation in the literature we have analysed (cf. Bourdieu, 1984). These considerations are most apparent in three main areas: references to professional film-making, discussions of realism and notions of creativity.

Learning from the professionals

As we have noted, becoming a serious amateur is seen to involve a learning process; and one key aspect of this entails the need to reflect on professional film-making practices. Improving one's work involves learning and applying 'film grammar' and techniques (such as the 'rule of thirds', the '180 degree rule', continuity, camera angles, lighting, editing) as well as paying close attention to planning and scripting. This is clearly seen as something that cannot be learnt simply through trial and error: in the words of one author, 'Cinematic rules are not so much a subject for "learning" as for studying and understanding' (Strausser, 1937: 7).

In these publications, film grammar is often taught in a formal manner using diagrams, drawings and photographs or screen grabs to explain specific techniques. This kind of formal study is seen to result in movies that will be more interesting, more artistic and of higher quality. For example, in Lescaboura's book, camera angles are discussed under a section entitled 'the hand of the artist' (1921); camera distance and angle are connected to the mood the film-maker wants to convey (Lovell-Burgess, 1932); close-ups are described as 'more attention grabbing' (Cleave, 1988); and jump cuts are referred to as a way to 'enhance the story telling process' (*Digital Video Magazine*, November 2005: 032). In a 2003 issue of *Camcorder and DVD Movie Maker* (July 2003), this formal approach even extends to a detailed semiotic analysis of the *Godfather* films (27–9).

Editing in particular is frequently referred to both as a downfall of poor quality home videos and an example of a technique one can learn by watching the professionals. Croydon (1951) suggests weekly visits to the cinema in order to learn about editing by studying commercial movies. Similarly, a feature in the first edition of *Camcorder User* (1988) suggests that readers turn off the sound and watch an episode of the UK soap opera, *EastEnders*, counting the timing for each shot and observing transitions and cuts. In recent magazines, sections with titles such as 'Hollywood Inspiration' discuss 'tricks of the trade' from current movies (e.g. *Digital Video Techniques*, October 2006).

Although editing has come to the fore in recent publications, with the advent of new digital editing software, it has consistently been identified as a defining characteristic of 'good' amateur film-making. Amateurs are repeatedly encouraged to cut irrelevant shots and to be ruthless about throwing out film that does not progress the story (e.g. Croydon, 1951). Again, editing is seen as a key to producing films that are more interesting for audiences and, like commercial films, tell a story. This is reflected not only in the chapters and feature articles on how to edit, but also in current advertisements. For example: 'VideoStudio 10 Plus helps turn hum-drum raw video footage into truly compelling movie productions' (*Digital Video Techniques*, October 2006: 002). By setting up a contrast between 'raw footage' and 'movie production' and describing these components as 'hum-drum' versus 'truly compelling', this advertisement makes clear the aesthetic quality the amateur is encouraged to achieve through editing, both in terms of process (a completed production) and purpose (to entertain).

The need for advance planning, both in order to ensure continuity and for structuring a film narrative, is another recurring theme. For example, a chapter in 1951 entitled 'Filming Baby on the Lawn' emphasises the importance of planning a sequence which includes a dramatic climax (Alder, 1951). Likewise, Cleave (1988) provides extensive details of planning and preparation for filming children's parties, weddings and vacations. In relation to filming parties, he writes: 'A children's party is bound to be a boisterous affair. But as movie makers, it's our job to try and bring order out of chaos, and one way we can do this is to make sure our video record has a firm shape – in other words, a proper beginning, middle and end' (111). One of the interesting aspects here is the suggestion that the portrayal of an event is *constructed* by the film-maker: the film needs to be 'shaped' in a way that belies the 'chaos' which is closer to the reality of the event.

Making it real

Despite this latter emphasis on the need for narrative 'shaping', realism has been seen as a key dimension of the preferred aesthetic of amateur film and video making. In the early publications, film is seen as preferable to still photography, precisely because of its ability to capture more realistic portrayals of people and events. Foretelling the advent of camcorders, Sewell wrote in 1938 'fully stereoscopic colour cinematography, allied with sound … [will] offer the most satisfactory method that has yet evolved of securing pictures of those persons and places that are near and dear to us' (115). Likewise, Grosset (1961) describes the switch from photos to movies as follows: 'Instead of awkward frozen gestures, people are demanding life and action – a living record of their family and friends, so they turn to movies' (7).

Even so, the film-maker is seen to play a proactive role in construct-ing a realistic portrayal of an event. As in Cleave's discussion of the children's party (cited above), film-making involves not just filming people and events, but carefully producing a construct which reflects a particular reality. Alder refers to ethical questions about this process: 'Some people doubt whether it is ethical for a family moviemaker to juggle with his lengths of film in order to manufacture a climax at the editing stage' (1951: 100). Yet he goes on to say that, on the contrary, editing produces a more realistic portrayal of an event: 'what [viewers] require is, above all, truth' (100). Describing how people react self-consciously to the camera, and therefore do not portray themselves in a natural manner, Alder argues that editing is needed in order to capture only those moments that 'record events in an intelligent style. All we want is a factual story' (100). Similarly, Grosset (1961) places emphasis on capturing 'natural and spontaneous shots' and suggests that editors 'cut out the parts where [actors] hesitate, glance at the camera, over-act or look embarrassed' (67).

The aesthetic of capturing people in 'natural' poses – as opposed to self-conscious acting for the camera – is a recurrent preoccupation here. For example, Davies warns, 'DON'T let anyone talk or look at the camera. The camera should always remain impersonal because if your subjects constantly look and point at us, the audience, the illusion will have been shattered' (1951: 204, original emphasis). More recently, in 2005, *Digital Video* magazine's 'quick start tips' refer to the need to capture spontaneous and natural moments and avoid people talking directly to the camera. The aesthetic in these discussions defines the camera and film-maker as an invisible, 'fly-on-the-wall' observer. The observer gains objectivity partly through capturing 'natural' moments in which the subject is unaware of, or at least not 'acting up' to, the camera. This objectivity can be obtained through knowledge of the individuals concerned: Livingstone (1979) says that being involved in the action gives greater insight into the subject, while Grosset (1961) suggests: 'You may tell your actors what you want them to do, but make sure your requests are in character and based on your knowledge of the family' (43).

As we have noted, the primary purpose of amateur film is seen to be that of entertainment. The aesthetic qualities associated with entertainment preclude 'hum drum' family films, films with no dramatic climaxes or those of poor technical or cinematic quality. As Davies (1951) writes: 'All you have to do is translate everyday happenings that have given you pleasure onto the screen with, perhaps, a slight over emphasis of the salient points. The hen-pecked husband theme should be good for a dozen films …' (235). Thus, while there is a premium placed on capturing spontaneous, natural everyday events, there is also a sense that the film-maker needs to actively shape and construct those events as entertainment.

Constructions of creativity

One of the more elusive characteristics referred to in the literature on amateur film-making is 'creativity'. Although the term is never discussed or defined in any depth, film-making is repeatedly referred to as an artistic or creative endeavour. It is not simply about keeping a record of family life, but rather a form of art, designed to be viewed and appreciated by others. Thus, Wheeler (1929) emphasises the importance of considering composition and lighting when filming, describing the film-maker as 'the creative artist in colour', mentally viewing and planning camera angles, distances and composition. Alder more explicitly states 'movie making is an art', although he makes it clear that the purpose of the artistic endeavour is functional, asserting that 'art for art's sake can go hang' (1951: 100). Nevertheless, this artistry is not necessarily amenable to systematic instruction. The artistic quality of film-making for Alder is 'not so much knowledge as an attitude, a kind of awareness of the screen. It is extremely difficult to teach an attitude' (109). Similarly, Bomback (1953) distinguishes between technical knowledge which can be taught and artistry which can only be modelled: 'we can explain the technicalities but we cannot teach the artistic presentation of a story. We can merely point the way' (preface).

The role of film-making as a creative personal outlet is referred to across the literature, and Beal (2000) makes the connection to other forms of cultural production, stating that 'creative videography has its roots in creative writing' (91). As we have seen, in some cases the creative aesthetic of amateur film-making is contrasted with the formulaic approach of commercial cinema or television, which is believed to give rise to passive consumption. This is particularly apparent in more recent publications, where there is a familiar rhetoric of condemnation of 'couch potatoes' and the 'boob tube':

> The end-product may not be a masterpiece, but [the amateur film-maker] can say: 'It's mine. I made it. A few months ago, it didn't exist.' This is the joy of creativity … It's something inborn in most of us but today's push-button way of life inhibits it. We are conditioned to be observers rather than participators, slumping in front of the telly, while the world goes by on the little screen.
>
> (*Movie Maker Magazine*, 1982: 723)

Likewise, Beal's (2000) injunction to amateur video makers to 'take back the tube' (quoted above) is echoed in Barrett's description of the power of digital video: 'Thanks to DV we're now starting to see some really creative and personal films that can provide a welcome alternative to the bland formulaic stuff that comes out of Hollywood' (*Camcorder and DVD Moviemaker*, 2003: 15). By contrast with some of the arguments noted above, the emphasis here is not on learning from the professionals, but rather on challenging and going beyond them.

Yet as we have implied, much of this literature urges amateur film-makers to conform to a relatively conservative, or at least 'classical' form of cinematic realism, characterised (for example) by conventional continuity editing and the 'invisible camera'. The rapid development of technology – perhaps particularly in the area of editing – makes it easier to achieve this; although it may also be making it possible to develop an aesthetic style that goes beyond it.

Conclusion

We began this chapter with the idea that growing access to moving image technology is blurring or breaking down the boundaries between 'amateurs' and 'professionals'. Countering this argument is the claim that, far from being a democratising force, video technology has actually been recuperated within the home mode, and (more broadly) within the private sphere. While we are certainly sceptical of claims about the revolutionary impact of technology, we have also suggested that the home mode may not in practice be quite as naïve and limited as critics suggest – and that it is at least deserving of more detailed empirical investigation (see Chapter 4 and Buckingham et al., 2010).

On the basis of the evidence presented in this chapter, we cannot make significant claims about the actual practice of film- and video-making, or how it may be changing. Rather, our attention has focused on the ways in which it is defined and constructed within publications targeted at the amateur user. In line with Bourdieu's theory of 'fields', we have argued that the cultural field of amateur film- and video-making is characterised by ongoing struggles for power, legitimation and control (Bourdieu, 1993). Yet the material we have analysed does not tell a simple story. There are several unresolved tensions and contradictions – for example, between an emphasis on the accessibility of the technology and the need to expend time and effort on learning; between the insistence on realism and spontaneity and the emphasis on the creative intervention of the film-maker; and between the need to learn from the professionals and the call to create alternatives to mainstream media.

One of the abiding imperatives in the publications we have reviewed is the need to distinguish between the serious or committed amateur and the more casual everyday user. The serious amateur is defined to some extent in terms of social class and gender, but also through the 'othering' of the naïve everyday user, who is seen to remain forever trapped within the unreconstructed home mode. In Bourdieu's terms, the serious amateur is an autodidact, who dedicates time and effort in pursuit of their learning and creative activity. Bourdieu (1990) would almost certainly have categorised amateur video production, like amateur photography, as a 'middlebrow' activity – although we doubt that the value systems he uses in mapping out the cultural field are quite as clear-cut today as they were in France in the 1960s and 1970s. Even so, our analysis suggests that the identity of the serious amateur has historically been defined in relation to a particular hierarchical system of taste, and an aesthetic based on particular notions of cinematic realism.

This portrait of the field complicates several of the generalisations that recur throughout the popular debates with which we began. On the one hand, it challenges a simple binary opposition between amateur and professional; and it disputes the notion that technology in and of itself can act as a force of empowerment, for example by virtue of its simplicity and accessibility. On the other hand, it questions the monolithic construction of the home mode – at least in its contemporary form – as an essentially naïve practice, or indeed as inevitably conservative (either aesthetically or ideologically). Our reading of the contemporary publications would suggest that while distinctions between professionals and amateurs (and between various 'grades' of amateurs) undoubtedly remain, they are becoming more complicated and less settled, and that the increasing accessibility and diversity of amateur video production is making life more difficult for those who would seek to discipline or regulate it.

Acknowledgement

An earlier version of this chapter was published in *The Journal of Media Practice* 8(2), 2007.

Note

1. Books referenced in the chapter are in the list of references. Magazines specifically referenced are: *Camcorder and DVD Moviemaker*, May 2003; *Camcorder User*, Spring 1988; *Digital Video Magazine*, November 2005, November 2006, March 2007; *Digital Video Techniques*, October 2006; *Home Movies*, 1951; *Movie Maker Magazine*, November 1978, December 1982; *Video Maker*, June 1986; *What Digital Camcorder*, April 2005, November 2005, December 2005, October 2005; and *Which Digital Camera*, November 2005.

References

Alder, R. (1951) Family movies outdoors. In R. H. Bomback (ed.) (1953) *Handbook of Amateur Cinematography*. pp. 100–44. London: Fountain Press.
Amateur Cinema League (1940) *A Guide to Making Better Movies*. Amateur Cinema League: New York.
Baum, G. (1991) 'Private eyes'. *Los Angeles Times*. July 25.
Beal, S. (2000) *The Complete Idiot's Guide to Making Home Videos*. Indianapolis: Macmillan.
Bomback, R. H. (ed.) (1953) *Handbook of Amateur Cinematography*. London: Fountain Press.
Bordwell, M. (1962) *Amateur Cinematography*. London: Oldbourne Book Co.

Bourdieu, P. (1984) *Distinction: A Social Critique of the Judgment of Taste*. London: Routledge.

Bourdieu, P. (1990) *Photography: A Middle-Brow Art*. Cambridge: Polity.

Bourdieu, P. (1993) *Outline of a Theory of Practice*. Cambridge: Cambridge University Press.

Broderick, P. (1964) *Amateur Film Making*. London: Cox and Wyman.

Buckingham, D., Willett, R. and Pini, M. (in press) *HomeTruths? Video Production and Domestic Life*. Ann Arbor, MI: University of Michigan Press.

Cameron, J. R. (1928) *Amateur Movie Craft*. London: New York: Cameron Publishing.

Chalfen, R. (1987) *Snapshot Versions of Life*. Bowling Green, Ohio: Bowling Green State University Popular Press.

Cleave, A. (1988) T*he ABC of Video Movies: Getting the Best from your Camcorder*. Manchester, New Hampshire: Morgan Press.

Cleveland, D. (2007) 'Filming The Family' from 'The Way We Were: 100 Years of Family Film'. East Anglian Film Archive. http://www2.angliatv.com/thewaywewere/filmingthefamily.shtml (Accessed 29 March 2007).

Croydon, J. (1951) Editing and titling. In R. H. Bomback (ed.) *Handbook of Amateur Cinematography*. pp. 245–80. London: Fountain Press.

Davies, D. (1951) Filming indoors. In R. H. Bomback (ed.) *Handbook of Amateur Cinematography*. pp. 196–238. London: Fountain Press.

Fauer, J. (2001) *Shooting Digital Video: DVCAM, Mini DV and DVCPRO*. Oxford: Focal Press.

Grosset, P. (1961) *8mm Movie Making for Pleasure*. London: Fountain Press.

Hobbs, E. (1930) *Cinematography for Amateurs: A Simple Guide to Motion Picture Taking and Showing*. London: Cassell.

Katelle, A. D. (2000) *Home Movies: A History of the American Industry: 1897–1979*. New York: Rochester.

Kodak (1966) *How To Make Good Home Movies*. New York: Kodak Publications.

Lescaboura, A. (1921) *The Cinema Handbook*. New York: Munn and Co.

Livingstone, C. (1979) *Film-Making for Pleasure and Profit*. New York: Macmillan.

Lovell-Burgess, M. (1932) *The Amateur Cine-Movement: A Popular Account of the Amateur Film Movement in Great Britain*. London: Marston.

Ouellette, L. (1995) 'Camcorder dos and don'ts: popular discourses on amateur video and participatory television'. *The Velvet Light Trap*. 36(Fall): 33–44.

Reyner, J. H. (1939) *Cinematography for Amateurs (3rd edn)*. London: Chapman and Hall.

Sewell, G. (1938) *Amateur Film Making*. London: Blackie and Son Ltd.

Sony Electronics (2007) 'Why choose Sony Handycam® camcorders?' http://www.sonystyle.com/is-bin/INTERSHOP.enfinity/eCS/Store/en/-/USD/SY_ViewStatic-Start?page=static%2farticles%2fhandycamguide%2eisml) (Accessed 29 March 2007).

Squires, M. (1992) *The Camcorder Handbook*. London: Headline Book Publishing.

Strausser, A. (1937) *Amateur Movies and How to Make Them*. London: Edward Evans.

Wheeler, O. (1929) *Amateur Cinematography*. London: Pitman Press.

Zimmerman, P. (1995) *Reel Families: A Social History of Amateur Film*. Indianapolis: Indiana University Press.

4
Inside the Home Mode

Maria Pini

Despite their occasional pretensions to more ambitious forms of video production, the advice manuals and consumer magazines examined in the last chapter implicitly recognise that, for most people, video is primarily a means of recording family life. In *The Camcorder Handbook* (1992) Malcolm Squires writes:

> Perhaps one of the most enjoyable uses to which you can put the camcorder is making an ongoing record of your family. You can include all sorts of activities, depending on what you like to do as a family. In this way you will also build up a permanent record of your children as they grow and develop over the years.
>
> (p.102)

This chapter focuses on the practices of camcorder users who do little more with their cameras than video their family and friends. Richard Chalfen (1982) uses the term 'home mode' to refer to the amateur photographer's or film-maker's representation of the private world of the family (see Chapter 2). The category of home mode video footage comprises the kind of material made, if not necessarily *within* the home, then dealing primarily *with* 'the home', the domestic and the familial. Such material tends to be thought of as 'private' and as such, its significance closely resembles that of the traditional family photo album.

Home mode imagery can be distinguished from representation which follows an established set of formal codes, tends to be shaped by commercial interests and is intentionally produced. In Chalfen's words, it is:

> [C]onceptually and pragmatically distinct from the professionally produced forms seen in advertising, photojournalism, art or museum

exhibitions, feature films, education, film festivals, and the like ...
[It is] generally produced by nonprofessional photographers using
inexpensive, mass produced cameras.

(127)

Such video commonly tends to be considered insignificant as a form
of cultural production: it is generally deemed banal, uninteresting,
unimaginative and unremarkable. The common tendency is to think of
such practice as the work of the excited new parent, or the 'emotional'
video-maker simply and unthinkingly collecting records of their 'nearest-
and-dearest'. Of all the various identifiable functions of the amateur
film or video camera, the category of the home mode undoubtedly
carries the least of what Bourdieu (1984) calls 'cultural capital'. Like
family photography, home mode film- and video-making is commonly
viewed as reinforcing rather than challenging a particular familial
ideology. As we have seen in Chapter 2, authors as diverse as Pierre
Bourdieu (1990) and Susan Sontag (1977) have argued that domestic
photography serves to sustain a representation of the family as integrated and cohesive, which tends to belie the increasing fragmentation
of contemporary family life. Such representations are typically accused
of erasing tensions and conflicts in favour of bland and superficial
images of 'happy families' – images which are of course also strongly
reinforced in the advertising and marketing materials associated with
these technologies.

Much the same is true with regards to family film and video. From a
wide range of perspectives, such 'ordinary practice' is dismissed as the
very least creative, interesting or meaningful use of the amateur film or
video camera. As we saw in Chapter 3, from buyers' guides, through critical reviews of amateur film history, to camera owners' *own* descriptions
of their practices, the home mode is commonly viewed as, at best, a
simple, naïve (in terms of its lack of formal codes) and relatively uncreative practice, and at worst, as a practice perpetuating an oppressive and
very selective image of 'the family'. According to Patricia Zimmerman
(1995), for example, the mass marketing of home film technology and
practice has historically encouraged precisely this 'narrative spectacle of
idealized family life' (46), and thereby stripped amateur film and video
of its more radical potential:

From 1897 to 1962 [the period of her study] amateur film discussion
incrementally relocated amateur filmmaking within a romanticized

vision of the bourgeois nuclear family thereby amputating its more resistant, economic and political potential for critique.

(x)

This sense of disappointment with amateur film and video is thus very familiar. Instead of being mobilised in the development of more radical modes of representation and communication, photographic and film technologies have, in their more 'ordinary' uses, been seen to bolster very particular versions of society and family life. Despite its radical potential, and the hype which accompanied its development, home video is regarded as a vehicle for the representation of 'happy', fun-loving and ultimately non-threatening, family units (Ouellette, 1995).

Discourse surrounding amateur film- and video-making therefore tends to construct home mode production as one of the least significant uses of these media. As discussed in Chapter 3, handbooks, magazines and manuals aimed at amateur film- and video-makers often acknowledge that the family is likely to be the dominant focus; and yet they frequently urge their readers to move beyond what are seen as the limitations of this mode. The implied reader of such material tends to be the 'enthusiast' who is interested in the aesthetics of amateur film and the range of new visual representational technologies, rather than the film-maker who is simply using the camcorder as a means of keeping records of their nearest and dearest. Very definite distinctions are thus reinforced between different kinds of practice and different kinds of practitioners. The home mode producer – to a much greater extent than the enthusiastic amateur or the 'hobbyist' – is constructed as the *other* to the video professional or the video 'artist'. So powerful and recognisable is this view that family film-makers *themselves* commonly position their practice accordingly, acknowledging its lowly cultural status and insisting, as the two typical interviewees quoted below do, that there is very little of significance about their camcorder use:

It's just for having a memory. Nothing beyond that.

(Phil)

Oh, it's nothing really. It's not creative. It's only for the children and the family and for us keeping ... It's memories really. No planning. Nothing like that.

(Kate)

Beneath the surfaces

Despite this generally dismissive view of home mode production, it is precisely what very many, if not most, camcorder owners actually do with their camcorders. At the very least, it seems much too sweeping to dismiss the makers of home mode video as necessarily or inherently uncreative or unambitious in their practices. On the contrary, it is important to look more closely at what is at stake and what investments are being made when home mode video is produced. As Chalfen argues, more detailed analysis 'is especially important in an area defined by stereotypes, or where the behavior is mistakenly thought to be so simple as to be beneath comment' (1987: 131). Our wider study (Buckingham et al., in press) points to the great diversity of what families actually do with video, and the different purposes for which they use it. However, this chapter deals specifically with the 'emotional' or 'affective' aspects of the production and consumption of home mode video. My aim here is to explore what goes on when home mode video is produced and consumed, and to look 'beneath the surfaces', so to speak, of home mode representation.

While very little has been written about such issues in relation to film and video, there is a body of work on photography that does provide important insights into issues surrounding the visual representation of self and family. In particular, a variety of feminist writers have, in their different ways, sought to move beyond a simple assertion of the limited range of self-representations involved in family photography. Such readings acknowledge a much more active subject, raising questions about the motivations underpinning both the production and the consumption of family photography. From Jo Spence and Patricia Holland's (1991) critical explorations of family photography to Annette Kuhn's (1995) analysis of the myths embedded in the family photograph, to Valerie Walkerdine's (1990) examination of her own desires in relation to family photography and Marianne Hirsch's (1997) deconstruction of the family album, emphasis has shifted towards issues which can be termed more 'affective' or 'psycho-social'. These are questions about the constitution of subjectivity, fantasy, desire and memory, and the relationship between photography and the physical embodiment of (or the failure to embody) what might be called 'identity fictions'.

As Jo Spence (1991) has argued, one of the main conventions of the conventional family album is to function as a store for acceptable, respectable and 'happy' images: images serving as 'evidence' of normality and success. In developing a form of phototherapy, Spence therefore sets out to explore the effects on memory, family history and subjectivity of these conventions. This is done by attempting to make visible, through the production and contemplation of photography, the otherwise hidden psychic and social processes involved in the construction of identity. By exploring what lies beneath the surfaces of family photographs, what is presented and what is 'erased' or denied, Spence raises centrally important questions about subjectivity-in-culture. As she puts it, in a later work (1995):

> While the media are saturated with stories of victims, unhappy families, disasters, the family records we keep for ourselves are decidedly lacking anything more than celebrations. Why is this so? The reasons are surely more profound than the fact that the advertising of companies like Kodak encourages us to have very limited types of snapshotting practices.
>
> (191–2)

In a similar vein to Spence, Valerie Walkerdine (1990) examines certain family photographs of herself as a child, discussing their power to evoke and 'hold' particular fictions of femininity – fictions that are both desirable and reviled. Her aim is to explore:

> The relation between acceptable and unacceptable images – the ones we tear up or hide away in cupboards – and what lurks behind them.
>
> (147)

Walkerdine discusses the particular emotions her family photographs evoke in her, and what these emotions might say about much more general fictions of femininity and class, and about acceptable and 'subjugated' knowledges.

Annette Kuhn (1995) similarly foregrounds the forms of fiction and myth (but importantly – and like the other writers referenced here – not as things opposed to 'fact') involved in the production and consumption of family photography. As Kuhn argues:

> Although we take stories of childhood and family literally, I think our recourse to this past is a way of reaching for myth, for the story that is deep enough to express the profound feelings we have in the present.
>
> (1)

For all these authors, family photography (and I'm including filmic representation here) functions *not* as means by which to neutrally 'capture' some pre-existing reality, but rather as part of the means by which the 'reality' of the family is actually constructed – in particular ways, at particular times and to particular ends – in the first place. We can say that such constructions typically create a sense of what Stuart Hall (1996) calls 'belongingness', and by extension, a sense of collective identification.

In surveying a range of anti-essentialist conceptions of 'identity' and 'identification', Hall reiterates the impossibility of the coherent, self-sustaining and unified model of 'self' that lies at the center of post-Cartesian metaphysics. This bounded, originary individual with an 'identity' of its 'own' has been critiqued from a variety of approaches informed by Lacanian and feminist psychoanalysis, deconstructionism, Althusser's model of ideology, Foucault's genealogical method and Butler's work on performativity. Drawing from all of these, Hall argues that identification is not in fact about the 'total merging' it seems to imply (this is simply a fantasy of incorporation) but a 'fictive unity' that requires work to construct and maintain. Discursive practices of various kinds play a crucial role in this construction; and it is here that we can apply Hall's ideas to family photography and video. I am suggesting that these forms of (self-) representation function in terms of such fantasies of incorporation, and thereby serve to constitute a family identity. We might say that the family photograph or the piece of family video footage functions to tell or remind members of their 'place', their 'belongingness'. It contextualises them within not only a particular material setting, but within a particular discourse about 'the family'. As Hall puts it:

> Identities arise from the narrativization of the self, but the necessarily fictional nature of this process in no way undermines its discursive, material or political effectivity, even if the belongingness, the 'suturing into the story' through which identities arise is partly in the imaginary (as well as the symbolic) and therefore, always, partly constructed in fantasy, or at least within a fantasmatic field.
>
> (1996: 4)

These writers provide a useful backdrop for a consideration of home mode video. It is their emphasis on the fantasies, the myths, the acceptable and unacceptable fictions embedded within family photography, which is most useful here. My focus in reading the data collected for this chapter, then, is upon the various processes through which 'family identity' is constructed. Although, as Anrette Kuhn (1995) has pointed out, family identity is commonly taken as a given, what is highlighted here is some of the work (both physical and psychological) which goes into its production and maintenance.

The following sections of this chapter contain an analysis of data collected from semi-structured interviews conducted with 11 parents whose use of their camcorders revolves primarily around home mode video making.[1] The central questions which shaped all of these interviews are as follows: Why is the home mode video produced? What role does such footage play in relation to senses of personal and family history? How does it perpetuate family memory? What fantasies, fears and desires appear to be invested within the home mode video? A fuller exploration of these questions would require a depth of inquiry which is beyond the scope of the present study, and might perhaps entail the kind of methodology developed within phototherapy. From one angle, what follows is rather more of a 'surface-skimming' of the data, although the aim here was never to attempt an in-depth psychoanalytic reading. Rather, my aim is simply to identify and discuss some of the key emotional themes emerging, paying particular attention to the ways in which home mode production works to construct a sense of 'family identity' – albeit one that may well be incomplete and partly constituted in fantasy.

The uses and significance of home mode video

Tim is a 42-year-old single father. His son, James, is almost 14 and has been videoed since he was less than a week old. As James has grown older, Tim has videoed him less and less. Indeed, the last time he did so was nearly two years ago, on James's 12th birthday. Like many of the parents I interviewed, Tim has used the camcorder much less often as his child has grown older. Below, he describes videoing his son for the first time with his newly acquired camcorder. This was just as James, Tim and James's mother were leaving the maternity hospital after the birth:

> We did it in the street outside the hospital and some at home with him and some of the new room, his new room. I really remember that bit of video ... all quite happy times, before things went wrong. I did it a lot for me and ... my mum likes to watch it too. When I split from his mum, she took all the cassettes, which was a real

blow, 'cause you know, there were the nights when I was on my own, no James around, finding my feet, new place, feeling down and not even a video cassette of him. She was being really difficult about it ... James was with *her,* so where's the problem? ... I don't do it much now 'cause he's much older and he doesn't like it ... I do get the tapes off her sometimes to watch them back though.

Tim is now separated from James's mother and says that during the separation, ownership of the video tapes caused a lot of argument. Eventually, he left these with James's mother, although he says that he still believes this to have been unfair because his mother lives with James and Tim doesn't. When asked to elaborate on this sense of injustice, Tim claims that having these tapes would have made the separation easier at the time, as though the footage might have filled the empty space left by James's departure.

Tim is touching on a very familiar theme, which emerges again and again from these interviews. Although he doesn't own the video tapes, Tim does borrow them from time to time. When I ask him to say more about how he feels when watching them now, he says that he feels sad because when he sees the footage, they all (him, his ex-partner, her adult son and James) look so happy. He says that the footage shows a time 'before things went wrong'. Significantly, when asked why his photo-album (which he *did* have with him) was not adequate in filling the perceived gap left by James, Tim, like virtually all of the other interviewees, says that video is just more 'realistic' than still photography.

Tim's interview brings up three interrelated (and in many respects, impossible to separate) themes which emerge from the interviews as a whole. The first two of these relate to notions of 'absence' and 'presence' – the role of video footage as a substitute for an absent loved one, and as bringing an absent place into 'the here' and an absent time into 'the now'. The third relates to the 'realism' of representation seen to be afforded by video. Taken together, these themes point to some of the ways in which home mode video footage serves to construct a sense of family identity.

Substituting for an absent loved one

Tim is completely typical among my interviewees in feeling that his video footage could have acted as a substitute for James's presence. In a similar way many parents produce video footage of their children to send to their own parents and family living abroad. Here the footage is seen to 'stand in' for, or somehow 'embody', the children. One interviewee, Kate, explains her videos of her young daughter in this way:

> Well they [her mother, father and brother in Ireland] can see how she's growing and what she looks like and my dad hasn't met her yet. So when they do meet, it's like he'll know her already.

Jocelyn makes a very similar point:

> I like just going out and filming 'a day in the life of us' to send to my family back home. It's as simple as that.

Like Tim, Bob is separated from his two children (a boy of three and a girl of seven) who now live with their mother in France. He too says that at certain points, he takes this footage out to watch. It brings him, he explains, both pleasure and pain: pleasure because he simply likes watching them and it's as though they're 'there with me'; and pain, because he is reminded that they are *not* with him. Bob talked at considerable length about the extent to which this video footage seems to bring his children 'back' to him, and remind him of when they all lived together. It clearly affords Bob an almost visceral connection to his children and to a 'past'. Far from being merely a trivial pastime, such footage often seems to carry considerable emotional power.

So much is home video footage seen to 'stand in' and embody an absent person that Kate describes the extreme difficulty of showing videos of her now-dead grandmother to her mother. She says:

> She [her mother] can still not bear to watch the film [of her own mother]. Well, it's like she's back there. Back in the room with us ... But, she's not, is she? But it's like she *is*.

Obviously, no matter how much such statements seem to be referring to a 'past', what they highlight is the absolute centrality and importance of the material present in giving meaning to this footage. The significance for Kate's mother of this piece of video is totally bound up with the present, a present wherein her mother is dead. So the footage may suggest a presence, but one which only reinforces absence. And the significance of what is perceived to be a 'past' is completely saturated by its situation within the 'here-and-now'.

Tim says that part of the difficulty he experienced during the times when he viewed videos of James as a baby came from the act of remembering:

> The little things you forget when they're not around. You're watching and suddenly all these tiny things you've forgotten come back, you know, like a twitch or how he sucks his fist and – especially at the beginning of the split, that was dead hard. It was so real watching these things that you just know so well, but you forget and you just want to reach out and pick him up.

For these interviewees, video footage allows them to feel that an absent person is 'here', yet it also reminds them that they are 'not here'. As such, the footage carries the potential for both pleasure and pain. Its force is double-edged. Tim is *not* with James. Bob is *not* with his children. And significantly, when Bob talks of watching footage of his youngest child, he says 'it's great to watch, but it's never like touching him, is it?'

Roland Barthes (1981) writes of photography:

> If I like a photograph, if it disturbs me, I … look at it, I scrutinize it, as if I wanted to know more about the thing or the person it represents … I want to enlarge this face in order to see it better, to understand it better, to know its truth … I decompose, I enlarge … I *retard*, in order to have time to *know* at last. … Alas, however hard I look, I discover nothing: if I enlarge, I see nothing but the grain of the paper. … Such is the photograph: it cannot *say* what it lets us see.
>
> (99–100 emphasis in original)

Bob and Tim can look, but they cannot touch. To adapt Barthes, their footage allows them to see, hear and otherwise 'sense' a space wherein their children appear to be, but they can only go so far. The children appear to *be* in the footage, but they are not.

Or to adapt Jacques Derrida (1988) writing on photography, this video footage can somehow 'hold' or 'contain' a concept – a person, place or time. Yet the material actuality to which that concept refers can never actually or properly inhabit it. As he puts it:

> That concept … belongs to it without belonging to it; it never inscribes itself in the homogenous objectivity of framed space but instead inhabits it, or rather haunts it.
>
> (266–7)

Tim's, Bob's and Kate's footage is similarly 'haunted'. All illustrate how the video footage of an absent loved one can appear to 'embody' a presence. The trace or 'ghost' of that person can be brought into the present, yet always accompanying this 'presencing' is the reminder of its absence.

Here and there

One function of this 'presencing' of an absent loved one is the construction and maintenance of links across both temporal and geographical space. It is the parents living far away, either from their own parents or from their children, who make this most clear, as illustrated by Kate and Bob for example. But these interviewees are by no means unusual. Geographical and temporal spaces are fundamentally important to all of the home mode video practices I looked at. Such links clearly play a crucial role in consolidating a sense of family identity and 'belongingness'.

Kate sends videos of her daughter to her parents in Ireland. In doing so, a familial connection is reinforced. Moreover, she has shown her children home mode video footage made and sent by her brother who is actually living in Ireland now. This footage shows Kate's nephew and niece playing, singing and 'just larking about'. Through the video, Kate's daughter is shown her family and situated in terms of a family identity. Siobhan, her daughter, is six and has met these cousins once, but over a year ago. When asked what she tells Siobhan while playing the tape, Kate says:

> I explain who they are and stuff like … say, who they are and how old they are and oh, where they live and things like: 'that's your uncle and auntie and that's your cousins'. She loves it and always asks to see it.

As well as reinforcing a sense of family identity, Kate indicates that in reviewing the footage sent by her brother, she is also establishing the basis for a form of national identity. For Kate, it is important that Siobhan knows about Ireland. On several occasions, she mentions showing her footage of Irish dancing and singing and emphasises Siobhan's enjoyment of this.

Another mother, Jane, regularly shows her children footage she recorded when she visited her 'home' in Poland with her five-year-old daughter. Viewing her video footage with her children (Isabel and her one and a half-year-old brother, Owen) is similarly about placing these children in relation to a Polish family context:

> Of course, it's important for them to see where their parents come from and who's still there, and how it's different from London. Isabel has very vague memories I think, but Owen has never been there and it's important.

As Gillian Rose (2003: 11) notes of photography, 'the more distant people are, the more important photographing becomes.' Rose's argument certainly appears to be evidenced by many of my interviewees. Home mode video appears to function for many of them as a way of connecting dispersed family members. As we have seen, footage can stand in for an absent person; and often, this absent person is brought into a 'here and now' in the construction of a linked chain constituting a coherent family unit. In the process, a sense of family identity is constructed. This sense of membership and continuity (between generations and between dispersed family members) works to bring into being a set of 'imagined communities' (Anderson, 1983) involving a host of identifications including familial and national identifications.

Gender identifications may also be at stake here. Interestingly, Mariya describes showing her daughter footage of her own wedding day, and in speaking of her daughter's love of this video says, 'Because I'm in a white dress, she probably identifies with it.' One could argue that such viewing plays a part in Mariya's daughter's constitution as feminine: she is invited to identify with the 'white dress'. Alternatively, we could argue that in reading her daughter's viewing in this way, Mariya projects her *own* desires. (I shall come back to Mariya's account shortly.) Kate says something very similar about her daughter Siobhan's viewing of her Irish cousins' dancing:

> She loves seeing all the costumes and watching them dance like that. They're girls so you know, they love all that dressing up and dancing around. And she loves dressing up and showing off and singing and watching it back. She likes seeing herself dressed up.

The theme of family identity and the sense of belongingness are also apparent in Jane's account of videoing her children:

> It makes me feel closer to mum and dad at home so ... they [her parents in Poland] can see them [her children] and so, you know ...

it's like we're all together again. It's important for us to have the contact like that. They're so far away. For my mum it's like she can be part of the, you know, that really important growing-up stage – that important stage in their life.

The role of home mode footage acting as some kind of historical and geographical 'glue' is, therefore, a common theme. Video is used to forge links across towns, countries, continents and across generations. Through such footage, these links are 'storied' into being and a sense of belongingness is made real.

This process may also involve forms of autobiographical narrative, perhaps particularly for children. Thus, some parents describe watching old footage together with their children, while describing to them what is going on, and detailing what these children were like as babies. For example, Jane says:

> She [her five year-old daughter] loves it when I explain, and she now sees herself in the cot. And she says 'oh, how cute I was. How nice I was'. She really enjoys it. She even asks to see the baby-films of herself. It's like they don't believe they were babies. So I put it on.

Speaking of reviewing old footage with her now seven-year-old daughter, Mariya says:

> And she watches it. She enjoys watching it. That's a bonding moment. Sometimes she may be in a bad mood or ... and if we all watch the videos when she was [a few] months old. Every time it sets such a cheering-up thing for a family. We just all sit down and then watch it and love it and we all cheer up and are in a good mood.

Such instances appear to provide particularly obvious illustrations of the 'interpellation' involved in achieving a sense of belongingness and identity. These viewing children are 'hailed', invited to recognise themselves as unique individuals, and as part of a *particular* situation.

The repetition of the video viewing which Mariya, like many of the other interviewees, refers to, further consolidates a family identity. By being told again and again what they are watching, where the footage was shot and what they were like as babies, children are situated and asked to recognise themselves within an already-established context. Alongside such verbal 'anchoring' or running commentary is the fact that video is commonly shared and reviewed in family groups, providing a further consolidation of a community identity. Like Mariya, Shanta describes how much her children enjoy watching both old and recent videos of themselves. In Shanta's case, tapes are passed around a large extended family network and viewing this footage is clearly part of sustaining a wider group identity, which is partly defined by ethnicity and religion.

Such examples illustrate the significance of the verbal or discursive dimension that accompanies home mode imagery. As Chalfen (1987) points out, a clear set of conventions surround the exhibition of home mode footage that are fundamentally important to meaning-making:

> Complete silence during a home mode exhibition event is socially inappropriate behavior – viewers and exhibitors are expected and conditioned to say something. These accompanying remarks appear to be as conventionalized as the imagery itself.
>
> (124)

There are, then, particular ways of watching and speaking about, and hence constructing meaning from home mode imagery. Such talk works partly in the construction of a sense of family continuity and belonging. To return to Shanta:

> So for example, myself, my family and their uncle's family and their grandma, we'll watch it together and the sisters. And us and the grandma, we will sit together, which is five families ... And the others like, would probably get it passed around to.

Such rituals function as a 'glue' cementing a sense of belongingness to a particular time, place and community, as Chalfen (1987) argues:

> Home mode activity serves to reify and strengthen previous and ongoing social-bonds. New photographs bring people together to maintain preferred and regulated social relationships. While participants view their ties with the past, with deceased relatives, or with relatives living in other regions of the world, they proceed to produce new evidence of cross-generational and intrafamilial relationships.
>
> (141)

Now and then

As I have implied, a form of history-making is central to the production of home mode video footage. Many of the parents interviewed here claimed that their footage was consciously being produced for their children to watch when they are grown up. They repeatedly said that they thought it would be important for their children to see the footage when they are adults. One father, Billy, is typical in this respect. He says:

> Well I think basically I'd say it's kind of a historical record for when Ella [his daughter] is older, so she can look back at it, or we can look back at it ourselves and see when she was younger, really.

Kate says that one of the most important reasons for her videoing her daughter is that she will be able to keep seeing this footage as she (Kate) gets older:

> I just want to be able to see all her movements and how she looks. When I'm much older and she's flown the nest, I'll have her on the video.

As Hirsch and Spitzer (2006: 125) have written of photography: 'Photography interrupts, actually stops time, freezes a moment, is inherently elegiac.' Hirsch and Spitzer's argument very much applies here, and although they are referring specifically to still photography, the notion that a moment has been 'caught' or 'captured' on video is a common one. There is a sense that through reviewing footage, the viewer can somehow re-embody that place and time, and return to that moment. Mariya offers a particularly clear demonstration of this theme:

> I just miss the past. So every time you know, the moment is gone. So my idea of photographs and video is sort of freezing the moments, the pleasure of life. I am really enjoying life. And one day if it's not there … And I want my daughter to see how things are and were … I think she will really appreciate it when she grows up to see what life was like now. So I am trying to get … capture what I feel about life; what to me life is. The beauty of it and the beauty of places and simple things. So I am really excited. I'm taking it [the camcorder] around with me anywhere, any time really.

A further clear illustration of the 'freezing time' theme emerges when parents speak of videoing newborns. I mentioned earlier that Tim now videos James far less frequently than he did when James was younger.

This is the case for many of the parents interviewed. On one level, this is straightforward: the newborn is videoed precisely because it *is* 'new'; a novelty. But what also comes through many of these accounts is a desire or a need to 'hold onto' the baby, and a fear of losing them. All of the parents interviewed here appear intensely aware of how quickly their babies are changing, growing into new phases of their lives. Before their eyes, these children are quickly becoming 'not babies'. By contrast, older children and adult family do not appear to be surrounded by this sense of fast-approaching loss. Hence the need to 'capture' or 'freeze' appears to be at its most intense when parents describe videoing their babies:

> They're kids and its over in a flash you know, even from you know a year ago, they've changed.
>
> (Leslie)

> My mum tells me on the phone, 'do more! Film him before he changes.'
>
> (Jane)

Gillian Rose (2003) makes the same observation in commenting upon the interviewees from her own study. These women are talking about their family photographs, and Rose quotes one mother saying:

> Well you sort of look at your children and they grow so quickly and it's … I struggle to remember everything … Time moves on so quickly and they're growing and they're changing and it makes me feel a little bit sad that it's gone, you know – those happy moments.
>
> (12)

A similar sense of urgency around 'capturing' a moment arises in relation to references made to death (to aged or dead family members, for example). Kate, when asked how *she* feels about watching the footage of her grandmother, which her mother cannot watch, says:

> It's important to have it. I know what mum feels but … personally, I treasure film of my family and especially when … especially the older generation, I want film of them. I want to have it. I'm sure it'll be hard to watch if they're gone, but I treasure it … My uncle's sick, very sick, in Ireland now and it's really important to me to have him on film before he dies.

For Teresa, her camcorder footage is seen to enable her recently widowed mother in Italy to see her grandchildren. In this case, it is significant that her mother is alone and overseas now. Through receiving this home mode video footage she can, *at least,* see her grandchildren:

> Oh, we bought the little camera when our first child was born ... yeah, because we were having children, and my dad died when I was pregnant with my first child and ... so we thought to send some videos to my mum ... She's in Italy. And we thought she's away, she's on her own now, but at least she can see the children. We do it for my mum.

Teresa bought her first video camera after the death of her father, when her first child was born. Although I'm not suggesting that Teresa is consciously making an association here between birth, death and camcorder footage, the description says a lot about the significance of home mode camcorder footage more generally. Indeed, Chalfen (1987) refers to this aspect of home mode representation as the 'defeating death' motivation behind its production. He notes the observed tendency for people to photograph more during times of rapid change:

> By increasing the frequency of picture-taking during times of change, people could be said to be slowing down the inevitable process of change and development.
>
> (134)

He goes on to quote one home moviemaker who says:

> One thing I've noticed about us is that these movies are taken less frequently when the kids get older, obviously because the kids don't change as fast. You want to preserve the babyhood because it goes so quickly.
>
> (135)

Likewise, Mariya tries to 'freeze' moments. She imagines that through videoing the beauty which she sees, and which excites her in the present, she will be able to re-experience this sensation in an imagined future. More than this, as a 'container' for her own emotions, this footage will hold her feelings intact so that they will be accessible to her daughter, who, in reviewing this footage, will be able to experience the same.

Realism and video

The realism associated with video footage is absolutely central to all of the themes discussed above. For many of the interviewees, video was seen to capture reality in a way that still photography could not. Many speak of video being more 'realistic', more 'authentic' and better able to 'capture' a person, place or feeling:

> It's different from still photography. Well, I think obviously here … the still photo doesn't capture the ulterior. It doesn't capture a whole occurrence … A regular stills camera, it just freezes a moment in time. It doesn't sort of have a continuity so you don't capture a whole event.
>
> (Phil)

> Well, you have the sound and the movement and all the kafuffle and so much more than you ever get with just a photograph. It's deeper. There's more to it. So, more realistic? Yes.
>
> (Kate)

> I like my photos, but the camcorder I would use more for when I want to hear and feel them, like sort of the moment, you know, which you can't feel with pictures. Because if you watch something, you get the feeling of the place you've been to whereas with photos, it's just like quick glances.
>
> (Shanta)

However, accompanying claims for the realism of their video footage are frequent acknowledgements by interviewees that the representations actually being presented are selective, partial, even contrived. Although video is seen to offer the 'having-been-there' quality which Roland Barthes (1981) writes about in *Camera Lucida*, interviewees are clearly quite aware of the selectivity involved, in terms of the actual ways in which the family or the self are presented. Choices about what gets videoed and what gets exhibited are not free, but regulated in various ways.

A distinction therefore has to be made between the video *medium* (seen to involve a technically 'realistic' quality) and the *representations* which are produced with it. What was videoed *did* take place. That videoed moment in time *did* happen. To return to Tim and Bob, the significance of their family video footage is centrally related to this: the evidentiality of video footage, its embodiment of a kind of 'having-been-there', is central. The significance of these events, however, is open-ended. As Barthes (1981) describes:

> Photography never lies; or rather, it can lie as to the meaning of the thing, being by nature tendentious, never to its existence.
>
> (87)

To return to my earlier arguments about the representation of family life, these video producers make quite clear distinctions between 'acceptable' and 'unacceptable' images of themselves and their families. In a thoroughly typical example, Jane, when asked if she would video difficult, tense or unpleasant family moments, says:

> Of course not. If I did, I'd erase it. Who wants to remember bad times? Or actually, who wants to show someone else your bad times?

Many other interviewees say something very similar. When asked whether they believe that they are constructing a 'realistic picture of family life', some interviewees laughed or giggled and many explicitly said 'no'. Many openly acknowledged that they are very selective in their videoing. In one (albeit quite unusual) case, Shanta details how within her own family's weddings, two different videos are commonly made. One is for 'public' (meaning wider, extended family and friends) viewing and one is for 'private' (meaning very close, immediate family) viewing. The former is far more formal whereas the latter shows the bride without full, formal dress and having fun with other female family members.

As I have suggested, the passing of either real or imagined time is absolutely central to home mode video production. A 'present' is videoed with the intention of being reviewed as a 'past' at an imagined point in the 'future'. For some of the interviewees (Tim and Bob for example), it is the passage of time (and all the changes to circumstance which it has brought) which brings pain. Irrespective of how realistic a sense of returning to the past might feel, reviewing footage is clearly *not* like being back with their children again. Footage is being viewed from a different present. The sadness they both mention comes not from the actual events and people they are watching and not even (in any simple way) from the fact that family reality is now very different, but because the 'present' completely shapes the way this 'past' is reviewed and hence, reconstructed. This reviewing brings to the fore something fundamental about the fragility of identity. Bob says of his footage, 'I really thought we were so happy and strong at the time. It's so disturbing and sad.' Footage *means* very differently when viewed in hindsight.

It is easy in the cases of Tim and Bob to understand why, when reviewing their camcorder footage, there might be sadness: their relationships have broken down and they are separated from their children. They were able to discuss (even quite critically) the 'happy families' representations they once constructed, and to recognise their footage as 'situated fictions' or visual 'stories', whose significance is entirely context-dependent. When asked whether he now believes that his footage shows a 'realistic' picture of that time, Tim says that 'it can't have been that happy really, because we were about to split.' Bob, on the other hand, says, 'Yes, it was real - at the time.'

All of this brings into question the 'realism' associated with video. For many of the interviewees, it is almost as if a quite conscious, knowing collusion with dominant representations of the family is going on. There is a level of play or (self-) mockery about the representations being produced – as is shown by the giggles, laughter or denial when asked if their footage showed a 'realistic' picture of family life. Gillian Rose (2003: 10) makes a very similar observation in her study of mothers talking about their family photographs. As she puts it, 'the cultural predictability of their family snaps was obvious to all my interviewees.' Importantly, this brings into question the notion that the home mode video maker is, as the stereotype would have it, naively and faithfully investing in the 'truth' of their video self-representations.

Constructing continuity and identity: Towards a conclusion

To close, I want to return to Stuart Hall's (1996) work on identity and identification, mentioned earlier. Hall's argument provides one useful way of understanding some of the central aspects of home mode video production. In addressing the concepts of 'identity' and 'identification', he draws broadly from a range of psychoanalytic and poststructuralist theory in discussing the many ways in which the 'fictive unity' that comprises an 'identity' is brought into being. Likewise, I have argued that much of what goes on when home mode video is produced constitutes precisely such an attempt to construct a sense of 'unity'. In other words, the representations of coherence, stability, continuity and integration, which home mode producers appear concerned to create, can usefully be seen as the means by which certain 'fictions' are brought into being – fictions which may prove comforting, meaningful and ultimately necessary to a sense of belongingness. Thus, Kate links her daughter Siobhan to her parents in Ireland: she is somehow 'sending' her there. Similarly, Teresa 'sends' her children to her recently widowed mother in Italy. Bob 'brings' his children from France into his current life in London.

Highlighting the levels of fantasy and the amount of work involved in the production of a family identity does not mean denying the very real purpose or effectivity of such an identity. Rather, it is about seeing identity (be this to do with nationality, gender, race or – as in the present case – the family) not as a given, but rather as something which must be brought into being, produced and continuously worked on. It is never complete; the work is never finished. In this respect, Kate's storying into being her Irishness is no more than what she might do in proclaiming herself a woman. Neither statement can be said to be untrue. But this truth is *made* rather than *given*.

Home mode video production can thus be viewed as an always-in-process bringing into being of a particular 'story'. Contrary to common critiques of the limited, conservative and ultimately insignificant nature of the home mode, it can be viewed as one of the many always-in-process operations involved in constructing a sense of identity and of one's place in time and space. What is very clear from the interviews here is the extent to which fantasy and desire are central to the home mode. Of course, the families abroad *do* exist, the distant countries *are* there, the baby *did* once exist as a baby and Bob *was* once 'really' happy in his family. The point is not that these representations are somehow false, but rather that the home mode video serves as a tool in the continuing work of producing images of coherence, permanence and belongingness – and hence of identity.

Note

1. These interviewees are drawn from a variety of sources. Five interviewees (Mariya, Shanta, Leslie, Jocelyn, Phil) form part of our much larger study of contemporary British camcorder use (see Chapter 1 of this volume). Two (Teresa and Billy) were contacted through a London primary school and constitute parents who use their camcorders primarily for videoing their children. Teresa is from Italy, and Billy is from Ireland; both hold Higher Education degrees obtained in the UK. The remaining four (two mothers – Kate and Jane, and two fathers – Tim and Bob) were recruited for more in-depth, semi-structured interviews concerning the emotional dimensions of their video-making. Tim and Bob (both of whom are British) were contacted through a mutual friend, while Kate (who is Irish) and Jane (who is Polish)

were contacted through a woman who had already been interviewed for the project. Tim, Bob and Jane hold no Higher Education qualifications, and Kate is currently studying for a diploma in Nursery Nursing.

References

Anderson, B. (1983) *Imagined Communities*. London: Verso.

Barthes, R. (1981) *Camera Lucida: Reflections on Photography*. Richard Howard (translator). New York: Hill and Wang.

Bourdieu, P. (1984) *Distinction: A Social Critique of the Judgment of Taste*. London: Routledge.

Bourdieu, P. (1990) *Photography: A Middle-Brow Art*. Cambridge: Polity.

Buckingham, D., Willett, R. and Pini, M. (in press) *HomeTruths? Video Production and Domestic Life*. Ann Arbor, MI: University of Michigan Press.

Chalfen, R. (1982) Home movies as cultural documents. In S. Thomson (ed.) *Film/Culture: Explorations of Cinema in its Social Context*. pp.126–37. Methuen, N. J.: Scarecrow.

Chalfen, R. (1987) *Snapshot Versions of Life*. Bowling Green, Ohio: Bowling Green State University Popular Press.

Derrida, J. (1988) On the deaths of Roland Barthes. In H. J. Silverman (ed.) *Philosophy and Non-Philosophy since Merleau-Ponty*. pp. 259–96. London: Routledge.

Hall, S. (1996) Introduction: who needs 'identity'? In S. Hall and P. du Gay (eds) *Questions of Cultural Identity*. pp. 3–17. London: Sage.

Hirsch, M. (1997) *Family Frames: Photography, Narrative and Postmemory*. Cambridge: Harvard University Press.

Hirsch, M. and Spitzer, L. (2006) What's wrong with this picture? *Journal of Modern Jewish Studies*. 5(2): 229–52.

Kuhn, A. (1995) *Family Secrets: Acts of Memory and Imagination*. London: Verso.

Ouellette, L. (1995) Camcorder Dos and Don'ts: Popular Discourses on Amateur Video and participatory television. *The Velvet Light Trap*. 36 (Fall): 33–44.

Rose, G. (2003) Family photographs and domestic spacings: a case study. *Transactions of the Institute of British Geographers*. 28(1): 5–18.

Sontag, S. (1977) *On Photography*. New York: Farrar, Strauss and Giroux.

Spence, J. (1995) *Cultural Sniping: The Art of Transgression*. London: Routledge.

Spence, J. and Holland, P. (eds) (1991) *Family Snaps: The Meanings of Domestic Photography*. London: Virago.

Squires, M. (1992) *The Camcorder Handbook: A Creative Course in the Skills of Home Video-Making, featuring Specially Developed Video Projects to help put Theory into Practice*. London: Headline Book Publishing.

Walkerdine, V. (1990) *Schoolgirl Fictions*. London: Verso.

Zimmerman, P. (1995) *Reel Families: Social History of Amateur Film*. Indianapolis: Indiana University Press.

5
Speaking Back? In Search of the Citizen Journalist

David Buckingham

> *Technology is shifting power away from the editors, the publishers, the establishment, the media élite ... now it's the people who are taking control.*
>
> Rupert Murdoch (2006)

'Citizen journalism' has become one of the feel-good slogans of the digital age. New technologies are believed to be giving ordinary people significant new opportunities to participate in media culture, and to represent their own perspectives and concerns; and in the process, they are seen to be revitalising democracy, and creating a more diverse and dynamic public sphere. Internet forums and discussion lists, weblogs (including video blogs), wikis, mobile cameras and message services, peer-to-peer networking and user-generated content sites – all are part of a new 'do-it-yourself' movement that is seen to be undermining and even directly challenging the power of big commercial media corporations. We can all be journalists now – or so the story goes.

In this chapter, I present a rather more sceptical analysis of this phenomenon. The term 'citizen journalism' is, in my view, generally ill defined and quite problematic. There is a significant gap between the rhetoric that surrounds this phenomenon and the reality. And the idea that such amateur journalism represents a fundamental challenge to the power of the dominant media is, I shall argue, very questionable. Looking at the ideas and practices of some amateur video 'journalists' will offer a rather more realistic sense of the possibilities and the limitations of this phenomenon.

Power to the people?

The notion of citizen journalism is one instance of a much broader set of rhetorical claims about the liberating and democratising potential of new media – claims that were aptly characterised many years ago by Richard Barbrook and Andy Cameron (1996) as 'the Californian ideology'. Contemporary advocates of this ideology such as Howard Rheingold and Dan Gillmor typically present the Internet as an inherently anti-hierarchical medium. Forms such as blogging are seen to offer an unprecedented degree of openness and accessibility, and thereby to generate new forms of social capital and community (Lasica, 2003). For some, the Internet represents the ultimate fulfilment of Jurgen Habermas's ideal of the public sphere, in which citizens spontaneously come together to engage in rational debate on the issues of the day; while others see it, in Al Gore's rather more capitalistic terms, as a 'free marketplace of ideas' (see Beers, 2006).

Dan Gillmor, founder of the Centre for Citizen Media in the United States, and himself a former professional journalist, is one of the most widely cited advocates of citizen journalism – or what he terms 'grassroots journalism, by the people, for the people' (Gillmor, 2006). According to Gillmor, technology – laptops, mobile phones, digital cameras and the Internet – is leading to a profound change in how people relate to news media. The gates that restrict citizens' access to the media have come down. News is no longer a lecture, but a conversation; and this 'open source journalism' is also leading to new forms of 'open source politics'. In using these new tools, 'the people formerly known as the audience' are developing new ways of communicating, and becoming better, more active citizens. Others argue that the editorial function hitherto confined to media elites has effectively been devolved to the individual reader or viewer (Rampton, 2007; Shirky, 2003). Some regard the Internet as an alternative, democratic 'mediasphere', which will fundamentally challenge the power of the oligarchy that controls 'Big Media' (Beers, 2006). Old, broadcast mass media are apparently being replaced by new, networked 'social media', which provide new forms of empowerment for the individual (Lilley, 2007).

Despite such claims about the subversive or challenging potential of citizen journalism, however, some of its most influential advocates have in fact been leading representatives of 'Big Media'. Endorsers quoted in the paperback edition of Gillmor's book, *We the Media*, include representatives from *Newsweek* and the BBC, as well as reviewers from mainstream newspapers and from *Fortune* magazine. One of the most influential advocates of this phenomenon is none other than Rupert Murdoch of News International, whose views about popular control of the media are quoted at the head of this chapter. Murdoch (2005, 2006) notes the decline in trust in newspapers, particularly among young people; and he appears to welcome the opportunities that the Internet offers for readers to generate their own content, and to engage in public dialogue. Representatives of the BBC have also been keen to celebrate the new forms of 'partnership' and 'collaboration' that are emerging in news journalism, particularly in the wake of the reporting of the London bombings on 7 July 2005 (e.g. Clifton, 2006; Sambrook, 2005). They argue that this approach is creating a renewed trust and 'intimacy' in the relationships between broadcasters and their audience. BBC Director-General Mark Thompson has even claimed that in an age of 'user-generated content', 'a publicly funded, monolithic broadcaster like the BBC looks increasingly irrelevant' (Thompson, 2006).

In practice, however, the claims made by such advocates of citizen journalism tend to be qualified by a recognition of the continuing need for professional journalism, and indeed for editorial control. Citizen journalism is more frequently seen as a complement to traditional journalism, rather than a replacement for it: it is part of a changed 'media ecosystem' rather than an alternative system in its own right. Indeed, as we shall see, there are distinct limits to the democratisation that is really being offered here.

Challenging the rhetoric

Despite the grand claims of such enthusiasts for citizen journalism, the concrete examples they cite are relatively limited both in number and in scope. Gillmor and others recycle a small number of well-known instances where bloggers have exposed political hypocrisy or corruption (as in the outrage that followed racist remarks by US Senator Trent Lott in 2002, and eventually led to his resignation as Majority Leader). Others cite the use of new media in the (failed) presidential bid of candidate Howard Dean in 2004 (see Trippi, 2004). In many instances, however, the examples cited could more accurately be described as 'witness journalism' rather than 'citizen journalism' – images captured in New York on 9/11 or in New Orleans in the wake of Hurricane Katrina, or (in the UK) of the tube bombings of 7/7, or the spectacular explosion of the Buncefield oil depot in Hertfordshire in 2005. As Samantha Henig (2005) points out, this kind of 'participatory journalism' is nothing new – there are clear precedents for the use of amateur footage in instances like Abraham Zapruder's film of the Kennedy assassination, or the video of Rodney King being beaten by the Los Angeles police. Furthermore, as she suggests, such material cannot really be described as 'reporting' or 'journalism', not least because it is typically embedded in reports produced and authored by professional journalists.

Aside from the limitations of citizen journalism in practice, there are several broader reasons for questioning the celebratory account of these developments. The undermining or devolution of the editorial function – if indeed it is occurring – could well be seen to generate significant problems in terms of the trustworthiness and credibility of news media. Critics of the 'blogosphere' argue that it is little more than a digital Tower of Babel – a chaotic 'dialogue of the deaf', in which the dominant voices are those of the 'flamers' and the 'ranters'. While new blogs are undoubtedly being generated at a remarkable rate, they are also being abandoned with similar speed (Bolton, 2007). As Nguyen (2006) points out, the blogosphere and other participatory platforms are generally dominated by socio-economic elites. It has also been suggested that very little of this user-generated content is actually read: most people appear to rely on established 'news brands' such as the BBC and CNN, and very few have the time or inclination to proactively seek out a range of sources.

For political activists, there is a danger that such material is merely preaching to the converted; and it is argued that if the aim is to produce broader social change, there is a continuing need for exposure in the mainstream media. Trish Bolton (2007) strongly challenges what she sees as the 'utopian' notion that online alternative journalism is likely to undermine the dominance of mainstream news media. She argues that access to such opportunities is still restricted by inequalities in literacy and cultural capital, and that the much-vaunted interactivity of online forums is decidedly limited. She suggests that in any case, the Internet is rapidly becoming a commercial medium, in which survival will depend on forms of advertising and promotion. Bolton notes that in practice many leading 'alternative' sites have abandoned open-access policies, not least because readers continue to need gatekeepers or editors whom they can trust to filter and interpret the mass of information.

This latter point is also a key concern for Andrew Keen (2007), whose criticisms of the 'cult of the amateur' were briefly addressed in Chapter 2. According to Keen, 'citizen journalism' is merely a euphemism for 'journalism by nonjournalists'. He accuses citizen journalists of offering up 'opinion as fact, rumour as reportage, and innuendo as information' (37). Unencumbered by ethical constraints, or a commitment to fairness and accuracy, or indeed any professional training, such individuals are fundamentally unaccountable either to government or to their readers. Far from revitalising democracy, the rise of blogging and citizen journalism could be seen as merely another symptom of a culture of individual narcissism – or perhaps exhibitionism.

Citizen journalism and big media

Keen's criticisms are essentially conservative, in the sense that they appear to resist any deviation from the current status quo in journalism. Nevertheless, his account clearly shows that the rise of participatory media is having destabilising effects on the basic business model of newspapers in particular. Advocates of citizen journalism such as Dan Gillmor explicitly acknowledge this, although the basis of any alternative business model remains unclear. Gillmor somewhat hedges around the failure of his own citizen journalism initiative, Bayosphere, although he does admit that the business model for citizen journalism is somewhat 'murky' (Gillmor, 2006: xvi).[1] One potentially fruitful approach here is that of 'hyperlocal' media, which has arisen partly in response to the steady decline in circulation of local newspapers, and is premised on taking locally based advertising. However, research suggests that the business model here is equally precarious, and there is little evidence of long-term sustainability. Even neighbourhood sites of this kind attract relatively few active contributors; and there is very little content on such sites that would be generally considered as 'journalism' (Boyles, 2006; Shaffer, 2007). (One relatively successful example of such an approach will be considered later in this chapter.)

Even so, the apparent enthusiasm of many in the media industries for this apparently challenging development needs some explanation. On the one hand, corporate or commercial interests have clearly become more significant in news journalism in recent years; and this has led to cuts in staff and resources, and a restructuring and casualisation of employment (Davies, 2008). At the same time, the advent of 24-hour 'rolling' news has meant a significant increase in the amount of screen time that needs to be filled; and many news organisations have also felt bound to develop their online presence, without necessarily having additional resources with which to do so. Meanwhile, there is evidence of growing public distrust of mainstream news media (Cappella and Jamieson, 1996; Nguyen, 2006) – a phenomenon that, as we have seen, Rupert Murdoch himself has acknowledged. In this context, 'citizen journalism' would seem to be an ideal means for news corporations to generate free content with reduced professional staff, while at the same time appearing to be empowering 'ordinary people'. In a casualised and highly competitive industry, there is likely to be no shortage of aspirant reporters who might well regard this as a useful means of building their portfolios. What might at first sight appear to be a form of democratisation could equally be interpreted as a way of reducing costs and simultaneously creating good public relations.

Gaining access

Even so, the opportunities for individual citizen journalists to gain access to mainstream media outlets are still very restricted and tightly controlled. As I have noted, professional journalists are often keen to proclaim the possibilities for 'partnership' with their citizenly counterparts, but in practice this partnership seems much less than equal.

In the UK, discussions of citizen journalism took off in the wake of the 7/7 bombings: the BBC reportedly received over 20,000 emails, 3000 texts, 1000 photographs and 20 mobile phone videos relating to the events, and its evening news broadcast used some of the latter footage. The Buncefield explosion later that year generated a similar flurry of material, with people apparently queuing at the BBC's news truck to deliver images and video footage (Clifton, 2006; Douglas, 2006a, b). The BBC subsequently established a 'User Generated Content Hub' with six staff to handle such material, verifying and checking sources (Eltringham, 2006). Similar initiatives have been established by other broadcasters: CNN, for example, has run its iReport service since 2006, while the news division of Independent Television (ITV) (the leading UK commercial terrestrial company) provides Uploaded, a video blog site for 'citizen correspondents'. Scoopt is an agency for citizen journalists who wish to sell their material to mainstream news outlets (it keeps 40% of the publisher's payment); and the mobile phone company Nokia has sponsored the UK Citizen Journalism Awards, run by the trade paper *Press Gazette*.

In practice, however, the nature of this material remains very limited. Much of it is the work of what the UK National Union of Journalists describes as 'witness contributors' (thereby, of course, excluding them from the honorific title of 'journalist'). For example, the winners of the 2006 Citizen Journalism Awards included footage of 7/7 and the Buncefield fire, while other featured entries covered fires and lightning strikes, extreme weather, natural disasters, armed police apprehending suspects and paparazzi-type images of celebrities.[2] A similar emphasis is apparent on other industry websites. Reuters' YouWitness site, run in collaboration with Yahoo, typically features footage of floods, plane crashes, explosions and firefighting, along with sequences of alligators or moose at large in suburban gardens.[3] The Scoopt agency also seems to focus on such material: as the website notes, 'the best, most valuable photos are those that capture a completely unexpected but sensational event, especially if the professional media are either not present or looking the other way'.[4] Footage of such 'off diary' events may ultimately find its way into mainstream broadcasting, but in practice it will be heavily packaged and edited, with voice-over commentary from professional journalists, and is unlikely to include any element of actual reporting on the part of those who have contributed it. Such contributions are likely to be one-offs, and it is certainly doubtful whether the majority of people who submit such material to the BBC or CNN would actually see themselves as 'journalists' in the first place. Indeed, some critics have termed such people 'citizen paparazzi', suggesting that events such as the London bombings led to growing numbers of people armed with camera phones vying with each other to capture the most gruesome images of the victims (Glaser, 2005).

The other dominant form on industry websites is that of the personal video blog, generally in the form of a 'talking head' speaking direct to camera. For example, ITV's Uploaded presents short vlogs on topical issues;[5] although like the BBC's 'Have Your Say' site, which is based around written submissions, it tends to be dominated by knee-jerk (and frequently reactionary) responses to events. CNN combines the two approaches, with a selection of fires, extreme weather and eccentricities of the natural world alongside viewers' commentaries on the day's news: a very short selection of these items is then packaged into a brief compilation on the main channel.[6] In this latter form, the fundamental continuity between the video blog and the time-honoured TV format of the 'vox pop' is readily apparent.

At present, it is hard to avoid the impression that, despite a rhetorical enthusiasm for the idea of citizen journalism, the broadcasters' actual commitment to it is very limited. Of course, this may partly be for very good reasons. As Peter Horrocks, the head of BBC Newsroom, has noted, the Corporation receives an increasing amount of user-generated material, but it leads to some difficult editorial dilemmas. While the use of such material might enable the broadcasters to reflect a wider range of views within society, there is a danger that its agenda can be hijacked by unrepresentative minority views: questions about journalistic ethics, taste and confidentiality – not to mention laws relating to libel and 'hate speech' – do not simply disappear when 'citizens' take charge

(Horrocks, 2008). In this situation, organisations such as the BBC are understandably reluctant to cede editorial control to contributors.

However, more apparently open public sites seem to be dominated by much the same kind of content. LiveLeak, whose strap-line claims that it is 'redefining the media', appears to focus primarily on violence, freaks of nature and spectacular events: videos of car chases and crashes, robberies, accidents and dangerous stunts sit alongside vast amounts of raw footage of detonations and bombing missions filmed by soldiers in Iraq and Afghanistan – footage that appears to hold a particular fascination for supporters of the invasion of those countries, who tend to dominate the accompanying forums.[7] NowPublic, a Canadian site that defines itself as a 'participatory news network which mobilises an army of reporters to cover the events that define our world', includes some videos produced by independent activist groups but is mainly dominated by items from the BBC, CNN, Channel 4 and Euronews, alongside out-takes from the *Big Brother* house, advertisements, film trailers and music videos.[8]

Of course, this all begs the question of what we define as citizen journalism in the first place. My interest here is in interrogating the claim that 'ordinary people' are somehow becoming journalists as a result of their access to technology (and specifically video technology). As such, I would want to distinguish between 'citizen journalism' and more organised, collective or institutionalised forms. Obviously, there is a long tradition of 'alternative media', a term that generally refers to the work of organised political groups: most of these are anarchist or left-wing in orientation, although there are also some on the political right (see Atton, 2001, 2004). Curated sites such as Ourmedia, Alternative Channel TV, the Open Media Network and the various Indymedia sites, as well as the 'non-profit' channels on YouTube, obviously contain a considerable amount of such non-mainstream media. However, much of this is produced by established activist, charitable or political groups: there seems to be very little material that is produced spontaneously by individual 'citizen journalists'.

The broadcasters' apparent enthusiasm for the idea of 'user-generated content' has also led to some important community outreach projects. The BBC's long-running Video Nation project is discussed in Chapter 8 of this book; and its Digital Storytelling projects, which are based on a model first developed by the Center for Digital Storytelling in California, have been widely influential internationally (see Burgess, 2007; Thumim, 2006). The BBC's local or regional sites also include some user-generated content (and it is worth noting here that the BBC generally avoids the use of the term 'citizen journalism'). BBC London Local, for example, contains several such contributions, some of which are very powerful and quite formally innovative. While most are drawn from funded workshop projects in which media artists or professionals have worked in schools, museums or community arts settings, some are 'authored pieces', produced from the collaboration between individual local people and BBC staff.[9] However, none of the material on the site can be considered to be 'pure' citizen journalism, in the sense that it emerged spontaneously and without any intervention or involvement in production on the part of the BBC. The BBC maintains editorial control of the site, and material is selected on the grounds of quality, although the advantage for contributors is that the BBC 'brand' confers a degree of legitimacy, and the site itself guarantees greater exposure than would generally be the case with an open-access site like YouTube. Even so, people's involvement in such projects is typically short term and one-off; and as with the BBC's Video Nation project Jo Henderson describes in Chapter 8, citizen journalism projects run by mainstream broadcasting institutions are bound to involve a compromise between individuals' interests and institutional imperatives.

By contrast, my interest here is in pursuing the claim that 'ordinary' individuals are now able to create their own journalism, outside such institutionalised settings. In fact, when we look beyond established 'indymedia' groups, organised workshops or educational projects, and the efforts of aspiring or semi-professional journalists, it is hard to locate actual instances of citizen journalism, particularly those involving the use of video. My requests to relevant BBC personnel for specific examples were met with suggestions that I should seek out footage of 7/7, Buncefield or the Asian tsunami – in other words, instances of 'witness journalism'. Identifying UK citizen journalists (and specifically those who are using video) proved extremely difficult. Nevertheless, in the following sections of this chapter, I present three descriptive case studies representing different forms of citizen journalism – although significantly, all three of the individuals concerned were somewhat wary about applying this term to themselves. In each case, my account is based on an analysis of productions and surrounding online commentary, as well as telephone or email interviews.

Vloggers, trolls and ranters

Aside from witness journalism, the most prevalent form of citizen journalism using video is that of the video blog, or vlog. Vlogs can, of course, address a range of topics, including intimate personal confessions – in which case they come closer to the video diaries discussed by Jo Henderson (Chapter 8). By contrast, the material considered here addresses social and political issues, and has its counterpart in the work of professional newspaper columnists, pundits or 'op-ed' writers. It typically takes the form of a commentary on news events covered by mainstream media, rather than news reporting per se. Vlogs require little more technical skill or specialist equipment than written blogs: many are recorded using built-in webcams, and they rarely involve editing. They generally last between two and five minutes, and can easily be uploaded to all-purpose sites such as YouTube or LiveVideo, or to sites specialising in social and political affairs such as LiveLeak. As I have noted, the leading UK commercial terrestrial channel ITV also currently hosts vlogs on its user-generated site Uploaded. Indeed, some vloggers argue that the use of video is much less time consuming and requires less preparation than written blogs – although written bloggers are sometimes rather contemptuous of vlogs for this reason. Yet in either medium, it is not necessary for bloggers to undertake their own research or check facts, as professional journalists are expected to do: the premium is on opinions, and – certainly in the case of video blogs – it would seem that the more strongly held and forcefully expressed such opinions are, the more likely they are to attract attention.

The world of political vlogs is certainly a long way from the communicative rationality of Habermas's idealised public sphere. While some vloggers prioritise humour, the most frequent approach is one of confrontational rhetoric. The next video is only a mouse-click away; and so vloggers often seem to resort to shock tactics in an effort to capture the viewer's attention. On sites like YouTube, vloggers are plagued by 'trolls', who respond to their work with deliberately inflammatory and abusive comments. The average readership for a written blog is frequently reputed to be around fifteen people; and while the figures for video may be higher, even the most popular and prolific vloggers get little more than a few thousand. Two of the most highly rated vloggers on YouTube, Kenrg and Warren26peace (the subject of the following case study), tend to peak at around 5000 views, while only rare celebrities such as the atheist commentator and self-described comedian, Pat Condell, regularly achieve views in the tens or, occasionally, hundreds of thousands.

Philip Warren, a 32-year-old mixed race British expatriate living in Canada, has achieved considerable notoriety for his vlogs, which began in 2006. As 'Warren25smash' and subsequently 'Warren26peace', he has posted around 200 videos, and his work has been briefly covered on MTV and in the press. His videos frequently attract a great number of written comments and several video responses. In 2007, he was the subject of a petition to get him ejected from YouTube, and of a 'Save Warren25 Campaign'. Warren's politics are consistently left-wing: his recurrent theme is opposition to US foreign policy (particularly the war in Iraq), although he has also vlogged on issues such as Zionism, illegal immigration, police harassment, privatisation, public health care, Scientology, homophobia and censorship. Warren's monologues are delivered direct to camera from what appears to be his living room. He does not seem to rely on cue cards or written prompts, and rarely hesitates or pauses. In an email interview which I conducted in July 2007, he described how he prepared stories using online news services, but felt that too much preparation would 'inhibit the expression of just what I think … keeping it as raw as possible seems to work for me the most effectively'.

The titles of some of his videos give a flavour of Warren's style: 'Iran is not a pussy America gets to fuck', 'Tom Cruise + Scientology = cunts' and 'Fuck the Zionist regime of Israel' being notable examples. The vlogs often rise to a crescendo of angry exhortation, although Warren rarely seems at risk of losing self-control. In our interview, he used the term 'rant' to describe his style, suggesting that he took particular inspiration from 'heavy music like rock and metal … loud performers with a simple and unyielding message like Rage Against the Machine and Soulfly'. As the above titles imply, cursing is a particular speciality; and this in itself has attracted much negative (and some positive) comment, including several artful YouTube mashups consisting entirely of Warren's most profane moments. There is certainly a misogynistic dimension here – most disturbingly in a video entitled 'Hillary Clinton – evil cun?' (*sic*), which dissents from the former First Lady's stance on the war in Iraq – although in general cursing seems to be valued primarily for its shock value.

Responses to Warren's vlogs are often equally vehement. While there is a good deal of positive feedback, much of the written commentary is infantile and abusive, accusing Warren of being 'retarded' and a 'dumb ass' or of participating in 'gay bumsex'. As a British citizen attacking US foreign policy, Warren has been routinely accused of anti-Americanism and of abusing US troops; and he has been a frequent target for right-wing vloggers on these grounds. Numerous US vloggers have challenged his right to comment on such matters, accusing him of being 'a racist fucking cunt' or alternatively a member of the 'Jihadi liberal alliance'.

One persistent adversary is 'Shrekhead', a supporter of the fascist British National Party who frequently appears in his vlogs wearing an England football shirt and ranting against Muslims, 'multiculturalism' and the European Union – although Warren's responses (as in the video 'Shrek you talk so much shit you make the sewers overflow') are not exactly models of reasoned political argument either. Some of the response to Warren has been a little more inventive, however, including some clever mashups and a 1950s-style fan video by 'Carole Morgan', whose flirtatious overtures to Warren were rebuffed, leaving her to conclude that he was merely a 'phoney' and a 'wanker'.

Warren's '25smash' account was closed by YouTube in late 2007, although (at least according to him) this was part of a general shake-up in response to charges of copyright violation threatened by the major US company Viacom, rather than straightforward censorship. Although he subsequently re-emerged on YouTube as 'Warren26peace', Warren has since diversified his output to other sites, most notably LiveLeak. In an early 2008 video 'You thought YouTube didn't suck?', he not only accuses the site of cutting videos and fixing statistics but also suggests that he has moved to other sites in an attempt to avoid the 'shitbrains' who have been attacking him. In our interview, Warren argued that vlogging offered a means of instant political protest that was at least safer than demonstrating outside Parliament and running the risk of being 'knocked unconscious by a policeman who feels threatened by my suntan'. Interestingly, while he was generally sanguine about what he called 'the movement towards net based entertainment and multiple nodes of information', he was careful to draw the line between his own work and 'citizen journalism' in a manner that is not too far removed from the criticisms of Andrew Keen (2007), discussed above:

> Cit Journalism sounds like a bubble that's going to burst and leave us with mass communication with no direct news sources any more able to corroborate a story but harder to hear about them and less centralised relay points. I think vlogging usurping the media is a nice idea but could have drastic consequences.

User-generated content

My second case study probably comes closer to the popular concept of the 'citizen journalist' – although it should be emphasised that he was one of very few such individuals that I was able to locate, despite a considerable amount of searching. Shola Ogunlokun is a father of four children, and is in his early 40s. Born and brought up in Nigeria, he has lived in London for 15 years. He works as a professional driving instructor, and video-making is one of his hobbies. Several of his videos can be found on the UK Current TV site, and some have also been shown on the Current channel, which is broadcast on Sky satellite in the UK. (Current TV, established by Al Gore and businessman Joel Hyatt, is known for its focus on the broadcasting of user-generated content.) Some are also posted on video-sharing sites such as YouTube and Revver. Shola maintains several websites, including one that details his experiences as a commuter on London's Northern Line and another reporting on his bid to fly a hang-glider around Britain.[10] Most of his videos posted on YouTube are short instructional films offering advice for trainee drivers, and are credited to UK Automobile Association Driving Instructor (UKADI), his online driving school.

Shola's interest in video-making originally grew out of his involvement in photography, and has now largely superseded it. He owns two video cameras, and has access to a third; and he claims to carry the smallest of these, a palm-sized model, with him most of the time. One of his websites contains some short films on particular cameras and other 'gadgets', suggesting that he is partly interested in technology for its own sake.[11] He edits his videos on standard domestic equipment, using Adobe Premiere and Avid. He initially learnt about video-making via a class held at his church (the tutor had worked for the BBC), and subsequently from Internet forums and websites. In the case of Current TV, he has been paid for videos which are selected for broadcast, although otherwise he defines this as an essentially 'amateur' activity.

Shola's videos are not simply 'witness journalism': as he put it, 'I tend to do a bit of research and go out of my way to actually look for the story, not just happen to be there when it happens.'[12] Those currently hosted on the Current site and on YouTube cover a wide range of topics. Some are close to local TV news: 'The London Tornado' focuses on the after-effects of a freak tornado that hit a North London street in 2006, while 'Wembley Stadium' features extensive vox pops of local residents' views about the building of the new football stadium. Some are drawn from Shola's holiday in Nigeria in 2007, including 'Corrupt Airport Officials?', which discusses the bribery of airport customs staff, and 'Nigeria's Fuel Crisis', which reports on the national shortage of fuel, despite Nigeria's position as a major oil exporter. Others have a more personal focus, including videos of Shola's hang-gliding activities, and 'Epic African Bike Ride', which describes an eventful 300-km bicycle ride he took as a teenager in Nigeria. Finally, some of the longer videos address broader social issues: 'Real Nappies' considers the alternatives to disposable nappies, 'An African's Voice' focuses on a protest made by an African organisation in London against the official commemoration of the ending of slavery and 'I'm a Survivor' explores the difficulties encountered by leukaemia sufferers from black, mixed race and Asian backgrounds attempting to find a matching bone marrow donor.

In an interview, Shola suggested that much of the impetus behind his work had arisen from the need to get 'exposure' or 'publicity' for particular issues or concerns: 'sharing with other people' was a key benefit of the Internet in particular. This was the case with his hang-gliding videos, which had first led him to make contact with Current TV; but, it was also evident with the videos on the abolition of slavery and on leukaemia, where specific issues affecting the black community were raised. In the former case, for example, he spoke about wanting to communicate specifically with 'younger people from the African-Caribbean audience', and helping them to be 'aware of history', while the leukaemia video was partly designed to help the African Caribbean Leukaemia Trust in their efforts to recruit more young black donors. By contrast, he said that the tornado story was probably a 'bad example' of his work: it was intended to inform the US viewers of Current TV about life in London, but otherwise it was not very different from 'normal' local news.

Interestingly, Shola initially refused my description of him as a 'citizen journalist':

> [T]hat word seems to be around a lot. And I don't know, there seemed to be an avid need for the so-called citizen journalists to actually get their work recognised, I mean, actually get their work out there … I don't know if I'm a citizen journalist or not. But I think that that term was probably coined by the mainstream media, to kind of differentiate them[selves] from people who are telling stories but are not paid to do it, or something like that. I don't know.

Like Warren, Shola claimed not to be interested in making a career as a journalist. Nevertheless, like Robert Stebbins' serious amateurs (see Chapter 2), he has a form of 'leisure career', which involves working in quite a focused and deliberate way to improve what he is doing. Perhaps more significantly, he has a longer-term commitment to reporting on real-life issues that concern him, and in communicating with an audience. To this extent, he did see citizen journalism as a means of drawing attention to issues that might not be addressed in the main-stream media:

> [I]f, for example, they would allow somebody like me to find a story that I think affects our community, and have the opportunity to actually tell it, without them censoring it, then that is what I would think is closest to citizen journalism … Because a lot of the time, to be honest, news … they carry it because it's going to make them more popular and therefore they make money.

Hyperlocal TV

Felixstowe TV (FTV), Britain's first web-based TV station, exemplifies the trend towards 'hyperlocal' or 'microjournalism' briefly mentioned above.[13] Felixstowe is a small town of around 25,000–30,000 inhabitants on the Suffolk coast in the south east of England: once a fashionable resort in the late Victorian age, it is now home to the UK's largest container port. FTV was founded in 2004 by Chris Gosling, a semi-retired PR consultant and freelance journalist. It was taken over in 2006 by Giles Meehan and David Jennings, two local residents who had worked with Chris. (Prior to FTV, Chris Gosling had been responsible for 'amdram', a leading UK site for those involved in amateur dramatics; and he has since become somewhat of an entrepreneur in the small-scale TV market, running The Caravan Channel and UK Boating TV, two web-based leisure stations that also have a broadcast window on Sky TV's Information Channel.[14]) Over the past few years, around 15 to 20 short video reports, averaging around 4–5 minutes, have been posted on the site each month, in addition to a weekly news round-up. As of early 2008, there were around 400 videos in the archive, and the site was receiving around 75,000 unique visits per month, representing almost half a million page or video 'hits'.

FTV is the main venture of a company, Really Local TV LLP, a limited liability partnership which is wholly owned by Giles and David: the company's website presents its work as 'part of the hyper-local community broadband TV revolution'. The aim is to serve the community of Felixstowe and its surrounding villages, as well as maintaining contact with 'expatriates' who have moved away from the area (interview-based items with such people form one running strand of its programming). Most of the video reports are produced by Giles and David, albeit sometimes in response to viewers' suggestions. A few are authored by, or in collaboration with, local residents, including some that campaign for or against planning decisions by the borough council. The website also incorporates forums for viewers' responses and online debates on local issues, alongside information about community events and a local business directory. Giles and David pride themselves on being able to respond to local news events much more quickly than national or regional TV stations.

The content of video items on the site largely reflects the staple topics of local journalism: they cover sports, local education services, charity fundraising events, local planning and renovation works, carnivals, fetes, festivals and dramatic or musical performances. Some stories have a more political edge, covering decisions made by the borough council, or the actions of local industry. In January 2008, for example, the station covered campaigns against the closing of a local convalescent home, events for Holocaust Memorial Day at a local school, and disputes over local traffic and planning regulations.

Giles and David are essentially self-taught video-makers, with no formal training: Giles had a career as a structural engineer, while David was formerly a musician and music teacher. Giles said that he had learnt largely through 'trial and error', watching broadcast news, and reflecting critically on his own work. The videos are produced on good-quality domestic or 'prosumer' equipment. Giles and David are aware of the need to produce video specifically for the medium of the web; and they are gradually becoming more ambitious, for example, in terms of using wide screen, captions and graphics, adding voice-overs and considering the overall narrative shape of an item. Equally, some productions remain very simple – a talking head interview or a sequence of images with captions may be all that is required for certain stories. The videos may not be formally very adventurous, but within the constraints of technology and resources, they are generally of very high quality.

For its founder and its current owners, FTV represents a new form of community-based media. Chris Gosling has argued that this kind of local TV is providing a unique service in a context in which commercial newspapers and television stations (and even the BBC) are increasingly being consolidated into operations that work on a regional, rather than a local, level (quoted in Kiss, 2006). In a posting on the FTV forum, Giles discussed the 'semi-anonymous character' of some Internet communities, and argued that services like FTV could 'bring us back to our real, local community again'. If there is a bias here, it tends to favour local residents and campaigning groups rather than centralised planners or businesses. Yet while there is obviously a strong identification with the local community, Giles also spoke of the need to represent the town fairly, and to show 'the good and the bad'.

However, FTV is not primarily a platform for 'grassroots' citizen journalism. In practice, relatively few stories are originated or submitted by viewers; and here Giles and David exercise an editorial function, checking the content with the sources and key authorities. Like the other case studies in this chapter, Giles was wary of the term 'citizen journalism', and clearly saw himself more as a semi-professional. Having the 'clout' of professional journalists representing a known organisation made it easier for them to speak to council officials, local politicians or representatives of businesses; and in the case of major local stories, it also meant that they would be taken seriously by professional competitors from larger organisations. In this respect, he argued, the station was able to combine 'the best of both worlds' – those of the amateur or citizen journalist and of the professional.

How financially viable is this kind of 'hyperlocal' initiative? FTV is principally funded through sponsorship and advertising: rolling banner ads on the site at the time of this research were primarily for small independent local businesses. This income is supplemented by occasional productions of promotional videos for local companies. It pays part-time salaries for Giles and David, the only two employees; and the station also uses volunteers, for example, as camera operators or as the weekly news presenter. The company does not generate profit as such, and Giles and David tend to work longer hours than those for which they are formally paid – although in this respect, the station is similar to many small start-up businesses.

Despite the apparent interest in such initiatives (the station has received quite widespread coverage in mainstream media, both nationally and internationally, and I was not the first researcher to contact them), there have been few successful or lasting examples of hyperlocal stations, at least in the UK. In an interview, Giles said that he had been expecting for some years that local web TV would eventually 'take off', but that there were still only two other such stations to his knowledge (in Kent and South Wiltshire). Local newspapers have attempted to use video in this way – for example, Archant, a leading regional newspaper publisher, which publishes Suffolk's *East Anglian Daily Times*, has included some video material on its website. However, the additional revenue generated from advertising around such material does not necessarily cover the costs of producing it, and such services are not expanding particularly rapidly at present. The longer-term viability of such locally focused services is thus far from clear: while the technology itself continues to fall in price, it will remain difficult to ensure a productive balance between specialist journalistic skills and practices, and commitment to the local community and to 'grassroots' participation.

Conclusion

It would be tempting to conclude this chapter by proposing that 'citizen journalism' is little more than a myth – albeit one largely perpetuated by the mainstream media industries for their own purposes. Jessica Ainley (2007) suggests that the term fundamentally misrepresents the motivations and intentions of people who are using such new media tools. She argues that the term 'citizen' mistakenly frames participants as having political motivations, while the term 'journalist' implies that they are gathering material with the primary intention of reporting news. Neither, she asserts, is generally the case. The notion of 'citizen journalism' represents a rather vainglorious attempt to appropriate the traditional mission of journalism – that of holding government to account, questioning policy, and reporting on civic functions and activities – to describe a practice that is fundamentally different in its methods and motivations.

Certainly, there seems to be a great deal more talk about citizen journalism than examples of it in practice, particularly when we focus on the medium of video. As I have suggested, espousing the rhetoric of citizen journalism enables the mainstream media industries to take on a superficial appearance of democratisation, while simultaneously reducing costs. Yet ultimately, the question here is about what *counts* as 'journalism'. Clearly, journalism is about more than reporting news – and in any case, what qualifies as 'news' depends very much on the person receiving it. 'Hyperlocal' initiatives and personal vlogs – however trivial or superficial they may appear to some – are no less examples of journalism than the work of Pulitzer Prize winners. Journalism in any medium is not necessarily always to be judged in terms of its rather grandiose sense of its own mission.

Furthermore, the limited nature of current citizen journalism should not necessarily be taken as evidence that it is never going to become more widespread. Even so, there are reasons for caution on this point. Access to technology is steadily becoming much less of an issue, although access to skills – in terms of researching and writing stories, interviewing and presenting, filming and editing – is much less evenly distributed. Editing in particular is a key skill that needs to be learned over time: while the mastery of a given software package is fairly easily acquired, the ability to make a coherent statement or construct a narrative in moving images generally requires a much more sustained process of learning.

Perhaps the most significant obstacles, however, are to do with the social context, and the motivation and purpose of such activity. In the case of video in particular, anything beyond simple blogging to camera requires a considerable investment of time, both in order to acquire the relevant skills and to create products that will be considered watchable, especially given the enormous range of competing material that is now vying for attention. It is hard to imagine why individuals would want to devote time, effort and money to such an activity if they are unlikely to reach a significant audience (which is not necessarily the same as a large one). The obvious danger is that such activities will be confined to the 'usual suspects' – to those who already possess the resources necessary to make their voices heard; and as such, the claim that citizen journalism represents a radical shift in the balance of media power seems rather less than plausible.

In these respects, the three case studies I have presented here are unusual, particularly in terms of the fact that they involve long-term engagement, rather than short-term or one-off productions. Much of the citizen journalism I have encountered in conducting research for this chapter is produced by people who are aspiring to become professional journalists or media producers. Other examples are produced as an offshoot of another activity, for example, as a means of sharing one's personal concerns or enthusiasms, or of campaigning for social change (for example, in the policies of local government). Once such aims are achieved, the producers will typically move on to other activities, or back to their primary interest. Such productions might well be seen as examples of citizen journalism; but their producers probably would not regard themselves as citizen journalists, or as somehow investing in this as a fundamental dimension of their identity. The people I have discussed in this chapter are different in this respect, even if they feel ambivalent about the term itself: Shola, in particular, is clearly motivated by his personal interest in the issues he covers in his videos, but the activity of making them, and of disseminating them to a wider audience, also constitutes a major source of motivation in its own right. While citizen journalism may become a more widespread practice over time, the 'pure' form of the individual citizen journalist, with a sustained commitment to reporting and commenting upon social issues, is likely to remain a comparative rarity.

Notes

1. Backfence, the company that bought out Bayosphere, itself also folded up in 2007.
2. http://www.citizenjournalismawards.com/ All web material gathered for this chapter was accessed between July 2007 and March 2008.
3. www.reuters.com/youwitness
4. www.scoopt.com
5. http://www.itv.com/News/uploadedarchive/default.html At the time of writing (March 2008), this selection had not been updated for some time, and it is not clear whether this service is continuing.
6. http://edition.cnn.com/exchange/
7. http://www.liveleak.com/
8. http://www.nowpublic.com/
9. http://www.bbc.co.uk/london/london_local/ I'd like to thank Dekan Apajee and Penny Wrout for talking with me about their work, and sharing their views on citizen journalism generally.
10. See shola.ogunlokun.com, www.meetbritain.org.uk and www.northern-line. blogspot.com
11. See www.ogunlokun.com
12. All quotations are taken from a telephone interview conducted in October 2007.
13. The material in this section is drawn from the FTV website (www.felixstowetv. co.uk) and associated sites, an analysis of videos accessed via the site archive, and phone and email interviews with Giles Meehan. This research was conducted in January and February 2008.
14. Gosling's company is called Serious Leisure TV, which may or may not be a reference to the work of Robert Stebbins, discussed in Chapter 2.

References

Ainlay, J. (2007) '"Citizen journalism" is full of incorrect assumptions'. *UK Press Gazette*. 5th October. http://www.pressgazette.co.uk/story.asp?storycode=39444 accessed March 2008.

Atton, C. (2001) *Alternative Media*. London: Sage.

Atton, C. (2004) *An Alternative Internet*. Edinburgh: Edinburgh University Press.

Barbrook, R. and Cameron, A. (1996) 'The Californian ideology' at http:// www.hrc.wmin.ac.uk/theory-californianideology.html accessed September 2006.

Beers, D. (2006) 'The public sphere and online, independent news journalism'. *Canadian Journal of Education*. 29(1): 109–30.

Bolton, T. (2007) 'News on the net: a critical analysis of the potential of online alternative journalism to challenge the dominance of mainstream news media'. *SCAN: Journal of Arts Media Culture*. http://www.scan.net.au/scan/ journal/display.php?journal_id=71 accessed October 2007.

Boyles, J. (2006) Grassroots Journalism in your own Backyard: How Citizen Reporters Build Hyperlocal Communities. MA Thesis. School of Journalism, West Virginia University, Morgantown.

Burgess, J. (2007) Vernacular Creativity and New Media. PhD Thesis. Queensland University of Technology.

Cappella, J. and Jamieson, K. H. (1996) 'News frames, political cynicism, and media cynicism'. *Annals of the American Academy of Political and Social Science.* 456: 71–84.

Clifton, P. (2006) 'Citizen journalism and its impact on news journalism'. Speech at Swiss Media School, Luzern. www.maz.ch/aktuell/news/242_Clifton_speech. pdf accessed October 2007.

Davies, N. (2008) *Flat Earth News.* London: Chatto and Windus.

Douglas, T. (2006a) '"Citizen journalism" moving mainstream'. *BBC News Online.* 25th January.

Douglas, T. (2006b) 'How 7/7 "democratised" the media'. *BBC News Online.* 4 July.

Eltringham, M. (2006) 'Citizen journalists challenge BBC'. *BBC News Online.* http://news.bbc.co.uk/newswatch/ifs/hi/newsid_4900000/newsid_ 4900400/4900444.stm accessed January 2008.

Gillmor, D. (2006) *We the Media: Grassroots Journalism By the People For the People.* Sebastopol, CA: O'Reilly.

Glaser, M. (2005) 'Did London bombings turn citizen journalists into citizen paparazzi?' *Online Journalism Review.* 12th July. www.ojr.org/ojr/stories/ 050712glaser accessed January 2008.

Henig, S. (2005) 'Citizens, participants and reporters'. *CJR Daily.* 8th July. www. cjr.org/politics/citizens_participants_and_repo.php accessed October 2007.

Horrocks, P. (2008) 'The value of citizen journalism'. 7th January. http:// www.bbc.co.uk/blogs/theeditors/2008/01/value_of_citizen_journalism.html accessed January 2008.

Keen, A. (2007) *The Cult of the Amateur.* London: Nicholas Brealey.

Kiss, J. (2006) 'Trad media turns on to broadband TV'. *Online Journalism News.* 19.01.06. http://www.journalism.co.uk/5/articles/51680.php accessed January 2008.

Lasica, J. D. (2003) 'Blogs and journalism need each other'. *Nieman Reports.* Fall, 57(3): 70–4.

Lilley, A. (2007) 'The me in media: participation, interactivity and the rise of the people formerly known as the audience'. Lecture at the Royal Television Society, London, September. www.magiclantern.co.uk/TheMeinMedia.pdf accessed October 2007.

Murdoch, R. (2005) Speech to the American Society of Newspaper editors. 13th April. http://www.newscorp.com/news/news_247.html accessed October 2007.

Murdoch, R. (2006) 'His space', by Spencer Reiss, interview in *Wired* 14:07. www. wired.com/wired/archive/14.07/murdoch.html accessed April 2007.

Nguyen, A. (2006) 'Journalism in the wake of participatory publishing'. *Australian Journalism Review.* 28(1): 47–59.

Rampton, S. (2007) 'Has the internet changed the propaganda model?' *Alternet Newsletter.* 22nd June. www.alternet.org/stories/54339 accessed October 2007.

Sambrook, R. (2005) 'Citizen journalism and the BBC'. *Nieman Reports.* Winter, 59(4): 13–16.

Shaffer, J. (2007) Citizen Media: Fad or the Future of News? The Rise and Prospects of Hyperlocal Journalism. Knight Citizen News Network. http:// www.kcnn.org/research/citizen_media_report/ accessed October 2007.

Shirky, C. (2003) quoted in J. D. Lasica 'Blogs and journalism need each other'.

Thompson, M. (2006) quoted in 'User generated content uncovered: power to the people'. *Campaign.* 25 August. http://www.brandrepublic.com/bulletins/digital/article/589413/usergenerated-content-uncovered-power-people/ accessed January 2008.

Thumim, N. (2006) 'Mediated self-representations: "ordinary people" in "communities"'. In S. Herbrechter and M. Higgins (eds) *Returning (to) Communities: Theory, Culture and Political Practice of the Communal.* pp. 255–74. Amsterdam: Editions Rodopi.

Trippi, J. (2004) *The Revolution Will Not Be Televised: Democracy, the Internet, and the Overthrow of Everything.* New York: Harper Collins.

6
Parodic Practices: Amateur Spoofs on Video-Sharing Sites

Rebekah Willett

A man in his 20s sits on a bed and turns on the TV, just in time to hear a news report which tells of a robbery that is taking place. The Spiderman theme tune comes on as the man – older, shorter and clearly not as fit as the original Spiderman – pulls a Spiderman outfit from under the bed. Having donned the outfit, 'Spiderman' runs down the stairs, pulls open the front door and is stopped in his tracks. Closing the door and grabbing his stomach, he groans that he has a stitch (a cramp in his side).[1] This is one of many spoofs produced by a group called 'bordominduced' available on YouTube and MySpace. The group joins tens of thousands of other video-makers in posting their amateur spoofs or parodies online, receiving comments from their audience and taking part in discussions about online videos.

On one level, these productions might be seen as part of a major change which is taking place in people's everyday media practices. Today, so we are told, more people are creating and watching a much wider range of moving image productions, and different forms of media literacy are developing. One of Britain's renowned film-makers, the late Anthony Minghella, claimed that YouTube contributors and audiences are 'film literate': they are sharply critical of mainstream films and are contributing to the current downward trend in cinema attendance (Hoyle, 2006). As we have seen in Chapter 2, academic interest in new forms of participatory media production has also highlighted the important role of fan cultures in creating new opportunities for consumers and producers to interact, and for diverse forms of knowledge to be developed, shared and legitimated; and it has been suggested that this is indicative of a broader change in the power relationships between media producers and consumers (Jenkins, 2006; Ito, 2008). On another level, however, these amateur productions can be seen in a more localised way – as simply a matter of groups of friends playing with a piece of technology and 'having a laugh'. This kind of creative play with media can of course be seen as a conduit for defining and performing identities, and for critiquing or merely 'holding a mirror' to dominant cultural practices; but it is important not to overstate its significance in terms of contesting the power of mainstream media.

The aim of this chapter is to analyse the different purposes and characteristics of spoofs produced by amateur video-makers. It specifically examines original video productions (that is, not compilations, re-edited versions or 'mashups' of commercially produced media) made by amateurs within the UK. I analyse spoof productions from video-sharing sites, looking first at a survey of over 120 spoofs, and then looking more closely at the text, audience and author of selected examples.

Defining spoofs

Although 'spoof' is the common term used by video-makers on video-sharing sites, it is effectively synonymous with parody and the terms are often used interchangeably by amateur video users in their tags or titles. (I will be using both terms, though in reference to online amateur productions I will use 'spoof'.)

Dentith (2000) defines parody as 'any cultural practice which provides a relatively polemical allusive imitation of another cultural production or practice' (9). This definition highlights the fact that parody does not just refer to texts, but also to cultural practices. Further, the inclusion of 'polemical' in the definition marks parody as being somehow contentious. Dentith goes on to say that the degree of contention varies enormously, with a range of aims: 'to attack, satirise, or just playfully to refer to elements of the contemporary world' (6). Genette (1982) focuses on the relation between the original text (or hypotext) and the transformed text (or hypertext), and defines parody in these terms, while also creating further categories. *Parody*, according to Genette, is a transformation of a text done in a playful manner. *Travesty*, on the other hand, transforms a text in a satirical manner. *Pastiche* is not a transformation at all, but rather a playful imitation which bears resemblance to an original text in style, without direct reference to form. And finally a *skit* also imitates a text, but with an element of satire.

Using these ideas, one could place spoof videos on a continuum according to the degree of polemic or critique, with texts one might label 'homage' on one end and those which are 'satire' on the other (see Figure 6.1). This continuum defines texts primarily in terms of the

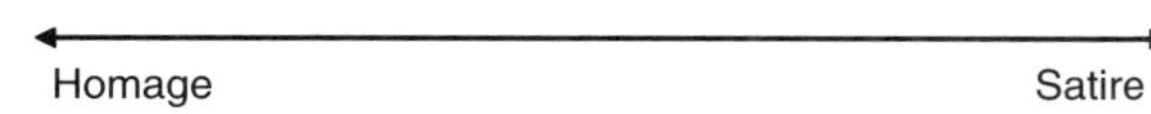

Figure 6.1   Continuum of spoofs

intentions of the author. The category 'homage', like Genette's pastiche and parody, therefore, refers to the relationship between the author and the original text – a homage imitates a text in a playful way, but the author enjoys the original text, takes pleasure in imitating or transforming it and is not critiquing it. The opposite end of the spectrum is satire, which is similar to Genette's travesty or skit. Here, the author clearly intends to problematise and criticise a text or practice. In contrast with homage, satire involves distancing oneself from the original text. In between these two categories is a large range of work which plays with texts as well as holding them up for critique to varying degrees.

This kind of categorisation is not unproblematic. To start with, the author's intention may be unclear and difficult to define. An author might give several versions of his or her intention, depending on the context of the discussion and how they want to position themselves (Buckingham and Sefton-Green, 1994). Furthermore, this leaves open the question of interpretation. For example, Dentith refers to texts which are 'just playful'; yet such texts may well be perceived as highly polemical, depending on the position of the reader. A playful reflection of particular aspects of the world through imitation or transformation, for some readers, might highlight questions about those aspects – even if, for the author, the play is not necessarily about raising questions, and might be more about pleasure. As such, different readers might place a given text in different positions on the continuum, or indeed in different positions simultaneously.

Parody can be seen as one 'tactic' which ordinary readers use to select and transform the meanings of cultural commodities in response to the 'strategies' of dominant institutions (de Certeau, 1984). More recently, these ways of 'poaching' texts have been seen as creating a new form of 'participatory culture' (Jenkins, 2006). According to Jenkins, fan practices attest to the power of the consumer to challenge dominant media industries: they create new relationships between consumers and producers, in which fans create new meanings, through elements such as parody, providing a critical take on mainstream media productions. Here, parody is more than just play for the sake of playing – parody is about redistributing power from the producer, allowing the consumer to contest, critique and create their own media, and to do so in a way which has an impact on big businesses. At the same time, there can be a form of 'convergence' here: Jenkins describes instances in which fan productions, ideas and ways of communicating and sharing knowledge are recognised by media industries and incorporated into their development and marketing of products.

By contrast, theorists such as Jameson (1984) argue that post-modernism is characterised by a culture of pastiche or 'blank parody', consisting of imitations of previous styles with no critical edge or ulterior motive. In Jameson's view, post-modern society is void of creativity, constantly rehashing the same ideas, images and quotations. Jameson's ideas raise questions about the intent of authors and the content of parodic texts as well as the extent to which fan producers, such as those described by Jenkins, are actually changing industry practices on any significant scale. The remaining sections of this chapter engage with these debates by looking at the texts themselves, as well as audience reactions and the authors' stated intentions.

Mapping spoofs

With tens of thousands of spoofs now at one's fingertips, narrowing the field down to make a manageable research project is necessary. Entering the term 'spoof' and related words into Google's search engine, I located specific types of spoofs on sites such as YouTube and Google Video, and ultimately collected over 120 spoofs from 68 different producers. (I did not attempt to gather a representative sample, and the sample is particularly limited in that most of the spoofs were labelled with the search terms I specified.) Given the focus of the wider project, of which this study is a part, I only included spoofs with original footage that were clearly made by amateurs living in the UK.

From the survey of 120 videos, the range of materials spoofed by amateurs can be grouped around particular genres: advertisements, sketch shows, music videos, cult movies or TV shows, and reality TV shows are the most common, although other genres with an amateur aesthetic such as pornography and vlogging are also present. I searched with the keywords spoof, parody, satire, homage, pastiche and mockumentary (separately). 'Spoof' brought up the most results by far, as featured in the title, tag or description. 'Parody', 'satire', 'homage' and 'mockumentary' brought up a smaller number of results, and 'pastiche' did not return any results within my defined area. The producers generally qualify their videos in the description, tags and sometimes titles, making it clear that the video is a spoof and not a serious imitation of a text. These qualifying statements also include labels such as fake, joke, comedy, funny, humor/humour, crazy, weird, stupid and silly. Furthermore, a number of producers make it clear that this is a project they did when they were bored or had nothing better to do. (This way of distancing themselves from their product is worth investigating, but I do not have the space to do so here.) A large majority of the authors of the spoofs surveyed were young white men, aged approximately 12– 25 years, and we can assume they have access to camcorders, editing equipment and broadband Internet. (Only 3 of the 68 producers were women, though occasionally women were included as actors. Only 4 of the 68 were obviously over 25 years, and all appeared to be under 40.)

Searching for amateur spoofs is complicated by the fact that one of the common aesthetic qualities of spoofs is precisely their amateurism. Commercially produced spoofs, therefore, often recreate the 'home-made' look through hand-held cameras, exaggerated acting, and low-budget props and costumes. On the other hand, amateurs increasingly have access to editing equipment and cameras which are similar to those used for commercial productions. This blurring between amateurs and professionals in terms of the achievement of a particular aesthetic makes the creation of spoof productions which look 'professional' easier for amateurs to achieve. In turn, this leads to particular texts becoming more liable to being spoofed. Programmes such as *Ghost Hunters,* which features low lighting and hand-held cameras, provide an aesthetic which the amateur can easily copy. Television shows or movies with an amateur aesthetic (comedy sketches, reality TV shows, documentaries and low-budget films such as *The Blair Witch Project*) are thus commonly spoofed on video-sharing sites.

Professional spoofs also provide models in terms of content. Common content in amateur spoofs such as sexual references, language/accent and cultural references (e.g. class-based stereotypes defined by cloth-ing and appearance) are also exemplified in professional spoofs, par-ticularly current sketch shows such as *The Catherine Tate Show* or *Little Britain* in the UK or *Saturday Night Live (SNL)* in the US. Although ama-teur videos clearly draw on sketch shows, comments on some videos indicate that it is problematic to spoof a spoof: as one commentator states, 'why spoof something that is already a joke?' Such comments clearly define a spoof as something that makes fun of a serious text (which is not already making fun of something itself). In this instance, the commentator is also saying that he/she considers the producer to be misreading the original text – taking it as something that is serious and can be made fun of. Importantly, this shifts our focus from the form to the content. However, whether something is serious or not is partly a matter of interpretation on the part of the viewer; and in some cases the original texts are ambiguous. Televised talent shows in which contestants mimic various performers and judges critique the performances can be seen to involve a parody of the genre, the original performer and the judging process. The shows are not, however, labelled as comedy; and the seriousness of the show, therefore, leaves it open to spoof.

In some cases, it is clear that the form has a crucial impact on the content of the spoof. As well as aiming primarily to spoof a particular cultural phenomenon, some producers use well-known media forms in order to make points about the content that is represented. A holiday film of a family in a seaside caravan, for example, is shot as a spoof of *Big Brother*, with snippets of mundane daily activities and each family member coming to 'the boiler room' to tell about their relations with other members of the family.[2] In spoofing *Big Brother*, the genre is offering a particular way of commenting both on the holiday activities themselves and on the voyeuristic conventions of reality TV. By using the form of *Big Brother*, one could argue that the text holds up the form for critique. Forcing someone to sit in front of a camera (in the diary room) and interrogating them about their actions, attitudes and feelings; getting people to comment on their relationships in private and then broadcasting those comments publicly; non-stop filming of everyday interactions – these are forms that one might well critique. However, the spoof is also saying something about a caravan holiday – it is like the situation of being stuck in a house with very little to do except analyse one's relationships with each other, and with someone creating activities for everyone to take part in. Therefore, the video could be read as a parody of both the form (reality television) and the content (confessions, family activities, caravan holidays).

As this implies, spoofs are likely to have multiple meanings for different authors and readers; and these meanings may be fluid and difficult to pin down. The next section, therefore, looks more closely at three spoof producers, examining statements from the authors and their audiences about particular productions. The data discussed in this section were collected through phone or email interviews and through the comments posted by viewers on the video-sharing sites. The cases typify a majority of the 120 spoofs surveyed, being produced by groups of friends, with young men predominating.[3]

Random Loaf – 'a surreal British sketch show of meaningful and non-meaningful sketches'[4]

Eighteen-year-old Martyn Lomax started the film-making group Random Loaf in 2005, creating 'spoof, random and comedy' sketches which are grouped together into a series of four episodes. *Stoke-on-Trent – Wish you Weren't Here* is a 3 minutes 15 seconds video described on YouTube by Martyn as a 'Light hearted spoof travel show from the midlands'. *Wish You Weren't Here* refers directly to a TV travel show, *Wish You Were Here*, using the form of the original text but transforming the content from a luxurious holiday destination to an ordinary town in the UK, emphasising both its ordinariness and also its more run-down and seedy aspects. The video attracted considerable criticism and debate among commentators on the site; and these responses raise significant questions about its intentions.

References to crime, homelessness and disorderly behaviour invite an interpretation of the piece as critique. However, one could argue that it is common to make fun of the place where one lives, just as it is common to make fun of friends or family in an affectionate way. It is hard to imagine a comedy spoof that would genuinely celebrate the benefits of living in Stoke. The spoof, therefore, may also be read not as a critique of the town as much as an example of a range of familiar social practices – making fun of where you live, spoofing a TV show, larking about with your friends.

The video includes very detailed elements of the form to create the impression of a travel show. It starts with fast-paced music matched in rhythm with cutaways from the video, then zooms in on the presenter who is standing at an entrance to a shopping mall. He says:

> Welcome to *Wish you Weren't Here*. Today we're in Stoke on Trent, the holiday equivalent of visiting a landfill site. Home to more than 238,000 unlucky individuals, Stoke on Trent offers some of the shoddiest, dirtiest sights and sounds in the UK.

The background muzak continues through this introduction with more cutaways (a landfill site, people walking in the shopping area). The presenter's intonation is upbeat, which matches that of holiday show presenters. Here one can see direct reference to holiday shows in the types of visuals, music, dialogue and presentation style. The description of Stoke is particularly reminiscent of holiday shows – almost as if the authors had copied the opening line of a holiday show and changed the analogy (landfill site) and adjectives (unlucky, shoddiest and dirtiest). This detailed transformation of a holiday show continues throughout the video, with occasional interruptions to the style, such as when a masked young man attempts to mug the cameraman and presenter.

In a telephone interview, Martyn said, 'I've lived here all my life, I'm happy really, but you can be critical about anywhere ... so I just think that's what it's all about ... I'm not being overly critical, I'm not slating it.' Martyn highlights the complexity of the critical nature of spoofs: he wants to be critical without being seriously (or overly) critical. Also, although there is an element of critique in the spoof, it is unclear where that critique is aimed and to what degree the town itself or the format of holiday programmes is being critiqued. It is obvious that holiday shows are a source for the spoof – but it is not obvious that the authors are critical of holiday shows. As Martyn describes, 'The format that it's filmed in is a spoof of a travel show ... filmed in a kind of cheesy corny way.' The 'cheesy corny-ness' highlights the slight critical take on travel shows, but one could argue that the form itself is not their primary target. The content, however, is more obviously critical. Muggings, homelessness, boarded up shops and homes, car theft, 'hooligans and boy racers' are all portrayed; and the video ends with a travel tip: 'Remember not to bring any valuables to Stoke on Trent as they will be stolen and taken to Cash Converters to fund organised crime and personal drug addiction.' Again, although Martyn says he is not 'slating' Stoke, that might be a response to the situation of being interviewed by a university researcher and being at the centre of an online argument about the nature of Stoke. Even so, it is not clear to what extent the authors are critiquing these social problems, and if so, who is the target of their critique – the council or the residents (which includes themselves). Another interpretation could be that they are parodying debates about social problems – highlighting the view that all robberies are a result of organised crime or drugs, for example. Alternatively, one could argue that the piece is more of an observation than a critique: as Martyn says, 'to create a good spoof you've got to observe first what's going on, I think if you understand what's going on, and you can sort of twist it a bit and find the humorous side of it.' The argument here might be that observations are subjective – if Martyn's spoof is more observational than critical, then it reflects his genuine view of Stoke as a place suffering from social ills.

The audience response to the video is less ambiguous. Many angry messages were posted with objections to the negative portrayal of Stoke. These audience members indicated that they felt the spoof portrayed

Stoke unfairly, and therefore, they did not find it funny. The messages indicate that the spoof is read as a serious critique of Stoke, rather than a 'light hearted spoof travel show', as indicated in Martyn's description. Here authorial intent comes under question. Sample comments include:

> [S]toke iz a mint place dont take the piss.
> Hey Jackass what a stupid video, stoke is sound place and your video is not worth viewing if you haven't lived here.
> [M]e and the people i watched this video with found this offensive and unfunny … the people who made this video are a disgrace to stoke, dont care if it was intended to be funny.

The third comment above indicates that this audience member realises the intent is to be funny. However, a number of comments indicate that the film focuses on too many negatives, exaggerating the social problems in Stoke and failing to portray it accurately.

Martyn recognises the difficulty of creating spoofs which are not offensive to people. He says, 'some people obviously could take offence to it, and that's one of the things that I find you've got to be really careful of making videos, there's just this line that you can't cross.' According to Martyn, negative comments are common on YouTube, partly because a dominant social practice is to slate everyone else's work, but in some cases the negativity results when an individual interest is at stake. Martyn says that he checks the profiles of the people who criticise his videos, and he finds people are offended when something in which they are clearly interested is mimicked. One of the critics of the Stoke video, for example, has posted lots of videos of the Stoke football club, and obviously takes pride in the town. For this audience member, Martyn crossed the line by disrespecting his hometown.

Many of the other comments discuss the accuracy of the portrayal of Stoke in the video, and criticise other audience members for not seeing the video as funny. For example, one reader writes, 'stop dissing the vid. its meant to be ironic and its just piss take u losers.' While some comments took this point of view on board (e.g. 'dont care if it was intended to be funny'), most refer to the accuracy of the video, with some arguing that things are far worse in Stoke and others arguing the opposite. One comment in particular sums up the complexity of viewing such a video:

> Me n my fella have just watched this vid, fair enough stoke is a bit of a shit hole but it's where a lot of people live isn't it. Mind you,

> that isn't stopping us trying to move out of stoke :-) We figured it's
> a bit of a piss take, n most of the people we know who live in stoke
> do exactly the same!

As this clearly shows, a spoof can be interpreted in many different ways – as a reflection of reality ('Stoke is a bit of a shit hole'), a problem for people who have to cope with that reality ('but it's where a lot of people live') and a common social practice ('most of the people ... do exactly the same').

Martyn has achieved some degree of success by having his film shown on terrestrial television. He has been contacted by two digital stations as well, and his hobby of film-making is now driving a change in his career path from computers to film production. Martyn's activities fit well with the convergence culture to which Jenkins (2006) refers. One could argue that his film aesthetic, choice of 'random' humour and professional-looking website (which includes 30-minute sketch shows) reflect a broader change in the industry towards more user-generated content available on demand. As he states: 'now we've got the technology to broadcast yourself on the internet, TV lacks that a bit ... what it's trying to do is blend in, all media, I think, TV and the internet and with interactive TV. It's going to change the way we look at it.' However, although more home-made videos are being shown on TV all the time, it is not clear that this is changing the audience's relationship with the industry. One could argue that such material is merely providing a cheap way to fill the expanding amounts of airtime as digital channels proliferate. Home videos are designated to spots which are framed on national television as 'homemade', and even when integrated into mainstream programming such as news, they are clearly labelled 'amateur'.

Another component from Jenkins' argument which is missing in Martyn's activities is the presence of a new kind of knowledge formation. Martyn (like the other three spoof-makers I interviewed) has virtually no formal training, but neither had he networked with other video-makers to exchange information, as Jenkins describes (2006). Although Martyn has a strong following (people will recognise him on the street as 'the guy from RandomLoaf'), he says the film-making is restricted to a small group of friends. Instead of looking at Martyn's video-making as a challenge to mainstream media or a new type of social networking and knowledge exchange, it is perhaps more useful to see it as an essentially local and more individual activity. With this in mind, the next case study will examine video-making in terms of issues around the identities of the young producers.

MyPancakePlace[5]

Like Martyn, Richard Fox is a 17-year-old who has been making videos for several years, learning video-making on his own, and leading a group of friends in making projects which are broadcast on YouTube under the name 'MyPancakePlace'. Richard says he learns through the many professional movies he watches, and he is able to imitate techniques, such as camera angles, in his own videos. Two of Richard's videos are clearly labelled as spoofs – one of a public service announcement about piracy and one of the movie, *The Blair Witch Project*. Richard has an interest in things that are parodic – his YouTube site indicates an interest in *Twin Peaks*, and he has posted several videos of Michael Jackson which he has edited together. Richard mainly works with the same three (male) friends on his projects, and he positions his varying activities with these friends firmly within the rhetoric of creativity saying, 'we're always doing something creative.' By labelling his activities as creative, Richard is identifying himself (and his play) as having a prosocial side. We can also speculate that Richard's filming and editing constructs a positive identity through projects such as his broadcast of his school talent show, which was viewed over 1500 times. Further evidence of the positive identity Richard is constructing through his video projects can be seen in some of the comments. One person, responding to a Michael Jackson compilation, for example, wrote:

> THAT WAS AMAZING! I seriously have no words, I'm totally blown away by your talent for this, WOW.

Closer examination of questions of power and play will come in the analysis of one of his videos below.

Richard's use of spoofs centres mainly on entertainment both for himself and his audience. As opposed to the definitions of parody discussed above, for Richard a spoof is most effective when it refers directly to the original source. He says, 'if something is really successful or famous for a particular reason, then people will sort of do their version of that but make it ridiculous … I think what makes a spoof good is taking one part and really elevating it so that it does look completely ridiculous.' Richard's use of the word 'elevate' is particularly interesting. Here he is indicating that the practice of spoofing is about highlighting or holding up an established cultural reference – in this case a reference to a moving image production – in order to make it look 'ridiculous'.

One example of a spoof Richard made of a serious text is a short advertisement warning against video piracy. The connection to the original source is key – Richard mentioned that people may not find their work funny if the connection is not explicit enough or if the audience has not seen the original source. For Richard, the pleasure in making the spoof is more important than audience response. He says, 'it's just for pure entertainment ... I don't so much think of what other people are going to react to it, I just do it because I enjoy doing that kind of thing, but if other people enjoy it that's great.' With this approach in mind, and Richard's emphasis on pleasure, it becomes clear that his definition of a spoof is closer to homage than it is to satire. Indeed, Richard indicated that his videos of Michael Jackson are produced in the spirit of homage, using mixes of the songs 'Hero' and 'I like the way you move' to construct a compilation of Michael Jackson's dance moves. As a Michael Jackson fan, Richard was interested in producing a video that experimented with different rhythms, musical structures and dance styles. However, in the films that he labels 'spoofs', the practice of scripting, acting and editing allows a more creative and critical take on existing cultural practices.

MyPancakePlace's film, *The Brea Witch Project*, was produced as a project for a German class at school. The movie is over ten minutes long, including conventions such as opening credits and 'bloopers'. As Richard explained, the movie only loosely follows the story of *The Blair Witch Project*. In their spoof, two boys are making a film in a nearby wood, and when editing the film they notice that a stranger has appeared in the background on their footage. As they edit, the doorbell rings, and when they open the door an unknown man (identified in the credits as from the CIA) drugs them. They fall unconscious, and when they awake, they are interrogated by the CIA man, who transforms into an alien. All of the dialogue is in German, consisting of questions and answers from an introductory level language class (e.g. What's that? I don't know. What's your name? How old are you?). Different camera angles, editing (including special effects) and scenes shot several times indicate that the project took some considerable time. (In fact it took three days and was 'seriously rushed', according to Richard.)

In one sense, the project demonstrates 'learning by doing' – Richard says he learns by watching films, and the film shows that they experimented with techniques such as camera angles (putting the camera on the ground to film people walking, for example). In another sense, however, the project can be seen as part of the play activities in which the friends are engaging. Looking at *The Brea Witch Project* as a product of play, we can see the production process as a 'third space', a place where reality and fantasy overlap and afford different types of interactions (Winnicott, 1971). In the fantasy space of the video, the boys are able to play powerful figures (such as the CIA interrogator and alien). Furthermore, in the reality side of the third space, the boys can put themselves in powerful positions of director and producer. In Winnicott's notion of transitional or third space, where the experience of inner and outer worlds, of fantasy and reality, overlap, creative involvement with subjects and objects takes place. 'It is in playing and only in playing that the individual or adult is able to be creative and to use the whole personality, and it is only in being creative that the individual discovers the self' (Winnicott, 1971: 54). Media theorists have used Winnicott's ideas to discuss fan and gaming practices as important spaces for creative expression, for exploration of the meanings of cultural texts and for 'psychic health' (Dovey and Kennedy, 2006; Hills, 2002).

If we see *The Brea Witch Project* as a form of play, then the production is providing an important space in which the young men are not only exploring the meanings of media texts but also exploring them in relation to their own identities. As a form of play, the production allows the group of friends to demonstrate their friendship, their media expertise, their identity as educational achievers and their skill in using technology. From this viewpoint, the production process offers an important way for the friends to define themselves in terms of discourses around young men. Part of the discourse around masculinity which is present in many schools is that it is not 'cool' for boys to do well academically, especially if a boy works hard. In *Failing Boys? Issues in Gender and Achievement* (Epstein et al., 1998), several contributors describe how academic achievement is feminised, resulting in ridicule for boys who are academic achievers. By producing a video which demonstrates technical skill and draws on popular culture, as well as marking the video as a spoof (not serious), Richard and his friends are negotiating their position as both educational achievers and 'cool' boys.

One area beyond the scope of this research is looking at the *process* of the productions to see how identities are being performed and defined. I did not have access to all the discussions which take place as the boys work out a script and spend hours filming and editing, taking on different roles as actors, directors, cameramen and producers. However, Lissa Soep's study of a similar group of young men making a film in their basement shows how these off-camera interactions may run contrary to the 'hard-core masculinity' displayed in their production (Soep, 2005). Soep writes: 'their moment-to-moment interactions revealed a very different ideology – one coded in everyday life and scholarship as "feminine", characterized by intimacy, propriety and intense collaboration' (178). The next group I discuss also has an outward appearance of hegemonic masculinity in the films they produce. However, by examining the online discussions around the films, other aspects of their film-making emerge.

Bentley Bros

The Bentley Bros are a group of brothers and their friends, aged 14–20 years. All of the 15 productions online at the time of writing are labeled 'comedy', with the exception of one 'experimental horror' film. The comedy often centres on spoofs of thriller-type genres, and includes direct references to TV, videogames and movies, including *Resident Evil*, *Ghost Hunters*, *The Babysitter* and *Scream*. The productions vary from carefully scripted and directed 60-minute films, complete with rented costumes and props, which take over a month of intense work, through to short films shot in an evening which are improvised on the spot.

The film I focus on, 'Da Ghetto Boyz: A Documentary', is an early production and not typical of the group, as it has no direct reference to an original source text. Comparing the comments on all their productions, this is the most controversial of their films, receiving critiques and comments from a variety of viewpoints. The film is described on YouTube by the Bentley Bros as 'A parody of chavs in Britain.' The film depicts a group of four young men, labeled 'chavs' or 'ghetto boys' by the producers. ('Chav' is a derogatory slang term used to describe a stereotype of a particular youth subculture in the UK, identified through particular brands and styles of fashion, music and attitudes. The stereotype is often connected with white working-class youth, and is associated with poor education, resistance to authority and racist attitudes.) The film presents an exaggerated stereotype of 'chavs', following the group as they beat up younger boys and take their shoes, football and money, search for things to steal and sell, mainly to buy cigarettes, and damage personal property.

The film is framed as a documentary, starting with a view of one boy putting on his 'bling' (jewelry) in front of a mirror, then turning to the camera and saying 'what are you fuckin' looking at?' (a challenge that in various forms is a recurring refrain in the video). It then follows the group during the course of a day, interviewing the members as they go about their business. The film parodies a particular form – in this case a 'day in the life' documentary, shot with a hand-held camera. The parody highlights the class dimensions of such documentaries (with a clearly middle-class person behind the camera asking questions to the working-class youth) as well as representational issues (asking questions which embarrass the youth and cause him to get angry, thus feeding into the stereotypes being represented).

Here again, there is some ambiguity when considering who or what is being spoofed: is it particular kinds of documentary film-makers, the audiences who regard such documentaries (or reality TV shows such as *Brat Camp)* as realistic or unproblematic portrayals of a culture or are the Bentley Bros spoofing themselves (rural middle-class youth pretending to be urban working class)? More obviously the film parodies a stereotyped subculture. It is clear that the parody relies on producing a stereotyped version of the 'chav', but it is less clear whether it is a parody of the stereotype or whether the producers see 'chav' as an authentic subculture. One YouTube commentator argues that the Bentley Bros view chavs as a 'real' subculture, implying they should realise that 'chav' is a stereotype. The commentator says '[it was sad] that some thick, thick twats think these people are actually "real".' On the other hand, many of the comments on the video (on YouTube and on the forum on the Bentley Bros' website) indicate that 'chav' or a similar subculture is indeed seen to exist in different parts of the UK and in other parts of the world. However, within a discussion of 'wiggers' ('white niggers') that started on the forum, a debate about the labelling of subcultures erupted. Strong opinions about stereotyping and labelling were expressed and one of the members of the Bentley Bros posted the following:

> People stereotype, that's what they do. You aren't going to get past it …You were baggy clothes, talk like a black guy when you're white, and you listen to rap? wigga? Maybe. Stereotyped as wigga? Yes. You have to live with it. People are ignorant enough to not get to know someone's personality and judge them on how they dress.

In this statement, it appears that the producers see the film as a chance to hold up the stereotype for critique. However, others criticise the Bentley Bros for reinforcing the 'chav' stereotype. One person defends 'chavs', saying 'they're only a product of the system,' and another argues that the 'chav' stereotype has 'been hyped and twisted by the media' and that the producers should 'stop whining and start realising how bad the white working class have got it in the UK'. This second commentator addresses the Brothers as 'fucking middle class wannerbe scum bags', and this class divide also comes through in comments about the actors' accents – there are several critiques of middle-class boys putting on working-class accents.

Through this discussion, the intent of the authors is still unclear. Stuart Bentley maintains that humour is their main aim, and that a majority of the comments on their videos are positive, from 'people that know exactly what we are on about'. As in Martyn's comments about responses to *Wish You Weren't Here*, Stuart said there were responses which indicated the film had personally insulted an individual, such as this one: 'even though i am a chav, i feel pretty bad of what people think, i don't go around doing stuff like that to people, they're what you call pikey chavs, mugging for money.' Again, this relates to the issue of stereotyping – by producing a stereotype of a 'chav', the film simplifies and exaggerates its object of parody.

The focus on a cultural representation, the 'chav', which is known to all the members of the group, gives the Bentley Bros and their audience a point of discussion. Their other films are more clearly connected to specific media texts, and in scripting a parody, the group is engaging with the text as part of their film-making activities. Stuart Bentley describes this process in relation to one video game spoof: 'we all came up with ideas and gags based on the game for *Resident Evil 4*, and I personally converted them into our script mixed with the official script for the game.' Media are part of the social life of young people, and through discussing and producing media, friends are not only connecting on a social level, they are also making sense of the role of media in their lives (de Block and Buckingham, 2007; Willett, 2006). Furthermore, humour is a common element of 'mateship culture' as analysed by James and Saville-Smith (1989). Kehily and Nayak (1997), who look specifically at male humour in secondary schools, conclude, 'humour plays a significant part in consolidating peer group cultures ... offering a sphere for conveying masculine identities' (p. 67). The parody of media texts for the Bentley Bros, therefore, works to cement their relationships, giving them not only a common point of reference but also a way of processing media – making sense of media portrayals of 'chavs', representations of masculinity, 'violence' and horror in films, for example. On a different level, the production process is a way of displaying the knowledge they are gaining through their media consumption. As Stuart comments: 'we never really learnt from anyone except from the films we watch. But you need the knack to notice the work behind a film rather than to get drawn into it.'

Conclusion

Given the definition of parody as 'a polemical allusive imitation' (Dentith, 2000), one might expect a chapter on spoof videos to present examples in which film-makers are challenging mainstream culture, holding up particular practices for critique and making statements through their productions. Returning to the homage-satire continuum, my survey of videos and the more in-depth examination of several video-makers identified very few productions that could be contained firmly within the category of satire. In most cases, the critical or 'polemical' component of spoofs was highly ambiguous. Yet in contrast to Jameson's argument that we are a culture of 'empty parody', the analysis has shown that the spoofs serve particular 'localised' functions. The young men who dominate the category of UK amateur spoof producers are using media production as a space in which they can play with their mates, construct positive masculine identities, and in some limited respects, present challenges to mainstream culture. This space is largely outside the gaze of the older generation,[6] and is to some extent independent and autonomous.

Instead of evaluating such activities according to how challenging or critical they are, we need to look at how they work in tandem with existing practices. Video-sharing sites are giving the people I interviewed inspiration, a talking point with their friends as well as an outlet for their productions. As Dave, of bordominduced, stated: 'I am finding that a lot of people are talking about what they saw or found on YouTube last night as opposed to a year or two ago when people would chat about what was on TV the night previously. I'm not saying that all TV is rubbish ... but there are a lot more interesting things to be found on the internet.' This could be seen as a powerful challenge to the mainstream media, creating the participatory culture Jenkins discusses; but it might equally reflect the fact that young people are simply spending more time in front of multiple screens, with the Internet supplementing their other media viewing. For example, Richard says he still goes to the cinema to see big-budget movies that are elaborate, realistic and professional. Unlike Jenkins' examples of amateur media practice converging with mainstream industry practice, the young people in this study are working in parallel with the industry, concentrating on their immediate friendship group and learning by doing as well as from a small social group. Although Web 2.0 may be changing viewing habits, and creating opportunities for people to broadcast amateur videos, it would be wrong to overstate the ideological challenges to mainstream entertainment this might represent.

Notes

1. http://www.bordominduced.co.uk/
2. http://www.youtube.com/watch?v=TrMKYwmAwBY
3. Permission has been obtained to use names of the three case studies and publish URLs of their websites. Participants have had a chance to read and comment on the draft of this chapter.
4. http://www.randomloaf.com
5. http://www.youtube.com/profile?user=mypancakeplaces
6. Only 4% of over-45s in the UK report watching online videos more than once a week (Online video eroding TV viewing, 2006; Ofcom, 2006).

References

de Block, L. and Buckingham, D. (2007) *Global Children, Global Media: Migration, Media and Childhood.* Basingstoke: Palgrave.

Buckingham, D. and Sefton-Green, J. (1994) *Cultural Studies goes to School: Reading and Teaching Popular Culture.* Brighton: Falmer Press.

de Certeau, M. (1984) *The Practice of Everyday Life.* University of California Press.

Dentith, S. (2000) *Parody.* London: Routledge.

Dovey, J. and Kennedy, H. (2006) *Game Cultures.* Buckingham: Open University Press.

Epstein, D., Elwood, J., Hey, V. and Maw, J. (eds) (1998) *Failing boys? Issues in Gender and Achievement.* Buckingham: Open University Press.

Genette, G. (1982) *Palimpsestes: La littérature au Second Degré.* Paris: Editions du Seuil.

Hills, M. (2002) *Fan Cultures.* London: Routledge.

Hoyle, B. (2006) 'Minghella's democratic vision of cinema, but not as we know it.' *Times Online.* 28 October 2006. http://www.timesonline.co.uk/tol/news/uk/article615750.ece accessed 3 July 2007.

Ito, M. (2008) Mobilizing the imagination in everyday play: the case of Japanese media mixes. In K. Drotner and S. Livingstone (eds) *The International Handbook of Children, Media and Culture.* pp. 397–412. London: Sage.

James, B. and Saville-Smith, K. (1989) *Gender Culture and Power: Challenging New Zealand's Gendered Culture.* Auckland: OUP Australia and New Zealand.

Jameson, F. (1984) Postmodernism, or the cultural logic of late capitalism. *New Left Review.* 146(July–August 1984): 53–92.

Jenkins, H. (2006) *Convergence Culture: Where Old and New Media Collide.* New York: NYU Press.

Kehily, M. J. and Nayak, A. (1997) 'Lads and laughter': humour and the production of heterosexual hierarchies. *Gender and Education.* 9(1): 69–87.

Ofcom (2006). Ofcom media literacy bulletin. Issue 8, December 2006. http://www.ofcom.org.uk/advice/media_literacy/medlitpub/bulletins/issue_8.pdf accessed 26 April 2007.

'Online video eroding TV viewing' (2006) BBC World News http://news.bbc.co.uk/2/hi/entertainment/6168950.stm, accessed 3 July 2007.

Soep, E. (2005) Making hard-core masculinity: teenage boys playing house. In E. Soep and S. Maira (eds) *Youthscapes: the Popular, the National, the Global.* pp. 173–91. Philadelphia: University of Pennsylvania Press.

Willett, R. (2006) Poofy dresses and big guns: a poststructuralist analysis of gendered positioning through talk amongst friends. *Discourse: Studies in the Cultural Politics of Education.* 27(4): 441–56.

Winnicott, D. W. (1971) *Playing and Reality.* London: Tavistock Publications.

7

Skate Perception: Self-Representation, Identity and Visual Style in a Youth Subculture

David Buckingham

Visual representation has always been an important dimension of youth culture. Academic studies frequently make great play of the *style* of groups such as punks and goths, arguing that clothing and bodily adornment function as symbolic statements of their rejection of mainstream values (e.g. Hebdige, 1979). Even so, the early 'classic' studies of youth subcultures typically accused the media of merely co-opting or colonising their more subversive elements. It was not until Sara Thornton's work on club cultures (Thornton, 1995) that researchers turned their attention to the ways in which youth groups might positively *use* specialist or 'niche' media for their own purposes – not merely to disseminate information, but also to establish (and to regulate) collective identity.

This chapter explores one area of youth culture in which visual representation – in the form of photography and now video – has been a significant, long-running concern: namely, skateboarding. I consider the status of skateboarding as a form of youth 'subculture'; the particular functions and purposes of video-making within it; the ways in which video-makers learn their craft; and the typical content and form of skateboarding videos. The research is based on extensive viewing of the videos themselves, immersion in specialist websites and personal interviews (via telephone, email and face-to-face) with six young UK-based video-makers, recruited through both specialist and generic video-sharing sites.

Skateboarding as youth culture

For many skaters themselves, skateboarding is much more than merely a leisure pastime. It can justifiably be seen as a form of *youth culture*, in the sense that it has its own preferred modes of symbolic representation, its own aesthetic, its own ethical codes and rules, and its own ideology. To be a skateboarder is to be more than just a person who happens to roll about the city streets on a piece of wood. Being an accomplished skater, and knowing where and how to skate, is obviously part of the story; as is wearing particular clothes and accessories, having a particular hairstyle, listening to particular kinds of music and choosing particular products or brands. But the skilful use of these external markers also helps to define you as a member of a group that is presumed to share particular *values* – values that are to some degree defined in opposition to, or at least as an alternative to, those of mainstream adult society. Becoming a skateboarder entails a process of self-identification: it is about the assertion of an attitude, and the claiming of an identity, that is literally *embodied* in particular forms of visual appearance and physical style. And while this can be an important issue for quite young children seeking to establish their place within the peer group (Waerdahl, 2007), for its most committed older proponents it amounts to nothing less than a complete 'lifestyle' (Borden, 2001).

Like other so-called 'new' or 'extreme' sports such as snowboarding, windsurfing and parcours, skateboarding is less organised or institutionalised than mainstream sport (Wheaton, 2000). It is undoubtedly a highly competitive activity, although skaters will typically argue that the competition is more with oneself, or with one's past performance, than with other skaters. Certainly, it is opposed to traditional forms of competition, in which there are clear winners and losers. Skaters like to present their sport as one in which 'there are no rules, referee, set plays, nor coaches' (Beal, 1996); and it is typically seen as a co-operative pursuit, in which participants themselves (rather than external authorities) define their own criteria for judging excellence.

This process of collective identification is to some extent provoked by the often punitive responses of adult authorities. The outlawing or disciplining of skateboarding in public places has a long history, and the 'cat-and-mouse' game of evading police or security personnel is (at least for some) a key part of the pleasure (Nolan, 2003; Stratford, 2002; Woolley and Johns, 2001). Skaters seek to reappropriate and transform public space, colonising the 'left-over spaces of modernist planning' (Borden, 2001: 188), and finding new and playful uses for redundant architectural features; and yet they are persistently regulated, harassed and excluded (a theme that, as we shall see, is a recurrent trope in skateboarding videos). While the most overtly 'political' articulations of skateboarders are to be found in campaigns around public skateparks

(Weller, 2006), large numbers of skaters resist even such minimally institutionalised settings in favour of the more subversive, 'anti-social' thrills of urban street skating (Stratford, 2002). This leads some academic commentators, such as Iain Borden (2001), to regard skating as a kind of critique of the routinised efficiency of the modern capitalist city, with its 'zero degree architecture' – although he is bound to admit that most skaters themselves are 'largely unaware of the political nature of their actions' (2001: 206).

To state the obvious, this is very much a male-dominated culture. Despite the presence of what some commentators have seen as elements of 'non-hegemonic masculinity' among skaters, the forms of rebelliousness that are valued are nevertheless relatively aggressive (Beal, 1996). 'Skater girls' do indeed exist (Pomerantz et al., 2004), but female skaters are typically marginalised or excluded, albeit not always through overtly sexist behaviour. The commonsense definition of skateboarding as an essentially masculine realm can also be reinforced by the representations available, for example, in magazine advertising (Rinehart, 2005). Meanwhile, other studies suggest that skating is a relatively middle-class pursuit, and one that is largely shunned by non-white ethnic groups (Karsten and Pel, 2001; Woolley and Johns, 2001). While some commentators dispute this, arguing that the culture is more socially inclusive (e.g. Borden, 2001), these observations are very much confirmed in the sample of skateboarding videos that I viewed for this research.

Despite the apparently subversive stance of skateboarders, it is also important to recognise that this culture is unavoidably commodified. Since its first appearance in California in the early 1960s, celebrated in the film *Dogtown and Z-Boys* (director Stacy Peralta, 2001), there have been several waves of interest in skateboarding, with notable 'boom and bust' cycles in the early 1960s and again in the late 1970s. From the earliest days, skateboarding has had its own 'artisanal' economy of small shops and companies making boards, accessories and specialist clothing, as well as its own 'insider' media, in the form of magazines, videos and now DVDs and websites. Despite the appearance of 'independent' retailers, many of the key producers of skating commodities are in fact owned by larger companies (Borden, 2001: 157). In addition, multinational corporations have periodically 'bought in' to the phenomenon, seeking to sell skateboarding 'style' (particularly in the form of clothing) to the much wider non-skater market. Like other areas of youth culture, skateboarding is characterised by the constant interplay between developments that appear to arise from the 'bottom up', among young people themselves, and developments that are promoted from the 'top down' by powerful commercial interests.

Skaters themselves are frequently critical of the involvement of big companies, but they also recognise that this creates opportunities that would not otherwise be available: several 'star' skaters are sponsored by large clothing and equipment manufacturers, enabling some, at least, to earn a wage and to travel the world. For example, Liam, one of my interviewees, was quite ambivalent about the 'big-business' aspect of skateboarding, although he also saw it as offering an important form of public recognition. Jon, another interviewee, argued that skaters would not respond well to feeling 'exploited', and were able to 'see through' marketing that was not 'genuine'. However, he also noted an important distinction between the 'core market' of skaters and the wider market: larger companies such as Vans (a shoe manufacturer) would never make a significant financial return by selling to skaters alone – they needed to reach out to a wider market, using their association with skating in order to establish their credentials as a 'cool' brand.

Media play a crucial role in defining the identity of the skateboarder. Through magazines, photographs and posters, videos and websites, skaters write their own history, create their own self-images and produce their own self-sustaining mythology. In these media, skateboarding is often linked to other forms of youth cultural activity or expression – most obviously fashion, music and other so-called 'extreme sports'. There is a common focus on the notion of *independence* that cuts across these different forms. This is apparent in one publication I consulted, the book *Declaration of Independents* (Baccigaluppi et al., 2001): here, the editors of *Heckler* magazine create what the book's subtitle terms 'an intersection of cultures' – specifically, snowboarding, skateboarding and 'indie' rock music – in seeking to document 'the formation of an independent era'. 'Independence' here is partly about constructing an alternative to corporate capitalism (a stance that in practice may be at least ambivalent); but it is also about proclaiming a kind of personal or collective autonomy, a freedom from constraint – an attitude that is flexible, individualistic and expressive, rather than rigid and conformist.

Nevertheless, it would be wrong to assume a straightforward or compulsory 'homology' between these different elements. Put simply, not all skaters like the same music or wear the same brand-name clothes. There are significant divisions within the skating culture, for example, between 'old skool' and 'nu skool' skaters, or between punk and hip-hop skaters, which are apparent in styles of skating, and the design of boards and shoes, as well as in fashion and musical preferences (Hunter, 2003). On a more interpersonal level, the acquisition and display of 'subcultural capital' is a crucial means of establishing one's authority and identity as an *authentic* skateboarder (cf. Thornton, 1995; Widdicombe and Wooffitt, 1995). The growing popularity of skating 'style' (if not necessarily of the activity of skating itself) within mainstream commercial youth culture, and the growing involvement of large corporations makes this establishment of authenticity an increasingly intense preoccupation. In this context, it becomes vital to distinguish between 'real' skaters and 'posers', between those who are genuine and those who are 'fake', who 'sell out' or who merely affect the attitude. (And it should also be noted here that the distinction between skateboarders and in-line skaters is stark and absolute.) In common with other youth cultures, there is an official rhetoric of openness here (anyone can join), but there are also strong tendencies towards exclusivity, hierarchy and competition within the culture itself: membership of the culture depends not just upon the committed acquisition of skating skills (and the risks that entails), but also upon displaying the right *signs*.

As Belinda Wheaton and Becky Beal (2003) suggest, the media also provide an important arena for the circulation and maintenance of subcultural capital. Reading and discussing specialist magazines, as in their study, are means through which hierarchies of status and credibility are established among participants. The magazines are used as a valuable source of information – particularly by relative 'beginners' – but criticising the magazines also provides opportunities for the display of 'insider' status and authority. While their interviewees were generally critical of what they perceived as the commodification of skateboarding, they also distinguished between 'fake' brands and 'authentic' brands with a longer-term association with skating culture. Even so, the 'alternative' constantly threatens to become part of the mainstream; and as it loses its exclusivity, the meanings associated with it also begin to shift. Several of the 'underground' skaters of earlier decades are now managing directors of the leading skateboarding companies; and in the case of video in particular, the 'indie' style has undoubtedly become more commercially viable with the success of television series and films such as *Jackass* and *Dirty Sanchez*.

The notion of 'subculture' has been widely questioned within recent work on youth culture (e.g. Bennett, 1999; Hesmondhalgh, 2005); and there is certainly room for debate here about whether skateboarding can usefully be seen as a form of subculture. Some might regard it merely as a 'taste culture', with little wider social significance, although some proponents of skateboarding are inclined to characterise it as a fully fledged 'counter culture', which critiques and challenges the economic rationality of the modern capitalist city (Borden, 2001). In Bennett's (1999) terms, skateboarders might perhaps be better seen as a 'neo-tribe', or as participants in a 'scene' – terms that seek to encapsulate the more fluid, even nomadic, nature of contemporary youth cultures. Yet either way, it is clear that skateboarding encapsulates some of the fundamental tensions inherent in contemporary youth cultures – between the assertion of individuality and the drive to affiliate with the group, between the desire for inclusiveness and the operation of social distinction, and between the autonomous expression of youthful identities and the pressures of commodification.

The role of visual media

The visual documentation of skateboarding has a long history. The documentary movie *Dogtown and Z-Boys* incorporates a wealth of film material gathered during the initial skateboarding boom of the early 1960s, and also features the work of some of the celebrated early photographers such as Glen Friedman. Iain Borden (2001: 114–16) tracks the evolution of this practice, focusing on the use of photographic action sequences (reminiscent of the work of the Victorian photographer Eadweard Muybridge) to capture innovative moves, and the role of specific technical features such as motor drives, stroboscopes and wide-angle lenses. Still photography remains a key aspect of skateboarding culture, with leading magazines like the UK's *Sidewalk* regularly featuring large, high-quality displays of action shots.

In recent years, the focus of this activity has shifted much more strongly towards video, which is distributed both on DVD and via the Internet. Skateboarding shops typically stock a very wide range of DVDs, and numerous 'DVD zines' such as *411VM* (which typically include a DVD with a magazine, a poster and a product guide) are published on a regular basis around the world. Short videos or trailers can be viewed or downloaded at most specialist skating websites, and the US-based site skateperception.com is a large site dedicated specifically to skating photographers and videographers, which includes facilities for mail-order shopping. To give some indication of the scale of this site, at the time of this research (spring 2007), it had over 11,000 registered members and over 1.2 million postings: its leading posters had more than 4000 individual postings. The site features its own selection of streaming videos, while individual postings also contain links to other videos available on generic sites such as YouTube as well as individually run and company sites. (Even so, it was notable that several interviewees also described public screenings (as in the case of Paul, whose publicity materials are reproduced in Figure 7.1).)

As this description implies, the culture of skateboarding video-makers does not sustain a clear boundary between the amateur and the professional. While larger skateboarding companies such as Powell-Peralta and Blueprint have diversified into video production, there are many smaller companies and individuals producing and distributing videos on a not-for-profit basis. The more dedicated participants on the Skate Perception website, who appear to be mostly in their late teens and early twenties, often describe this work as a 'career'. There is a good deal of emphasis in the interviews featured on the site about the need for

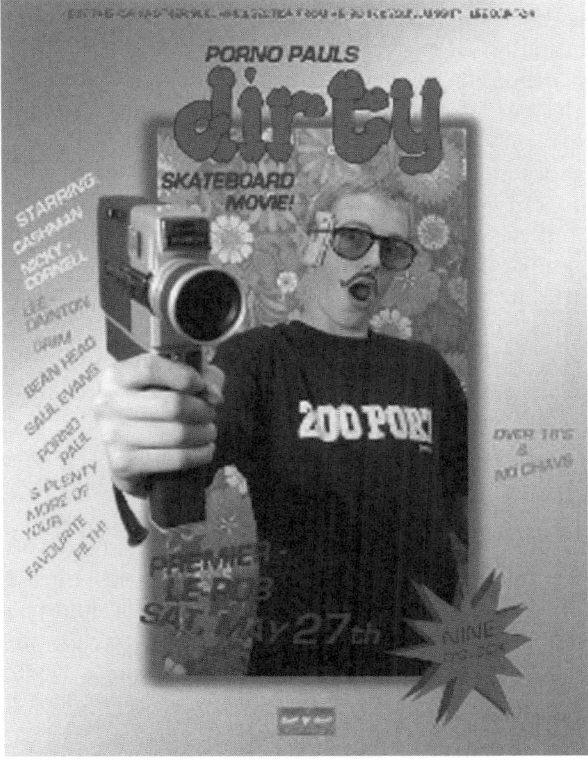

Figure 7.1 Publicity flyer for 'Porno Paul's Dirty Skateboard Movie'

aspiring video-makers to 'work their way up the hard way', starting with videos of their friends before moving on to more well-known skaters. Older video-makers featured on the site, such as Kyle Camarillo of San Francisco, are employed full time by skateboard and film companies such as Transworld. Others complain about the competition that is increasingly apparent: Mike Zorger of Washington, D.C. describes how 'you look behind your shoulder while filming fisheye on a certain trick and you have some little dude poaching the hell out of your shit' (skateperception.com, 2007). Meanwhile, some ambitious skaters explicitly request or commission videos of their work, in the hope of attracting sponsorship, in what are sometimes referred to as 'sponsor me' videos. According to some UK contributors, such as Sheffield's Matt Hirst, this commercial dimension is much more strongly developed in the United States (skateperception.com, 2007).

What role do these specifically *visual* dimensions of representation play in skateboarding culture? To some extent, they can be seen simply as a manifestation of the fact that – like many other forms of youth culture – skateboarding is highly 'image-conscious'. This is partly about the overt display of style. Particular types of clothing (baggy trousers, hooded tops, cut-off shorts, band t-shirts), logos, keychains, hairstyles, hats and shoes are used to create specific 'style ensembles' that mark out identity and group affiliation (Hunter, 2003). While some of these aspects could be seen as functional (the physical activity of skating effectively calls for baggy clothes and specialised shoes), the embodiment of 'attitude' (your posture, how you *wear* your clothes) is also critical. The graphic designs on skateboards themselves are also important as a means of differentiation, given that the basic technology of the boards remains fairly constant (Borden, 2001: 26); and skating is also often associated with graffiti art.

However, the drive to represent skateboarding on video obviously derives primarily from the fact that it is about *movement*. 'Style' in skateboarding is not simply a matter of technical ability: it is not just about the moves you make, but also about *how* you move. Discussions among skateboarders frequently struggle to encapsulate these elusive but vital qualities: skateboarding is not only about elegance, fluidity and effortless ease but also about aggression, about defying gravity – and perhaps above all, about what I have called *embodied attitude*. I will return to some of these aesthetic qualities in considering the videos themselves more directly.

This display of style in movement partly serves an instructional function. Videos can be used as a source for learning new moves and tricks, which is particularly important for new skaters. Skaters may also watch videos of their own performance, in seeking to improve particular aspects, or look back on what they have achieved. As Matt, one of my interviewees, put it, video 'is the main media that shows how people are progressing', while Liam argued that 'it's a good way of pushing yourself and everything, but it's also to look back on everything … and progressing, seeing how far you've come.'

Along with other media such as zines, video also serves as a means of community building, and of sharing 'insider' knowledge: it can offer a form of contact between isolated groups, which is crucial in a rapidly evolving culture in which preferred skating sites (or 'spots') and moves are constantly changing and evolving. The videos help to inform viewers about the architecture of the spots themselves – cityscapes, squares, industrial parks, corporate malls – as well as the configuration of the space – the particular combination of rails, stairs, benches, curbs and so on, as well as the manufactured half-pipes and other 'furniture' of established skateparks. Skating videos typically feature locations recognisable to viewers, and serve to mark out local territory, which can play a key role in the nomadic pursuit of skaters by the authorities. For example, Liam, an 18-year-old living in a rural village, spoke about the role of video in building connections across a wider community of skaters in neighbouring towns – which was also apparent from the flow of messages on his MySpace site, where several of his videos were posted. Meanwhile, as Jon (an older skater) noted, there was a considerable element of competition here among the more commercial videographers: choosing original spots and showing original tricks were at a premium in a crowded market.

For the video-makers I interviewed, the making and viewing of videos seemed to have provided them with a greater sense of purpose and motivation. In some instances, this was relatively immediate: Mike, for example, talked about watching videos 'to pump you up' before going out skating. In other cases, however, it appeared to be more long term. Liam spoke about video-making as a way of 'getting something more out of skateboarding', while Matt described video-making as 'rewarding':

There is no better feeling than working hard for a trick and then getting it on tape. And there is also no better feeling than premiering your video to a crowd and hearing their reactions. Some people say videos are ruining skateboarding and taking the fun away because all people want to do is film everything and stress out about landing crazy tricks. And yes, some do do it for the wrong reasons. But for me and my friends, it's kind of our motivation for each year. It gives us a goal and purpose. That sounds cheesy, but it's true.

To some extent, terms such as 'representation' and 'documentation' rather underestimate the significance of these image-making practices – at least if this is taken to imply that they are merely secondary to the primary activity of skating itself. On the contrary, for many skaters, visual representation is an indispensable aspect of the culture: it is itself a statement, a form of symbolic action, not merely a record of something else.

Learning cultures

These video-makers learn their craft in a variety of ways. Relatively few have any formal training in video-making, and in most cases, they learn through individual experimentation and trial and error. At the same time, there is a strong sense of participation in what the educational theorists Jean Lave and Etienne Wenger (1991) call a 'community of practice' – in effect, through forms of apprenticeship, in which specialised knowledge and skills are passed from more established members ('old timers') to relative beginners ('newbies') (see Chapter 2).

My interviewees spanned a fairly broad age range: the youngest was 12 years old and still at school, while the oldest were professional video-makers in their mid- to late-twenties. Most appeared to have begun by using the family video camera. Jacob, the 12-year-old, had learnt initially from working with his father (who had a more 'artistic' interest in video-making), and from watching skating videos, of which he claimed to have an extensive collection. Developing his skill as a video-maker involved copying particular techniques, such as mounting the camera on a board to allow for travelling shots at ground level, as well as acquiring new items of equipment, such as the fisheye lens that is a ubiquitous feature of skating videos. His first video, made with his father, involved large amounts of slow motion, although Jacob was currently seeking to make his videos 'faster' and hence (in his view) 'more professional'. He was still using a basic editing package, but was looking forward to achieving more complex effects with Final Cut Pro, a professional package widely used among skateboarding video-makers.

As I have noted, video-makers often have a sense that there may be a progression between amateur and professional status. Paul, for example, described how his involvement had moved on from simply 'filming my mates', largely because of the involvement of an older professional mentor: 'I met Lee Dainton, who was filming at the time for his skate company video. He started taking me on filming trips and he started teaching me techniques with filming, filming angles etc … from this I have filmed other stuff than skateboarding and have recently had my name credited in *Dirty Sanchez*, the movie, for additional filming.' Jon and Matt, both in their twenties, had come to making skating videos only in their late teens. However, both had since used the skills they had developed to find work in the mainstream media industries: Matt was a television editor, while Jon had since moved into running his own video production company, and both attributed their success to having started with skating videos. Jon had also been particularly inspired by the work of Spike Jonze (who moved from skating videos to becoming a Hollywood director) and on a more personal level by another mentor, Dan Magee of Blueprint Films.

According to Jon, the making of skate videos had significantly expanded in recent years: 'for every good skater out there, there's a camera, a kid with a camera behind him.' This was, he argued, largely a matter of access to technology; but it was resulting in a younger generation with significantly greater technical skills:

> Now I can see that there are fourteen, fifteen-year-old kids who have got the same sort of technical skills as someone about twice their age who has been working in TV for years, and that's purely 'cause of skating, because they're just obsessed with getting the right kit. You know, they spend hours learning the editing software and … learning the after-effects software …. These kids are going to have such a leg up whenever they enter the work market, if they want to do that, because those sorts of skills I think will be in real demand.

Even so, Jon was less than optimistic about the current economic climate for aspiring video-makers. With so much material available free online, skaters were unwilling to pay for videos; and the 'core market' itself was small, and increasingly crowded with new products. The best option today, he argued, would be to acquire sponsorship in order to distribute a video as a cover-mount on a magazine. As this implies, the opportunities for 'mid-range' producers may be declining, as the gap widens between amateur or non-profit video-making and the large-scale commercial industry.

Websites are also playing an increasingly important role in terms of learning. The Skate Perception website provides extensive resources for skateboarding video-makers. There are instructional videos on a wide range of specialist topics – 'vector painting', repairing cameras, lighting set-ups, slow motion and rotoscoping; product reviews evaluating 'prosumer' camcorders and other technology, with specific reference to their advantages and disadvantages for filming skateboarding (including issues such as weight and stability, the placement of controls and battery life); and advice pages and discussion threads providing detailed information on topics ranging from fitting lenses and file compression to 'vignetting' and other post-production effects (at the time of this research, there were over 3000 subtopics relating to fisheye lenses alone).

Skate Perception also runs competitive 'assignments', mostly focused on the evaluation of specific shots – 'best handrail shot', 'best fisheye stairset shot', 'best rolling longlens handrail shot' and so on. However, perhaps the most interesting area in terms of learning is the critiques, where members submit their work for frank but generally supportive commentary by 'SP's panel of video judges'. The advice here is partly of a technical nature (to do with issues such as lenses, colour balancing or eliminating camera shake), but much of it is also focused on aesthetic issues. Video-makers are encouraged to 'get creative' and to go beyond 'point and shoot', by varying their angles, moving in closer, avoiding overuse of the fisheye lens and using manual settings rather than automatic exposure. Here, for example, 'Biggie11' offers feedback to one aspiring video-maker:

> Filming stationary fisheye on flat ground ledge tricks hardly ever looks good, so I would advise filming long lens for that. You should shoot the single ledge tricks long lens. As for settings, it was pretty easy to tell they were all on auto. I'm not sure what camera you were using, but try to utilize even the most basic settings such as exposure. You also need to use the rule of thirds for the fisheye shots. Unfortunately, with such a minimal amount of wideness on that fisheye, it's hard to make the filming look spectacular. Just keep filming, and build up your experience so one day you can invest in some better equipment. I see kids on here all the time that buy three chips for their first cameras, and their filming is horrid because they have no experience. Keep filming, and you will build up your experience and skill.

As this comment shows, aspiring video-makers are encouraged to follow some conventional forms of 'film grammar' (the 'rule of thirds'), and to use manual rather than automatic settings in order to achieve greater control. While there is an aspiration towards 'better equipment', this is not an end in itself: the feedback is principally about aesthetics (about what 'looks good' or 'spectacular'), and not merely about technology.

Even so, technology does appear to matter, and in quite particular ways. According to Jon, there are now more specialised 'subcultures' among video-makers, at least partly based on the kind of equipment that is being used: 'there's this real following of fashion and trends within what cameras to use, and some cameras have got real kudos and others don't … And it gets almost farcical really when you get these twelve-year-old kids wandering around with cameras that are worth about two grand.' In the discussion boards on Skate Perception, participants are keen to define themselves in terms of their technological kit. When I interviewed Paul, aged in his late teens he offered me the details of his set-up as follows: 'I used Panasonic NV-GS 400 with a Raynox 0.3X Semi-Fisheye for most of the video and when filming inside skateparks I used Jessops VL-35 light. For some of the video I used Sony vx2100 with a Century .3x Ultra Fisheye Adapter. To edit the video I used Adobe Premiere Pro.' The Sony VX1000 camera, in particular, seems to enjoy an almost mythical status among skateboarding video-makers: it is a relatively heavy camera that is no longer manufactured, but is believed to have particularly good colour quality. Likewise, the Mark 1 Century Optics fisheye lens – known among skaters as the 'Death lens' – is also widely regarded as the essential brand, again despite the fact that it is no longer manufactured (at least in the Mark 1 version).

Representing skating

The content of skateboarding videos inevitably reflects the composition and the preoccupations of the culture. Among the scores of videos I have seen, the focus is predominantly on urban skating, rather than on the more institutionalised environment of skateparks (which, as I have noted, are viewed somewhat ambivalently by skaters). Confrontations with authority are a recurring theme: 12-year-old Jacob's film *Get Out!* features a typical scene in which the boys are ritualistically expelled from a particular skating spot by a gesticulating security guard, who is filmed from a safe distance in long shot (cf. Burn and Parker, 2003). Across this fairly large sample of videos, gathered primarily through specialist and generic video-sharing sites, I have encountered not one example featuring female skaters, and only very rare appearances by non-white skaters (principally Asian-Americans).

To the outsider, the majority of skateboarding videos might well appear predictable and formulaic in terms of both style and content. The typical structure entails a simple sequence of individual skaters performing moves or tricks. Each skater is introduced in turn via a caption (sometimes with a freeze-frame), and then shown in action. Jon, one of my more experienced interviewees, used a very appropriate analogy to describe this:

> I always see skate films as a bit like porn. Like, they are all about just like the money shot [the orgasm shot]. Like people just want the best trick. Like, with no storyline. That's all they want. They want, like ... bang-bang, like massive tricks done by the best people that they've never seen before and it's just about building up on that. So all the skate films that you'll have seen, it will just be like trick, trick, trick, trick, intro to a bloke, trick, trick, trick, trick ... next bloke, and so on.

Nevertheless, as Jon pointed out, such apparently repetitive sequences of tricks would 'speak volumes' to the specialist viewer. Viewers would typically pay close attention, not just to the tricks themselves, but also to the locations: particular well-known 'spots' recur in a range of videos. At the same time, there is a premium on innovation here. As Jon put it, 'you can't go to the same spot and do the same trick as somebody else had done in the same spot in your video, you have to do something different. You know, there's all this sort of politics that goes on beneath the surface that you won't know about until you get into the scene.'

As Janine Hunter (2003) points out, skating is an activity in which learning is carried out almost exclusively in public: there is no 'backstage' practicing. Skating videos frequently attest to this by including 'bails' (or failed manoeuvres) as well as successful ones; and in some cases, this extends to sequences in which participants display their wounds or injuries, or simply vent their frustration by smashing up their boards. To some extent, this might be read simply as a kind of macho confirmation of the risk-taking that successful skateboarding entails, although there could be an element of male masochism here too.

Nevertheless, the overriding focus of the videos is simply on capturing successful tricks. Like dance, skateboarding is about the spectacle of bodily movement; and while this is partly a matter of physical skill or technique – of agility, strength, timing and reflexes – it is also about aesthetics and 'style'. Such qualities are very hard to capture in words: terms like grace and elegance, or aggression and daring, can only begin to identify the embodied nature of the experience, and the particular ways in which the body, the architecture and the board itself are related. These qualities are in turn reflected in the visual style and the editing of the videos.

For most of the video-makers I interviewed, the camerawork was the most important element here, while the use of music and editing played a somewhat secondary role. One email interviewee, Mike, for example, wrote as follows:

> I believe that the camera angle, the style of the skater, the music, and the surroundings have a major part in making a skate video. I try to get buildings in the background, some shots of the sky, stuff like that. I like artsy shots. Maybe like a silhouette of a shadow skating down the road or something to that effect. But I think that the camera angle is the most important in the style of a skate video. If you have a good angle anything can look good.

Jon, likewise, argued that skateboarding was 'all about shapes ... some of the shapes that skateboarders make when they're skating are just amazing, and a lot of it comes from capturing that.' The frequent use of low-angle shots in particular serves to exaggerate and dramatise these spectacular geometric shapes.

The specific role of the fisheye lens is worth noting here – particularly in contrast with the use of the telephoto lens that is typically used in much other sports photography. The fisheye has greater depth of field, and exaggerates the height as the skater flies through the air, and the angularity of the body shape. As Borden (2001: 128) notes, it also enables the camera to capture not just the skater but also the surrounding architecture and the community of other skaters who are often seen observing the trick. Similar points could be made about other characteristic aspects of camerawork. The long-lens tracking shot, where the camera follows the skater – known as the 'Fred', after Fred Mortagne, who first perfected it – heightens the sense of risk, while also positioning the camera operator (and hence the viewer) as a fellow participant. The low-angle shot with the camera mounted on the board at ground level exaggerates the sensation of speed, while the occasional use of still frames and slow motion also serves to accentuate the angularity of the shapes, and the skater's defiance of gravity (while simultaneously allowing for close study).

Editing is obviously crucial in contributing a sense of pace and rhythm, and music plays a key role here in lending an overall coherence to the piece. Among the video-makers I interviewed, there were different approaches to combining images and sound: some began with a track and edited images to accompany it, while others edited the images first and then fine-tuned when they had added a selected track. Liam, for example, spoke about adjusting the pace of the editing and the movement to accompany the quieter passages of the music.

At the same time, music also made it possible to establish connections with other youth cultural styles. Liam talked of using music to reflect the 'image' of the skater ('if they have a bit more of a rockish style, then we'll use that'), and about using specifically 'English' music to reflect their location. As Matt explained:

> One thing that you need to do is find a song that suits the type of skating. You have no idea how many bad videos I see where you know the person was just thinking 'oh, this song is rad, let's use it', but the song does not fit the skating at all, and it just ends up looking stupid. Sometimes, I hear songs I don't like, but put to the right skating, it can be amazing. But yeah, you don't want to use a fast metal song to a skater who skates slow, and vice versa, although there are always exceptions. Sometimes I'll edit a video part to 5 or 6 different songs to find out which one works the best.

In fact, the styles of music used in skateboarding videos are quite diverse. Across the sample I viewed, the music ranged from relatively mainstream indie rock (Arcade Fire, Coldplay, At the Drive-In) to commercial R+B (Janet Jackson) and rap (Nas) to anonymous techno breakbeats and even mainstream pop (including the notable 'PJ Toxic Remix', in which the Britney Spears video is combined with skating footage). Significantly, however, the music rarely obliterates the live sound – the noise of skate wheels, the slap of the board as it lands or the scraping as it grinds along a kerb or rail, all contribute to the sense of immediacy and participation.

Despite the apparent similarities among the videos in terms of content and structure, other elements contribute to creating a more individual 'feel' – which may partly reflect the style of the skaters, but may also be the original 'signature' of the video-maker. The use of different fonts in captions, for example, or of special effects such as 'vignetting' and 'vector painting' (topics of considerable discussion on the Skate Perception site) also play a role here. Some skateboarding video-makers argue that style – or indeed the ambitions of the video-maker – should not detract too much from content. Likewise, elements of narrative, documentary (such as interviews) or comedy are often seen as a distraction from the action. Jon, for example, admired some more comic skating videos, but argued that comedy would ultimately 'undermine' what the skaters were doing.

Nevertheless, several interviewees, and indeed some contributors to Skate Perception, were critical of the rather relentlessly 'serious' approach of some skate videos. Jacob, for example, talked about how he deliberately included 'little random bits in between' the skateboarding (such as close-ups of people or local landmarks), while Liam argued that it was good to include more comical elements in order to have 'a little break' and to 'make it the most entertaining'. Likewise, one critique posted on Skate Perception by 'Ryan', one of the resident video judges, urges the film-maker to introduce more variety in his approach:

> Focus on composition and things like that in these shots. You were sorta close with it, with the reaction of the guy clapping, but like I said try and make it a little bit more interesting composition-wise. You could have also gotten some things like timelapses and stuff that would have made the montage much more interesting. The key thing here though is variety. Don't just have skating skating skating skating skating skating skating skating skating skating and then that's the end. Mix it up! Make it more interesting!

Paul, another interviewee, argued that it was vital to have a 'unique style' – achieved in his case through the use of a particular font for captions, and especially through comedy. Under his nickname 'Porno', he has made a series of videos that combine skateboarding with parodies of 1970s-style pornography, as is apparent from the publicity flyers he produced for one public screening (see Figure 7.1: note the fake moustache, floral wallpaper and 'retro'-style video camera).

While these elements are individually important, they also have to be combined into an effective overall ensemble. As Jon put it, describing the work of one of his heroes, Dan Magee:

> [H]e was the first guy that I came across that really made skate films look incredibly beautiful ... And he was using the same raw materials that everyone else was. I mean, the skating in his was better, but ultimately it was skate footage. And he just cut it in a way with the music and the colours and the rhythm that just made it look phenomenal, really ... It's all about creating a final package that really works with the skater and the spots and everything. It's all got to ... It's quite complicated making it work right.

Conclusion

This case study illustrates some of the functions that video-making serves in representing and constructing a specific form of youth culture. However, it also exemplifies several of the broader themes that run through the other studies in this book. The production of skateboarding videos is a developed and self-reflexive practice, with particular forms of social organisation. Through both face-to-face and online interactions, these video-makers are establishing their own aesthetic and stylistic conventions. They are using a variety of means and opportunities to learn, both about technology and about the 'language' of video as a medium. Amateur practices overlap with the professional production and distribution of videos to a point where the distinction itself becomes quite blurred. The practice of video-making is a key part of the way in which the culture represents itself, and how the identity of the participants comes to be defined. In common with the other camcorder cultures we have analysed, this is a practice that is simultaneously personal and social, economic and aesthetic.

References

Baccigaluppi, J., Mayugba, S. and Carnel, C. (2001) *Declaration of Independents.* San Francisco: Chronicle Books.

Beal, B. (1996) 'Alternative masculinity and its effects on gender relations in the subculture of skateboarding'. *Journal of Sport Behavior.* 19(3): 204–20.

Bennett, A. (1999) 'Subcultures or neo-tribes? Rethinking the relationship between youth, style and musical taste'. *Sociology.* 33(3): 599–617.

Borden, I. (2001) *Skateboarding, Space and the City: Architecture and the Body.* Oxford: Berg.

Burn, A. and Parker, D. (2003) *Analysing Media Texts.* London: Continuum.

Hebdige, D. (1979) *Subculture: The Meaning of Style.* London: Methuen.

Hesmondhalgh, D. (2005) 'Subcultures, scenes or tribes? None of the above'. *Journal of Youth Studies.* 8(1): 21–40.

Hunter, J. (2003) '"Flying-through-the-air magic": skateboarders, fashion and social identity'. MA Dissertation. Sheffield: University of Sheffield. www.shef.ac.uk/socstudies/shop/7hunter.pdf accessed 1st June 2007.

Karsten, L. and Pel, E. (2001) 'Skateboarders exploring urban spaces: ollies, obstacles and conflicts'. *Journal of Housing and the Built Environment.* 15: 327–40.

Lave, J. and Wenger, E. (1991) *Situated Learning: Legitimate Peripheral Participation.* Cambridge: Cambridge University Press.

Nolan, N. (2003) 'The ins and outs of skateboarding and transgression in public space in Newcastle, Australia'. *Australian Geographer.* 34(3): 311–27.

Pomerantz, S., Currie, D. H. and Kelly, D. M. (2004) 'Sk8er girls: skateboarders, girlhood and feminism in motion'. *Women's Studies International Forum.* 27: 547–57.

Rinehart, R. (2005) '"Babes" and boards: opportunities in a new millennium sport?' *Journal of Sport and Social Issues*. 29(3): 232–55.

skateperception.com (2007) Spotlights. http://skateperception.com/spot/ accessed 1st June 2007.

Stratford, E. (2002) 'On the edge: a tale of skaters and urban governance'. *Social and Cultural Geography*. 3(2): 193–206.

Thornton, S. (1995) *Club Cultures: Music, Media and Subcultural Capital*. Cambridge: Polity.

Waerdahl, R. (2007) 'To be or not to be: commodified expressions of group affiliations and individuality'. Unpublished paper. University of Oslo.

Weller, S. (2006) 'Skateboarding alone? Making social capital discourse relevant to teenagers' lives'. *Journal of Youth Studies*. 9(5): 557–74.

Wheaton, B. (2000) '"New lads"? Masculinities and the "new sport" participant'. *Men and Masculinities*. 2(4): 434–56.

Wheaton, B. and Beal, B. (2003) '"Keeping it real": subcultural media and the discourses of authenticity in alternative sport'. *International Review for the Sociology of Sport*. 38(2): 155–76.

Widdicombe, S. and Wooffitt, R. (1995) *The Language of Youth Subcultures: Social Identity in Action*. Hemel Hempstead: Harvester.

Woolley, H. and Johns, R. (2001) 'Skateboarding: the city as a playground'. *Journal of Urban Design*. 6(2): 211–30.

8
Handing Over Control? Access, 'ordinary people' and Video Nation

Jo Henderson

> Video Nation hands over control to you. If you are unhappy about a finished video, you can suggest changes or choose not to have it shown. That way you are free to shoot first, decide later.
>
> (Video Nation, 2008)

Video Nation is a well-established participatory video-making project run by the BBC: it operates on national and various local websites, as well as providing material for television and radio broadcasting. Participants are invited to submit self-filmed video diaries on a range of self-selected or BBC-defined themes and subjects. On its website, the project presents itself as a neutral platform where 'ordinary people' are encouraged to represent their 'views and experiences on camera and online' (Video Nation, 2008). After agreeing to take part in the project, participants are lent video cameras and shown their basic functions, or they request or agree to an 'assisted shoot'. The footage is edited by the BBC into a two-minute short that, once approved by the participant, is uploaded onto the project website and archive. As indicated in the quote above, Video Nation claims that the participant has ultimate control over the finished video in the form of a veto that may be enacted at any point.

This chapter interrogates the claim that the BBC 'hands over control' to the 'ordinary person' (in this case, the Video Nation participant), and sets this in the context of broader questions about the relationship between broadcasting institutions and 'ordinary people'. Data include archival materials from the BBC's Written Archives Centre (WAC), interviews with Video Nation participants and BBC producers involved with the project, a survey of 100 videos and close analyses of selected examples. The focus of this chapter is on the points of institutional mediation – the selection of participants, the filming and editing processes, the commissioning procedures and the archival practices of the website. I suggest that despite recent claims about the democratisation of media (discussed in Chapters 2 and 5), the range of positions available for 'ordinary people' to represent themselves on Video Nation has in fact decreased significantly since the project moved from a broadcast to an online platform.

The BBC and access television

For more than 80 years, the BBC has been built around the Reithian edict that it should educate, inform and entertain its audience. Historical research suggests that the relationship between the Corporation and its audience has changed significantly over time, yet it has always remained a point of difficulty and sometimes contention (e.g. Born, 2005; Burns, 1977). Since the advent of commercial television in 1955, the BBC has been bound to compete to maintain its share of the popular audience, and hence to justify the continuation of the licence fee, the form of compulsory taxation through which it is funded. At the same time, its public service mandate has required it to reflect all elements of society, including minority groups and interests.

The history of access programming at the BBC began as far back as the late 1960s. The emergence at that time of new forms of documentary film-making – 'direct cinema' and 'cinema verité' – appeared to offer new possibilities in terms of representing the lives and perspectives of ordinary people. Many of the BBC trainees who had 'developed during the upsurge of 1968' were influenced by these new forms, as well as by the principles of access television developed in the United States (Thomas, 2008). Meanwhile, the synch sound facility and lower light requirements of both portable film equipment and the emergent technology of video were encouraging producers to consider the possibility of making programmes 'in the real world', outside of television's ritual space of the studio.

As a response to these developments, the BBC produced new guidelines (*Principles and Practice in Documentary Programmes*, 1972) aimed at standardising practice across factual programming (Vaughan, 1999: 11). Producers were advised to 'keep themselves, their opinions and their equipment out of the picture' (Thomas, 2008). However, the guidelines were open to different interpretations, reflected in programmes such as *The Space Between Words* (Roger Graef, 1972), *Swallow Your Leader* (Colin

Thomas, 1973) and *The Family* (Paul Watson, 1974), which in various ways challenged the apparent neutrality of conventional documentary. *The Family* was one of the earliest examples of the *factual* representation of domestic life on UK television (as opposed to fictional forms such as soap operas), and its transmission raised serious ethical issues relating to the participation of ordinary people and the notion of celebrity.

Rowan Ayers and Mike Fentiman, producers of the BBC2 current affairs programme *Late Night Line-Up*, also experimented with new forms and subjects in factual programming. One of their programmes featured a live segment in which Guinness workers in a Glasgow factory were asked for their opinions about television programming. According to Peter Humm the factory workers argued 'that the BBC would not be interested in the opinions of ordinary viewers and that anything they did say was bound to be edited to fit BBC prejudices' (Humm, 1998: 229).

This critique led the BBC2 Director of Programmes, David Attenborough, to suggest to the Board of Governors that a form of 'community programmes' could introduce 'new editorial attitudes that do not derive from the assumptions of the university educated elite who are commonly believed to dominate television production' (WAC, 1972a). However, it was not only the Board of Governors who needed persuading about the benefit of such programmes. The 'closed-shop' (union labour only) conditions of TV studios had until this point ensured that the amateur and substandard format of domestic video was restricted to special circumstances in news production. (Professional video was already being used for both news and repeat transmissions.) It was the amateur status of the non-union producers, rather than the technology of video per se, that the Association of Cinematograph and Television Technicians (ACTT) found objectionable.

By framing community programming as experimental and waving the regulatory stick at the unions and governors, Attenborough was able to set up a new Community Programmes Unit (CPU) in 1972. The CPU was put in the hands of Paul Bonner, an experienced BBC documentary-maker who later became the first programme controller at Channel 4, the second commercial television channel in the UK. Under the CPU's auspices, community or special interest groups could propose an idea for a factual programme based on their interests and activities. Provided they met certain conditions, they were able to choose from existing televisual formats (actuality/location shoots, investigative reports, studio discussions or debates) and participate in the editing of a programme about themselves. As the 1974 BBC Handbook reiterated, 'The groups are given technical facilities and professional advice by the BBC, but themselves decide the style and content of their programmes, subject to limitations of cost and the legal requirements of broadcasting' (WAC, 1974: 37).

As part of the application process, the groups had to agree to certain conditions: the resulting programme had to be free from advertising, obscenity, libel, incitements to riot and politics (WAC, 1972b). However, as Dovey argues, 'Successful ideas for programmes were almost always those submitted by groups involved in social action campaigns or cultural development – constructed by the Unit as the representatives of "the unheard, the rarely heard, and the socially inarticulate"' (Dovey, 1993: 165).

The CPU series aired at the end of each day's schedule under the title of *Open Door*. (The originally proposed title *Open House* was rejected, perhaps because it inferred too much access.) Each programme featured up to three groups, sometimes resulting in unfortunate combinations (for example, one paired the British Association of Retired Persons and the Society for the Rescue of Destitute Animals). Each series included at least one feedback slot where studio and remote audiences could respond to previously aired programmes.

In 1983 *Open Door* evolved into *Open Space*, with two main differences: firstly, the programmes moved to an earlier transmission slot, which necessitated higher production values to appeal to potentially larger (and more mainstream) audiences. Secondly, the output concentrated on individual voices rather than ideas from groups. Nevertheless, the individuals involved continued to have editorial control, thus preserving the principle of access originally envisioned for the CPU. According to Jeremy Gibson, then head of the CPU, the unit was 'developing a "freedom of speech" editorial policy rather than a practice based on any shared set of political principles' (quoted in Dovey, 1993: 167).

Video Diaries

This 'freedom of speech' policy led to the development of the highly regarded *Video Diaries* series, the immediate forerunner to Video Nation. Unlike *Open Space*, in which groups applied to participate, the producers of *Video Diaries* actively sought out individuals with interesting stories to tell. As executive producer Bob Long explained, the BBC received around 3000 applications for each series of eight programmes, and while four of these were selected, a further four were invited by the BBC (quoted in Humm, 1998: 233).

Successful applicants were loaned a video camera for anything up to a year, in order to produce an hour-long or feature-length programme.

As well as the loan of the camera, the participant was assigned a BBC producer who would offer training in the use of the equipment and feedback on the footage. Self-filming enabled the participant to experiment with the camera uninhibited by anyone else's presence. The extended one-to-one relationship between the participant and the producer, particularly in the editing process, enhanced the possibilities for the participant to contribute meaningfully to the construction of the programme.

The first series of *Video Diaries* was broadcast on BBC2 in 1990. These often poignant, first-person accounts frequently dealt with difficult subject matter which had not previously been represented on television. For example, in the first series a young man returned to Belfast at the time when concurrent broadcasting restrictions made any representations of the province potentially problematic; a woman confronted her father about the abuse she was subjected to in her childhood; a young gay man 'came out' to his strict religious parents; siblings recounted their traumatic upbringing; a convicted prisoner reconsidered the attitudes and actions that led to his 12-year jail sentence; and a disability campaigner protested about the lack of access to public transport for wheelchair users. The mode of address employed in *Video Diaries* was also unusual. The first-person monologue direct-to-camera is a privileged form, then rarely used in television: its conventions were reserved to signify unimpeachable content such as the Royal Christmas Message to the nation. Factual material featuring everyday domestic settings was also still rare (apart from occasional clips in the domestic disaster show *You've Been Framed*, which started in the same year as *Video Diaries*).

The series made for captivating, innovative and award-winning TV. The entire second series won a BAFTA for 'innovation' in 1992, and an individual programme, *Gary Lineker and Me*, won the BAFTA Flaherty Documentary Award the following year. In Dovey's words, 'Here, the critics agreed, was something genuinely new and fresh in the arid schedules of network TV' (1993: 168). Part of the uniqueness of *Video Diaries* was that the programmes were entirely made from amateur footage. The series also marks the point where a domestic video format (Hi8) reached the minimum quality set by the ACTT Union (Dowmunt, 2001). *Video Diaries* opened the door for new forms and new representations of domestic reality that *The Family* had only hinted at.

Video Diaries transmitted at 10.30 pm on Saturday nights, and although individual programmes sometimes attracted audiences of up to nine million, the series as a whole did not achieve consistently high figures. The unpredictability of viewing figures, along with the extended producer input and exceptionally high shooting ratios (sometimes 500:1), became increasingly problematic in a deregulating domestic television market. The series and its offspring, *Teenage Video Diaries,* ceased to commission new programmes in 1994, although the production time and scarcity of slots extended transmission to 1999 when the final programme, *Spit It Out,* was broadcast. In total 60 programmes were broadcast under the strand, with less than half offering examples where 'ordinary people' had applied for access. As an indication of changing times at the BBC, the CPU was diminished and proved itself unable to survive within the constraints of the internal market system, eventually closing in 1998 to make way for the rolling news channel BBC24 (Born, 2005: 439).

Video Nation – the broadcast project

In 1992 Alan Yentob, then head of BBC2, approved a proposal for Video Nation, a new project in which 'ordinary people' would submit self-filmed accounts or vignettes of their everyday lives. In keeping with some of the aims of the CPU, Video Nation would 'continue to offer remarkable insights via self-portraits by individuals from diverse walks of life, extending the representational range of British television in unparalleled ways' (Born, 2005: 439). The project was seen as a way of extending access to 'ordinary people' who were under-represented or misrepresented within mainstream broadcasting, while 'building on the success of the *Video Diaries* series' (Rose, 1994/5: 9). However, a substantial difference between the Video Nation project and its predecessors, *Video Diaries, Open Space* and *Open Door* was that it was based on the principle of editorial *approval* rather than editorial *control.*

Video Nation's commissioning as a project rather than a series freed it from the annual round of slot or series commissions and meant that content was produced without the guarantee of broadcast. The project aimed to 'provide material to a diversity of programmes that had not been developed yet' (Carpentier, 2003: 15), while simultaneously forming an archive based at the British Film Institute (BFI). The material would offer fragmentary glimpses into the contemporary experiences of 'ordinary people', including 'sequences on subjects they chose plus material shot in response to "briefings" and questions sent out by us' (Rose, 1994/5: 10). Early suggestions from the project for topics included Your Least Favourite Thing, A Favourite Place, Friday the 13th, Spare Time, Cultural Identity, Money and Holidays. The only defined usage of the material was the inclusion in the BFI archive; and as there was no commitment to broadcast, the content could, in principle, be freely chosen by the participant.

The production team of Bob Long, Chris Mohr and Mandy Rose aligned Video Nation with the Mass Observation project, an independent sociological research initiative founded in 1936 by Tom Harrison, Humphrey Jennings and Charles Madge. Mass Observation volunteers were asked to submit anonymous written accounts of their everyday experiences on the 12th day of each month and to respond to contemporary events such as the Abdication Crisis and the coronation of George VI. Jennings was the most acclaimed British documentary film-maker of his time and also one of the organisers of the 1936 Surrealism exhibition in London, and it is his influence that is perhaps most apparent in the Mass Observation archive. Submissions to the archive cover topics such as dreams and weather reports, the regularity of bowel movements and the price of fish, reflecting Jennings's interest in the surreal juxtapositions of everyday life. In aligning itself with this element of Mass Observation, Video Nation solicited the submissions of 'ordinary people' regarding their mundane, everyday experiences and their personal responses to public events. According to a BBC press release 'Our contributors are the 1990s equivalent of the original panel of volunteers. The difference is that instead of writing they use up-to-the-minute camcorder technology to keep a daily record of their lives.' These 'ordinary people' were later defined by executive producer Bob Long as being 'non-media professionals' (Carpentier, 2003: 21), perhaps a hangover from the union discourse that had now lost its currency.

Seven thousand people responded to a general call for participants put out on BBC channels; and in addition, as producer Chris Mohr recounts, the project made 'grass roots attempts ... to reach underrepresented communities' (Carpentier, 2003: 25). From these responses, the BBC selected 57 contributors who undertook to submit 90 minutes of footage every two weeks over the course of a year. According to one of the other producers Mandy Rose, the participant selection aimed to achieve 'a multi-cultural group who would, broadly speaking, mirror the country in terms of income range, regional spread and political opinion, [although] we were clear that we couldn't represent the country' (Rose, 1994/5: 9).

Successful volunteers included an unemployed black youth from Birmingham, a member of the House of Lords, a merchant banker, a Myalgic Encephalopathy (ME) sufferer, a soldier, a house husband, a vicar, a single mum, a nun, a refugee and a new age traveler or 'hippy'. Of the 57, 43 were based in England (though not necessarily born there), seven were from Scotland, three from Wales and three from Northern Ireland (one dropped out). The youngest was a 12-year-old miner's daughter from Doncaster, and the oldest was a 73-year-old retired army officer from Devon. At least ten of the original participants were from non-British ethnic groups, and 30 were women. While attempting to be broadly representative, the selection process compounded some existing stereotypes (for example, the five unemployed participants included the only black youth) (WAC, 1994a).

In common with the *Video Diaries* series, participants were loaned a Hi8 camera for a year. Instead of developing a relationship with a BBC producer, the participants attended training days where they learnt the basic functions of the camera and took part in 'exercises during which people became accustomed to shooting "subjectively" rather than as silent observers of the "home movie"' (Rose, 1994/5: 10). Similar instructions were repeated in the project newsletter: 'Remember to include yourself in every sequence you shoot' and 'film at least two details (cutaways) of every sequence (ten seconds and still)' (WAC, 1994b). These tips still appear, in a different form, in the 'filming skills' section of the Video Nation website.

However, as I have noted, participants' access to production was reduced when compared with the forerunner projects, *Video Diaries, Open Space* and *Open Door*, as editorial control changed to editorial approval. Mandy Rose explained:

> [F]or logistical reasons we couldn't offer access to the cutting room, we did offer contributors a contractual right of editorial veto: to see any material we wanted to transmit in context and to say no if, for any reason, they weren't happy with it.
>
> (Rose, 1994/5: 10)

The small production team already had 57 participants submitting potentially 84 hours of footage every two weeks, which at least needed to be reviewed. Attendance at edits would have substantially increased project costs in terms of travel, expenses and BBC producer time.

The project experimented with a number of broadcast formats: themed compilation programmes such as *Money, Money, Money*; the annual *Video Nation Review of the Year*; and the transmission of the unedited 'rushes', *Video Nation Uncut*. By far the most popular and best remembered were the two-minute shorts that were broadcast on weekday evenings at 10.30 pm before the current affairs programme, *Newsnight*, on BBC2.

The first broadcast short was made for the suggested topic 'Your Least Favourite Thing' by retired Colonel Gordon Henscher, the oldest participant. *M-I-R-R-O-R* is an engaging one minute 14 seconds short, a simple and articulate reflection on the process of ageing and the subject's relationship with his reflection. The opening three cutaways show reflections from different mirrors accompanied by a piano soundtrack. From the cutaways it moves to real-time footage of the Colonel, in a collar, tie and cardigan, sitting forward in an armchair talking direct to the camera – as though 'we', the mass of singular viewers, were sitting there as 'guests' in his home. The monologue starts with the word 'Mirror' being spelled out and then spoken:

> There was a time when they were very useful, still are of course, I have to use them. But it's a ghastly thing to look and see your face, what it is now, and what you feel it should be inside you.
>
> (Video Nation, 1994)

At the end of his monologue, the Colonel leans forward and turns 'us' off, deliberately disrupting the effect of the mimicked face-to-face encounter.

Unscripted real-time (that is, unedited) monologues such as the Colonel's were rare; they depended on a participant's ability to speak articulately and 'perform' in front of a camera free from pauses, repetitions or stutters. As previously mentioned, *factual* domestic scenes had been rarely seen on television prior to this point. Video Nation shorts (and their predecessor, *Video Diaries*) offered viewers 'a chance to see inside people's homes and lives at a level of intimacy no film crew, however sensitive, could ever match' (Dovey, 1993: 168). This intimacy is particularly created by the proximity of the subject to the lens, which suggests a lack of mediation, thereby naturalising the pro-filmic events. Of course, the event is constructed for the camera, and therefore appears as a putative moment – as the event that would be taking place if the camera were not there. However, in the case of a direct address to camera, there is no equivalent experience that takes place when the camera is absent.

Between 1994 and 2000, 1200 shorts were broadcast as part of the Video Nation project. Audience figures for the televised shorts ranged between 1.1 million and 1.9 million, depending on the programmes that preceded and followed them. The weekly themed compilation programmes reached their audience peak of 1.6 million viewers for the *1994 Review of the Year*, broadcast on Christmas Eve (WAC, 1995).

Despite these positive ratings and the critical acclaim that *Video Diaries* and Video Nation had received, the project was axed from the broadcast schedule after the appointment of Jane Root as Controller of BBC2, apparently in the interests of a 'tighter evening schedule that would hold viewers' (Carpentier, 2003: 17). The project's final newsletter announced in May 2000, 'After a long period of uncertainty, the controller of BBC2 has finally decided not to recommission Video Nation for the future. While remaining extremely proud of the project she is now keen to explore and develop a new venture to take its place' (WAC, 2000).

Video Nation Online

The online archive was launched in 2001 when BBC Online recognised Video Nation as an ideal vehicle to demonstrate the potential of broadband technology. Chris Mohr, one of the original producers, stated, 'the shorts library provided a unique source of (relatively) cheap and copyright-free video-content ideal for broadband to demonstrate its potential. It was already cut into hundreds of segments whose duration and personal nature were perfect for the web' (quoted in Carpentier, 2003: 17).

Despite the project's suitability for broadband, it has in fact remained a narrowcast project: online access is restricted to people based in the UK (that is, license fee payers). The shorts are streamed and cannot be downloaded. In 2000, the Video Nation project began to produce new material for the BBC Where I Live websites, which are run by local BBC radio and TV stations (now relabelled as BBC Local websites). Currently, the project is run by a four-person full-time production team based at the BBC's Birmingham headquarters. The team is complemented by regional production staff comprised of local radio and regional television presenters, journalists, camera crew or web editors, for whom Video Nation accounts for approximately 10% of their workload. Some websites are centrally funded and may include a full- or half-time post, while others are incorporated into one of the 31 local websites which have Video Nation sections. The shorts appear on the BBC Local websites and may also appear on the main Video Nation website. Some of the shorts are selected for the *Your Stories* strand on the Community Channel on BBCi (and other digital TV platforms). Local news programmes may feature a Video Nation short as an upbeat item with which to end a programme, and the World Service has used them to demonstrate conversational English on their language-teaching site.

Audio tracks from Video Nation shorts have also been played (in their entirety only) as stand-alone radio features and have been used in human-interest talk shows, such as *Home Truths* and *Saturday Live* which are broadcast on Saturday mornings.

Some shorts are made to link with BBC-wide campaigns or project features. In these cases, the regional BBC producer finds participants who fulfill certain criteria and are prepared to speak on particular subjects.[1] The participants are allowed to represent themselves only in relation to a topic or theme that is predefined by the institution – such as *Abolition*, a series of programmes to mark the bicentenary of the abolition of slavery, or *White*, a BBC2 series about white working-class communities. The recent campaign *No Home* (2007), commissioned to mark the 40th anniversary of the housing charity, Shelter, produced shorts that featured in a documentary, *Moving On*. Extracts from some of these shorts were interwoven with the tale of the presenter, actor Ray Gosling's experience of homelessness. *Moving On* was broadcast in a post-midnight Sunday slot on BBC4 to an audience of 40,000 and won the Best Documentary 2007 at the Royal Television Society Midland Centre Awards.

Other contacts between the individual participants and the project come through another connection with the BBC – as a phone-in participant, a quiz competitor, or someone who has contributed images or comments to the BBC Local or BBC News24 websites. Participants, like the BBC producers with whom they work, display different attributes and competencies in terms of media literacy, production, communication and social skills. The producers' skills vary according to the other roles they fulfill within the BBC. All Video Nation staff are offered basic training (in line with the wider internal drive for BBC staff to write, present, edit and upload their own reports), although not all are able to take part in training due to conflicting work commitments. Some regional producers view Video Nation as the 'icing on the cake' of their job and consistently produce interesting and engaging shorts that perhaps reflect *their* competencies rather than those of the participants. For others, the project does not compare favourably with the faster environment of daily production and news schedules, although it is seen to provide good experience in production techniques. Long-term producers tend to be more committed to the original aims of the project and are less enthused by 'campaign shorts' (where there is pressure to deliver material in relation to a predefined theme). Newer producers are likely to have come to the project through a news role, and for them the shorter turnaround and deadlines are more in keeping with news production; for them, campaign shorts are quicker and easier than other kinds of material.

The content management system of the Video Nation website allows users to search for shorts by location (through the BBC Local websites), by category (the 42 archival categories include Happiness, Family, Belief, Community, Countryside, Values, Identity, Faith, Art and Media) and by title and participant name. As an archive at the BFI, the unedited footage of Video Nation participants may offer future researchers data similar in richness to the data in the Mass Observation archive, now held at the University of Sussex. The Video Nation archive reaffirms its alignment with the 1930s Mass Observation project in its intention to establish a 'citizens archive', but as with all archives, it suffers from out-dated taxonomies and classifications; and, as with all websites, information becomes inaccessible because of technical faults and broken links displaying the ubiquitous 'Error 404' message.

Video Nation: Two case studies

I focus here on the experiences of two participants whom I have inter-viewed and whose videos I have analysed as part of my broader research on Video Nation. These two case studies are in some ways a complete contrast: one might be seen as an ideal Video Nation participant, while the other's attempts to participate within the terms of the project have been thwarted at every stage. There is no suggestion that these par-ticipants are typical or representative of the wider project; rather, they illustrate two very different experiences, and raise some interesting broader issues.

Denise

Denise is a long-term participant who has made approximately 25 shorts for the Video Nation broadcast and web projects. She is described by the Video Nation website as family lawyer, and is now a partner in a legal advocacy practice in the West End of London.

Denise was recruited by Video Nation after making a pilot for Carlton Television (an independent commercial television channel) for a pro-gramme on dating. Even though she is well accustomed to speaking on other people's behalf in her role as a lawyer, Denise said that she would have found the idea of volunteering herself for the project 'off-putting'. Her motivation for participating in the Carlton pilot was that media production seemed 'exciting and glamorous'; Video Nation and inclu-sion in the BFI archive made it seem more substantial and 'out there'.

Denise has had a positive relation with the Video Nation project over an 11-year period. She has worked with a number of different BBC producers and produced shorts for both broadcast and web distribution. She has relished her role, is proud of her involvement in the project and has been happy to represent the Video Nation project at BBC events.

Eight of Denise's shorts were made for the broadcast project and the remainder, including two training videos that appear in the 'filming skills' section of the website, have been produced for the online project. At least two other shorts, including one entitled *Day of Atonement,* have been completed and approved by Denise but have been incorrectly archived, never put on the website or removed. One of Denise's shorts, *Edgeware,* was removed before broadcast transmission (Video Nation, 1997a). *Edgeware* is about a demonstration against the proposed closure of the hospital where Denise was born and leans towards a form of citizen journalism. Other shorts with a similar approach are *Transplant* (Video Nation, 1996) and *Coping and Hoping* (Video Nation, 2004a). The day before transmission, *Edgeware* was pulled because of a local by-election in the north of England that was being contested on the issue of hospital closures. The BBC was not concerned about the content of Denise's short, but lacked the time to offer a counter opinion that would have been legally required in order to demonstrate political balance.

Denise made her first short, *Transplant,* before she had attended the training days the project then ran. *Transplant,* like the shorts *Shoah* (Video Nation, 1997b) and *Auschwitz* (Video Nation, 2004b), explicitly references her Jewish faith in the web description:

> *Transplant* by Denise Lester
> Denise is in hospital where she is about to become a bone marrow donor. It is a slightly risky operation, but afterwards she feels it was worth it. Helping to save a life is the finest thing you can do as a Jew.
>
> (Video Nation, 1996)

The one minute 44 seconds short contains 15 edits, a long way from the direct monologue to camera that Colonel Gordon Henscher achieved in the first broadcast short. Visual edits are apparent, but cutaways are used to disguise edits in the audio track – reflecting what Brian Winston has described as 'the immorality of the cutaway' (Winston, 2008).

Certain themes run through Denise's output. For example, the theme of remembrance is present in *Shoah,* about the National Holocaust Museum; *Auschwitz,* about Denise's pilgrimage to the concentration camp;

Di (Video Nation, 1997c), about the death of Princess Diana; *A Long Day* (2005),[2] about a campaign on behalf of the victims of the London bombings on 7 July 2005; and *Two Years On* (Video Nation, 2007), about her professional involvement in the campaign. Another theme that she has explored is London cultural events: many of these shorts only appear on the London BBC Local website, although her shorts *Chelsea Flower Show* (Video Nation, 2003a*)* and *Marathon Man* (Video Nation, 2005) are on the national Video Nation site. Some of the content themes are apparent in the titles – although her film *Office Workers* (Video Nation, 1998a) that appears on the national Video Nation site is in fact about attending the Notting Hill Carnival and the fun and diversity of the event. Many of Denise's films are made on location rather than in her domestic or private space. Three feature her office, and at least three were made while she was on holiday, including *Coping and Hoping*, which is about the 2004 tsunami when Denise was in Thailand. Most could be seen to offer a private response to a public event rather than a private experience, although an exception would be *Sixteen* (Video Nation, 1998b) in which a younger Denise reflects on her life and her hopes when she was sixteen.

Denise's practice could largely be seen to reflect the idealised notion of 'citizen journalism' discussed in Chapter 5. In many respects, she is an ideal Video Nation participant: an articulate, committed, civic-minded legal professional, who is able to reflect on her personal experiences in a broader historical and cultural context. For the purposes of the project, she also speaks as a 'representative' of a particular ethnic and religious community. The fact that she was originally recruited, and that she is to some extent attracted by the possibility of 'glamour', does not undermine the fact that her central motivation is one of civic-minded action (a motivation that is also apparent in her choice of career and her religious work). Nevertheless, Denise did express some reservations about the project. Her (and my) inability to find her short *Day of Atonement* on the website left her wondering whether the cultural narrative promoted by Video Nation is only able to contain representations of Jewishness in relation to the Holocaust. In an interview with me, she said: 'It is as though my Judaism is defined by Auschwitz and my relation with Auschwitz, but not in relation to a festival that's meaningful. I hope that the BBC are not, in the current climate, engaged in some form of self-censorship and balancing act.'

Hamish

I was initially drawn to Hamish's work in relation to Ruth Holliday's research using video diaries as a way of analysing queer identities

(Holliday, 2004). Video Nation had lost contact with Hamish, so I contacted him through his Internet profile. His response to my initial email is as follows:

> Oh yes! The Video Nation extravaganza! It was shot about five years ago, maybe six … I'll not go into a lot of detail here but it is not at all as I planned it to be, and I am not proud of it.

Hamish is in his early 70s, and now describes himself as a professional kilt wearer and kilt collector. He takes particular interest in kilt etiquette and documents which kilts and accessories he wears to which events. He has worn kilts since his teens for the Scottish dancing that he practised to a semi-professional level. He has also been involved with amateur dramatics and radio productions, including a stint in radio drama at the BBC. He has continued to do what he describes as 'bits and pieces for radio and voice-overs' whenever he is asked; the weekend after we met, he was scheduled to compere a folk festival in Wales.

Hamish's singular short, *Kilts*, features under the categories of Happiness, Home and Values and is described on the website as follows:

> A few years ago, Hamish from West Sussex made an unusual decision. He decided to start wearing kilts and skirts instead of trousers. He's had to put up with a certain amount of ridicule, but he argues that they are the most comfortable thing a man can wear – and you don't have to be Scottish.
>
> (Video Nation, 2003b)

The film is a mildly camp account of some of the benefits of kilt wearing, in which Hamish extols the versatility and comfort of the garment while standing in front of the stone fireplace of his 1970s-style suburban bungalow. It opens with an establishing shot of the exterior of the house, over which appears Hamish's name and location. Then the film cuts to Hamish, showing him from the waist up in front of a fireplace, and he addresses the camera as though telling us a secret: 'what you don't know is that about four years ago I gave up wearing trousers – instead I've gone for the traditional comfort of the kilt.' From here there is a vertical pan to demonstrate that Hamish is indeed wearing a kilt, and then some cutaway shots to still images – one of Hamish in a white kilt and crimson shiny shirt, and another of a man – possibly Hamish – in a traditional kilt and walking clothes. Next is a short section of moving footage in which Hamish is seen placing something in the boot of his car and then getting in the driver's seat. (Hamish remembers that the producer was particularly keen to get a shot of him swinging his legs into the car.) The direct address is intermingled with a voice-over from another section of footage, so that as Hamish is shown outside the home, we are told that he has come to accept that 'children who know no better will yell out something obscene from across the street, but we don't worry about that, we can take it.' As we return to the direct address, Hamish suggests that wearing skirts is not uncommon for men and we would 'be surprised at the number of men who do wear skirts in the privacy of their own home and in the company of their friends and families. There's nothing sinister about that, there's nothing untoward about it, it's perfectly natural and straightforward.' The next dissolve leads to a shot of Hamish wearing a black leather kilt and shiny top, explaining to us in a cookery show hostess-style that he wants to show 'the type of thing you can do if you want to get away from the traditional materials'. He recounts how he wore this kilt to the theatre only a couple of weeks ago – 'not with this top, mind' – and as he completes his twirl for the camera, he shows clear signs of sexual arousal.

According to Hamish, the video came about in a slightly unorthodox way. He knew some of the people at BBC Southern Counties radio – 'they would get me in to read the weather or make short announcements.' One day the Video Nation producer at the station introduced himself and asked if Hamish would like to make a documentary about an unusual aspect of himself. Although he realised that a full-time male kilt wearer in West Sussex was 'obviously' unusual, Hamish felt flattered, and entertained notions of an hour-long documentary on BBC2. Having no previous experience of video technology, he was looking forward to experimenting with the camera and making his film, which he had decided would be about the heritage of etiquette connected with some of the kilts in his collection. In order to demonstrate that kilts were the ideal garments for men to wear for any occasion, from something as informal as a football match to a banquet at Buckingham Palace, he envisioned modeling certain outfits. His intention was to represent himself as an authority, an expert on all things kilt. The BBC producer he had been assigned had other ideas, however. She turned up, and, rather than (as Hamish was expecting) showing him how to work the camera and leaving it with him, explained that they were short of cameras and that the video would have to be filmed there and then. In Hamish's words, to make matters worse, 'the producer suddenly decided that she was going to take over and direct it – she was saying that it would be far more effective if we did this and we did that.'

The resulting film was uploaded before Hamish had seen it. Hamish had never been asked to sign a consent form or been given the opportunity to exercise his editorial veto. When he asked the radio station to remove this short, he was told 'no, they couldn't do that because it was getting more responses and feedback than almost anything else they had done.' The short generated 17 responses soon after it was uploaded, a substantial number in Video Nation terms. Hamish remains unhappy with the short: 'I have several times asked the BBC to remove it, but they are not keen to do so.'

Hamish's experience illustrates some of the ways in which the institution may constrain the representations made by 'ordinary people'. Far from offering him the opportunity to represent himself in any way he chose – or indeed as an expert – Hamish felt that he was represented as an eccentric. His short emphasises the camp elements of transgender clothing, a long-standing staple of English humour, rather than an informed and authoritative account of the Scottish cultural tradition of kilt wearing. Indeed, it would appear that the project may already have positioned Hamish as an eccentric in selecting him in the first place. More damagingly, the editing undermines Hamish's declaration that there is nothing sinister or untoward about wearing skirts or kilts by immediately following this with footage where his sexual arousal is evident.

Conclusion

Despite the obvious differences between these two case studies, certain similarities are also apparent. Firstly, when the participants were recruited by the BBC, neither were 'media virgins': Hamish had done his 'bits and pieces for radio', and Denise had come to the BBC's notice through her participation in the Carlton pilot. Secondly, both are accustomed to performing – Denise is used to 'taking the stage' through her work and Hamish is involved in amateur dramatic productions and his kilt wearing appearances. Thirdly, both are strong personalities who have participated in other forms of media production since their involvement with Video Nation: Denise offers comments from a legal perspective to a renowned Sunday newspaper and is now a script advisor on a long-running BBC hospital drama series, while Hamish has a growing Internet profile as a professional kilt wearer and plans to make a documentary with BBC Scotland. Outside the Video Nation framework it would be difficult to make a case for either of these participants to be viewed as 'ordinary people'.

However, it is also difficult to agree with the BBC's claim that control is somehow being 'handed over' in this context. Instead, the 'ordinary person' is recruited to fill a position predefined by the institution – albeit with contrasting results. In Denise's case, her professional status allows her to occupy the position of an expert, and to speak as a representative of a particular religious group. By contrast, Hamish is reduced to an individual eccentric, if not a positive deviant. Unlike Denise, Hamish does not have the institution's authority bestowed on him: the project does not afford him the position of the expert that he feels himself entitled to occupy.

My broader analysis suggests that there are numerous points at which the BBC continues to retain institutional control of the work of Video Nation contributors. Firstly, participants are most frequently 'recruited' on the project's terms rather than spontaneously volunteering themselves, which in turn reflects the project's priority, in a climate of 'branding and stranding', to contribute to wider BBC campaigns. Secondly, regardless of whether the participant has received training in filming (the project no longer runs workshops for participants), they may well be asked to reshoot their footage in particular ways, or the footage may be shot or reshot by the regional BBC producer rather than the participant. Thirdly, the participant is not present throughout the editing process, and the decisions referred to in the quotation at the start of this chapter – 'shoot first, decide later' – are in fact made by the producer, with the participant being required merely to provide approval. Lastly, the project's delivery via the website involves a further level of mediation: archival practices such as the titling, description, classification and categorisation of the shorts all serve to frame and define the participants' work in particular ways.

To this extent, it would be very hard to see a project like Video Nation as a contribution to 'empowering' ordinary people. Indeed, I would argue that the range of positions that the broadcast project represented has been retracted since it transferred to web delivery. The project has moved away from the access principles that formed the basis of the CPU; and yet in moving online, it has failed to capitalise on the potential of Web 2.0 technologies and the new opportunities they offer for participation and distribution. Production, in general, is far more frequently motivated and controlled by the institution than the rhetoric of the website suggests. As such, Video Nation largely supplements and reproduces the BBC's agenda rather than expanding or challenging it.

In the current context, it may indicate the limitations that will be faced by any national broadcasting institution in attempting to respond to calls for the wider democratisation of the media.

Notes

1. Information for this section has been gathered as part of my doctoral research. Data collection included attendance at Video Nation producer training days as well as interviews with selected producers.
2. No longer accessible online, as of 8 November 2008.

References

Born, G. (2005) *Uncertain Vision. Birt, Dyke and the Reinvention of the BBC*. London: Vintage.

Burns, T. (1977) *The BBC Public Institution and Private World*. London and Basingstoke: Macmillan Press.

Carpentier, N. (2003) Bridging cultural and digital divides. Signifying everyday life, cultural diversity and participation in the online community Video Nation. Paper presented at *New Media and Everyday Life in Europe*, European Media Technologies and Everyday Life Network Conference. London, 23–26 April 2003.

Dovey, J. (1993) Old dogs and new tricks access television in the UK. In T. Dowmunt (ed.) *Channels of Resistance.* pp. 163–78. London: British Film Institute.

Dowmunt, T. (2001) Dear Camera... Video diaries, subjectivity and media power. Paper presented at OUR Media conference. Washington DC, 24th May 2001. Retrieved from http://ourmedianetwork.org/files/papers/2001/Dowmunt. om2001.pdf on 10 November 2004.

Holliday, R. (2004) 'Filming "the closet": the role of video diaries in researching sexualities'. *American Behavioral Scientist*. 47(12): 1597–616.

Humm, P. (1998) Real TV: camcorders, access and authenticity. In C. Geraghty and D. Lusted (eds) *The Television Studies Book*. pp. 228–37. London: Arnold.

Rose, M. (1994/5) Real Lives Video Nation. *Vertigo* Winter: 9–10.

Thomas, C. (2008) Learning from – and rejecting – the British Documentary tradition. Paper presented at 'Documentary Now Conference'. London, 11 October 2008.

Vaughan, D. (1999) *For Documentary*. London: University of California Press.

Video Nation (1994) Mirror. Retrieved from http://www.bbc.co.uk/videonation/ articles/u/uk_mirror.shtml on 28 October 2008.

Video Nation (1996) Transplant. Retrieved from http://www.bbc.co.uk/ videonation/articles/u/uk_transplant.shtml on 28 October 2008.

Video Nation (1997a) Edgeware. Retrieved from http://www.bbc.co.uk/ videonation/articles/u/uk_edgeware.shtml on 28 October 2008.

Video Nation (1997b) Shoah. Retrieved from http://www.bbc.co.uk/videonation/ articles/u/uk_shoah.shtml on 28 October 2008.

Video Nation (1997c) Di. Retrieved from http://www.bbc.co.uk/videonation/articles/u/uk_di.shtml on 28 October 2008.

Video Nation (1998a) Office Workers. Retrieved from http://www.bbc.co.uk/videonation/articles/u/uk_officeworkers.shtml on 28 October 2008.

Video Nation (1998b) Sixteen. Retrieved from www.bbc.co.uk/videonation/articles/u/uk_sixteen.shtml on 28 October 2008.

Video Nation (2003a) Chelsea Flower Show. Retrieved from http://www.bbc.co.uk/videonation/articles/l/london_chelseaflowershow.shtml on 28 October 2008.

Video Nation (2003b) Kilts. Retrieved from http://www.bbc.co.uk/videonation/articles/s/southern_kilts.shtml on 28 October 2008.

Video Nation (2004a) Coping and Hoping. Retrieved from http://www.bbc.co.uk/videonation/articles/l/london_copingandhoping.shtml on 28 October 2008.

Video Nation (2004b) Auschwitz. Retrieved from http://www.bbc.co.uk/videonation/articles/l/london_auschwitz.shtml on 28 October 2008.

Video Nation (2005) Marathon Man. Retrieved from http://www.bbc.co.uk/videonation/articles/l/london_marathonman.shtml on 28 October 2008.

Video Nation (2007) A Long Day. Retrieved from http://www.bbc.co.uk/london/content/articles/2007/08/22/victims_video_feature.shtml on 28 October 2008.

Video Nation (2008) Take Part. Retrieved from http://www.bbc.co.uk/videonation/takepart/ on 28 October 2008.

Winston, B. (2008) Trust and other Naiveties: Documentary in the Digital Age. Nick Burton memorial lecture. Canterbury Christ Church University, 22 October 2008.

Written Archives Centre (WAC) (1972a) Confidential Memo. 12 July 1972. Caversham, UK.

Written Archives Centre (WAC) (1972b) Open Door Consent Form. 14 November 1972. Caversham, UK.

Written Archives Centre (WAC) (1974) *BBC Handbook*. Caversham, UK.

Written Archives Centre (WAC) (1994a) *Video Nation Newsletter*. February 1994. Caversham, UK.

Written Archives Centre (WAC) (1994b) *Video Nation Newsletter*. August 1994. Caversham, UK.

Written Archives Centre (WAC) (1995) *Video Nation Newsletter*. January 1995. Caversham, UK.

Written Archives Centre (WAC) (2000) *Video Nation Newsletter*. May 2000. Caversham, UK.

9
In the Bedroom: Sex on Video

Maria Pini

About 16 years ago, I bought my first camcorder. The idea of filming sex had never occurred to me, yet within a year, at least three people had asked me whether I had used it to make, in one man's terms, 'anything naughty'. It was soon obvious that the idea of owning a camcorder commonly connects with the idea of visually recording sexual activity. As Jon Dovey describes:

> Domestic video cameras have a way of finding their way into the bedroom at some point. If a camera is brought into an uninhibited social group, sexual innuendo will almost certainly be one of the discourses it generates.
>
> (2000: 69)

Years later, when I began working on the research reported here, and after encountering numerous references to the use of camcorders for recording sex, I telephoned the Deputy Editor of a leading camcorder consumer magazine to ask about this. I had two main questions. The first concerned the very general area of sex and camcorder use. The second was a question about why, within his publication, there was a monthly advertisement for the Omax 'Feminine Massager', a vibrating device which promises 'orgasm within sixty seconds' (this was routinely the only advertisement in the magazine which was not overtly connected with camcorder technology). In typically (for this area) enigmatic fashion, I was told with regards to my first question, to 'use my imagination'. When I inquired further, he said that 'obviously' many people used their camcorders to video sexual activity. With regards to my second question, he said that the magazine editorial did not want to be completely overt in making a connection between sex and camcorders. Nevertheless, the link was, in his words, 'obvious'.

Such anecdotes serve well in setting the background for this chapter. In short, there is a well-established and recognised connection between camcorders and the representation of sex, and it is here that both celebratory hype and concerned panic have been heard. On the one hand, there are animated personal accounts of the pleasures of the camcorder-as-sex-toy and excited claims about the fundamental threat posed to the sex 'industry' by amateur sex video production. On the other hand, there are feminist fears surrounding the normalisation and domestication of porn and general concerns about an increasing sexualisation of everyday life.

This chapter examines the discourses surrounding amateur porn production and analyses certain aspects of the practice itself, drawing on in-depth interviews conducted with five individuals who have used their camcorders during sex. It is centrally significant that none of the interviewees neatly fit the common image brought to mind by the term 'amateur porn producer' – a term suggesting at least some degree of organised production, exhibition or distribution. Instead, these are camcorder users simply using their camcorder as a form of sex toy for personal, private sex play, recording sexual material primarily for their own consumption. They must, then, be distinguished from the growing number of amateur pornographers who regularly post their productions on the Internet or exhibit at festivals such as the Indie-Porn festival CUM2CUT, and those with an eye to making money from their productions.

The interviewees discussed in this chapter are typical of the kind of camcorder users referred to by the journalist Libby Brooks (2002). According to Brooks, the camcorder is seen to provide 'ordinary' people with a safe and satisfying means by which to reclaim and recreate images of more 'ordinary' sex for their own, personal consumption. Brooks suggests that as video recording technology has become more accessible, private taping of sex has become the contemporary equivalent of the mirrored ceiling (Brooks, 2002). Likewise, Kevin Campbell, author of the 1994 how-to book on *Video Sex*, claims that camcorders are the most exciting sex toys available to couples. This suggestion forms the basis of Irvine Welsh's fictional work *Porno*, published in 2002, which casts contemporary Britain as a nation of do-it-yourself (DIY) porn-makers, addicted to voyeurism and sexual exhibitionism. For Welsh, DIY porn-making is our new drug of choice. It has become completely mundane and mainstream, like eating at McDonalds or enjoying Karaoke. Technology has simply made porn-making easier and 'normal'. Although fictional, the picture painted by Welsh is thoroughly familiar and is by no means limited to a British context. A 1991 article in the *Los Angeles Times*, for example, refers to 'the latest American trend: X-rated videos done by real people in their real homes with their own camcorders' (Perry, 1991). Likewise, in an Australian online news article from 2003, Nick Galvin identifies the spread within Australia of a fast-growing cottage industry in DIY porn.

The data discussed in this chapter reflect this use of camcorders 'in the bedroom' by 'ordinary' people (meaning people largely unconcerned with video technology, creative expression, commercial gain or the visually aesthetic). Such users may *not* spring to mind when thinking of 'amateur pornographers', and defining such users is by no means straightforward. As was illustrated in Chapter 2, across a range of activities, the term 'amateur' is often very difficult to define. On the one hand, such definition appears straightforward, referring to the practitioner who, unlike the professional, receives no financial payment. Yet, the existence of terms such as 'semi-professional', 'serious amateur' and 'Pro-Am' clearly muddies the waters. How then are we to define camcorder users who produce erotic material for their own private consumption? They are clearly not Pro-Ams in Leadbeater and Miller's (2004) terms – none of my interviewees expressed any interest or desire to move into 'professional' pornography or to make money from their practice. They cannot be defined as 'serious' or 'dedicated' amateurs working to professional standards – for example, none suggested that they critically evaluated their own work against 'professional' porn standards. And despite the fact that the practice was constructed in terms of a long-standing 'fancy' or 'desire' on the part of the maker, it was not something to which makers appeared especially strongly committed. Rather, the present interviewees are closer to Andrew Keen's (2007) notion of the 'rank amateur' or Stebbins's (2007) concept of 'casual' rather than 'serious' leisure. The video practices analysed in this chapter are about play, sensory stimulation and entertainment rather than 'serious' practices requiring long-term investment, a degree of training and dedicated commitment.

Defining amateur pornography

Amateur pornography has become an area of completely (and in many ways, deliberately) unclear distinctions and definitions. Although there has always been ambiguity – and even deception – surrounding the term (with 'pictured unawares', 'readers' wives' and 'girl next door' -type fantasies motivating many pornographic narratives), technological developments, including camcorders, digital cameras, mobile phone cameras and the growth of the Internet, have made this ambiguity more extreme. The majority of Internet porn is produced outside a relatively centralised studio system where traditionally the bulk of porn was produced; and as a result, distinctions and definitions have become even more blurred.

One definition of 'amateur porn' refers to video which is recorded for the purpose of pleasure and entertainment, as opposed to video produced for financial gain. According to O'Toole (1999), during the peak era for amateur production of low-grade pornographic videos (which he identifies as 1986–90), a trend developed for sharing home-made videos within circles of friends or within small trusted networks. Irrespective of how common such practice actually was, a discourse about such DIY video sharing developed. Today, the 'amateur porn' label is more fluid; for example, it is commonly applied to professionally produced porn which mimics 'amateur' work. Where once amateur porn-makers might have made attempts to make their work look 'professional', now professional producers often go to great lengths to make their work appear 'amateur'. 'Gonzo porn', for example, is a well-known 'professional' filming style heavily influenced by 'amateur' porn. This style is characterised by an attempt to make the viewer feel as though they are directly within the scene, with one or both participants filming and performing sex and with little regard for technique, narrative or direction.

The amateur 'look' – with its claims to 'authenticity' – clearly makes money. As Patterson (2004) explains, 'amateur porn' online takes its visual language partly from the amateur videos produced by couples during the period to which O'Toole (1999) refers. The success of such practices during the late 1980s and early 1990s alerted the professional porn industry, which was quick to copy the 'amateur look'. Much of what had previously been seen as drawbacks (such as bad lighting, lack of a narrative and wobbly camerawork) was turned into a deliberately crafted style. Such mimicry paid off. Not only did big companies purchase 'home-made' porn, they also began producing their own so-called 'amateur' videos, laying claim to the 'authenticity' associated with genuinely amateur productions. David Bennett (2001) describes how big companies began 'heavily investing their technical expertise in simulating the low production values of home-made erotica' (388).

This professionally produced 'amateur' porn involves either professional actors mimicking 'amateurs' or professionals filming and directing, with 'real' amateurs or relative newcomers to the practice appearing alongside an established 'professional'. Very often the narrative echoes this actual situation – with the newcomer being 'interviewed' on camcorder for the role. On one level, the appeal of the notion of the initiated amateur and, by extension, of amateurism, is completely obvious: it plays into well-established sexual fantasies of the corruption of innocence. Yet the situation also evidences what might be seen as a contemporary 'fetishization of the real': viewers' suspicions that what they are watching is merely simulated, artificially staged or somehow 'fictional' are very directly undermined. As Dovey explains:

> In this context, the scopophilic pleasures of the 'real' become undeniable – enormous numbers of men are paying for intensified sexual pleasure by buying porn that advertises itself not as weak narrative fantasy but as reality itself.
>
> (2000: 68)

The notion of 'amateurism' therefore operates at several different levels within the production of porn. Professionally produced 'amateur' porn is generally produced by the commercial porn industry, which has access to a range of marketing and distribution channels. It is also possible to identify *independent* porn, which is produced outside of this system and is generally available only by mail order through a catalogue or website, and *alternative* porn, which typically caters to specialised tastes (including those of female consumers) that are poorly served by the mainstream industry. Both kinds of material can certainly generate profit, although this is arguably not their primary aim. Truly 'amateur' porn would then be material produced not for profit, by individuals working on their own behalf; and if it is circulated at all, this happens within networks of friends or acquaintances. Yet despite these labels, distinct differences are very difficult to identify. Many producers of such material themselves disagree on definitions, motivations, sexual or political agendas, and so forth. In this context, 'amateurism' is a flexible and ambiguous quality, whose significance is open to a considerable degree of negotiation.

Understanding casual amateur pornography

The casual camcorder user who records sex for private consumption, as a form of play, sexual pleasure and entertainment is one type of amateur pornographer. Whether video produced solely for private consumption and erased after a few viewings properly constitutes 'pornography', or is even identifiable as 'media', is perhaps questionable. Here the producer and consumer (or audience) are one and the same, which would suggest that traditional 'sender-message-receiver' approaches to media analysis may be irrelevant.

Within academic discussion of the area, this particular kind of production is often ignored. Many of the reasons for this are clear: obviously, once material is exhibited, it can be 'counted'. If it is not posted on the Internet or copied for distribution, its existence remains hidden. Furthermore, this is a practice which few people discuss openly. More significant, perhaps, is the fact that such practice might not be recognised as 'porn-making'. Camcorder owners might videotape private sex, review their footage once, erase it and never classify what they have done as pornography: in many respects, this is far closer to a casual leisure pursuit. We have no way of gaining accurate statistics on the number of people using their camcorders to privately record sex. 'Everyone's doing it' headlines (Adams, 2006) may be common, but in terms of actualities, we simply do not know.

Dovey (2000) identifies just two forms of amateur porn: firstly, people not involved in the industry using their camcorders to record sex for pleasure and profit; secondly, professionals trying to emulate the amateur feel of the first category. Dovey's first category, however, includes those seeking financial profit. There is no detailed discussion or empirical analysis of those who may be video recording sex merely for their own consumption and entertainment. Instead (understandably given the problems of accessing casual porn producers, and also because it is not his aim to conduct an empirical study), Dovey analyses 'reality porn', firstly, in Freudian terms relating to scopophilic pleasure and, secondly, in terms of the growth in reality media genres more generally. Ruth Barcan (2002), on the other hand, distinguishes between sex footage made for private use and sex footage made for financial gain. Like Dovey, Barcan locates the growth of the former within what she sees as a far more general – and rapidly growing – 'taste for the ordinary'.

It is this practice – of 'casual amateurs' recording sex for private consumption – that is the focus of this chapter. The following analysis attempts to highlight how such DIY porn producers themselves articulate the pleasures they associate with these practices. Five participants, four men (Peter, Dylan, Dominic and Paul) and one woman (Lisa), were interviewed in depth about their making of amateur porn. Flyers were produced and distributed within a café/bookshop specialising in erotica based in central London. The same flyers were distributed at an event known as the London Alternative Market (LAM) which is held on the first Sunday of every month. The flyers asked producers of amateur erotica/porn video to volunteer for an interview. Anonymity was guaranteed and telephone interviews were offered where face-to-face meetings seemed inconvenient or inappropriate. Two interviewees were interviewed only once and by phone. Two were interviewed twice (once during our first face-to-face meeting at either the café or the LAM and once on the telephone). One (Peter), who was contacted via a mutual friend, was interviewed once in person. Interviewees were aged between 28 and 52 years. The four men identified themselves as heterosexual, while the woman said that she was 'mainly straight'. All interviewee names have been changed.

All of these interviewees fall within the category of those who videotape sex primarily for their own private enjoyment and consumption. Two, Lisa and Paul, have shared or posted their videos online, but in both cases, their faces were concealed or hidden from view. Also in both cases, the material was not shot with the intention of posting on the Internet; this was something they thought about much later, and they only posted short bits of film or a few digital still images. Dominic primarily films sex as part of a private practice with his partner, although he has also appeared in one video for a friend and his wife. Peter and Dylan have never shown their footage to anyone else. All interviewees stressed that the practice was just 'for fun' and interestingly, all of them suggested an 'emotional' side, as well as an erotic one, to the practice – constructing their footage as important 'keepsakes', or reminders of particular relationships, and emphasising the trust, care and respect necessarily involved in the practice. In what follows, I examine these interviewee accounts by elucidating the major themes to emerge, highlighting where appropriate, the extent to which these resonate with more general contemporary discourses around amateur pornography – to which I shall return in the conclusion.

'Everyone's at it'

A major theme to emerge from the data is the idea that video recording sex is a completely normal practice. Dominic says that the practice is:

> Incredibly common. Like Mr and Mrs Jones next door type. And Mr and Mrs Jones have got this boring, totally uninteresting life and in

secret they have this incredibly raunchy, horny life. A sexual secret kept from everyone else.

Other interviewees indicate similar views:

> Yes, come on, I reckon most people get their video camera home and after a bit, it must cross their minds, what it'd be like to get it out during sex. (Lisa)

> Oh, [it is] incredibly common. Any couple, any pair that has a camera will want to try it. It's incredibly common I imagine. Any couple that's communicating about sex will probably have experimented with their camera. Oh yes. (Dylan)

There is a general idea, then, that using the camcorder to record sex is a thoroughly common, almost 'inevitable' practice. As with the camcorder magazine editor I mentioned at the start of this chapter, the attitude is generally one of 'oh, come on!' Peter, Dominic, Lisa and Dylan all say that they bought their first camcorder precisely for this reason. As Lisa explains:

> Just straight after we bought the camera we filmed sex. In fact I think we even mentioned it before we bought it as one of the good reasons to get one in the first place.

These interviews support Dovey's (2000) argument that the camcorder *will* find its way into the bedroom. But perhaps, given the small sample size, it is more precise to say that a *discourse* or a set of expectations about camcorders in the bedroom is clearly evident. This discourse informs people's constructions of the camcorder, which in turn informs individuals' practices, and what they think of doing with their camcorders.

'Just a bit of raunchy fun': Play and performance

For all of the interviewees, recording sex was first and foremost about having fun: spicing up their sex, playing, experimenting, satisfying their curiosity, getting a 'buzz' and so forth. Indeed, several (four) went to lengths to 'defend' their practice against any potential 'misunderstandings', thus indicating an acute awareness of the suspicions commonly associated with recording sex. Dominic is typical in this respect: very early in the interview and with no prompting, he stresses that his videos are 'not for financial gain or anything. Nothing heavy, no S and M. Nothing heavy'. He explains:

> You have a little fun ... It was just a fun one. Just purely fun ... A bit of fun. Literally bit of fun in the bedroom. Not for financial gain or to sell them, to show them. Just for me and to show the lady I was with. It's a turn-on, to get you sexually aroused. That's it.

Dominic mentions 'fun' five times within this short space. Similarly, during my first interview with Lisa, she says that this practice needs to be written about because not enough people recognise it as 'harmless and normal'. Like Dominic, she chooses to point out that 'it's a bit of fun.' Other interviewees make a similar point, stressing the harmless, fun nature of the practice: this is about 'showing off', intensifying the sexual experience, 'having a giggle' and so on:

> Yes, at first it was simply us recording the sex, having a giggle, playing it back and getting turned on by it. Yes, and then, well once at least I remember, we would play games with it. Well just typical role-play stuff. Like he'd play at being this pornographer trying to persuade me to pose! That kind of thing. (Lisa)

> Yes, it's purely for fun. That's it. (Dylan)

The scopophilic pleasures of voyeurism and the related pleasures of exhibitionism are stressed within all of the accounts. As Paul puts it:

> It's a bit like having sex in front of a mirror I think. Because we are both voyeurs and exhibitionists at heart. My partner is a real exhibitionist and I'm a big voyeur. I love porn. I love to watch. So, I've got this added bonus of being able to watch the two of us. 'Cause when I'm in the middle of sex with my partner, I don't see myself. I see only her. I'm very close-up in a way. Being able, with a camera, to see yourself doing that, it allows you to step back, take a few steps back and watch the action. And because you make the action, it's your favourite thing that you're watching. In a way it's like custom-porn. (Paul)

It becomes clear from the data that comparing videoing sex to the mirrored ceiling (Brooks, 2002) is indeed appropriate. For all of these interviewees, recording sex, and the fun associated with this, is centrally bound up in ideas about watching and being seen as if from afar. Unlike with the mirrored ceiling, however, camcorder footage can be reviewed after sex has finished. Furthermore, and I shall return to this shortly, the material presence of the camcorder can in itself be seen to intensify sexual pleasure. Many talk about the 'thrill' of having a 'third person' present, and the camcorder coming to signify a human 'third person'. So even though there may be no intention of actually showing footage to a real, other person, the idea or some kind of 'trace' of that imagined 'third person' is there. As Dylan explains:

> There's something about being able to watch it later, like a third person perspective of me and my partner. It's very, very erotic. A third-person perspective is a major turn-on. Yeah, it puts the thought in your head 'I'm being watched'. There's certainly exhibition in it. Being watched. Even if you don't intend to share the footage, it's a turn-on.

This viewing entails a separation of 'the viewing self' from 'the self on screen' which intensifies the voyeuristic pleasure. The gap or split is 'sexy'. Dominic alludes to one aspect of this in describing a fantasy coming into play during sex, about being an actual 'porn star':

> You think, 'wow I'm a porn star'. But you're not. In your mind you're an international, hot-shot porn movie star. But you're not. Obviously, you're not. And you get a buzz out of it. You think somebody's watching me doing this and you do get a kick out of it. It's a bit kinky when you think you're doing this and being watched. It seriously is an incredible sexual turn-on.

Lisa also mentions this fantasy of being seen by a larger audience:

> It's erotic anyway – watching sex, irrespective of who's doing it. Then there's the curiosity of 'I wonder what I'd look like in a porn flick'.

All the interviewees spoke of the pleasure they experienced with their partners on reviewing their footage. For some, this review was a turn-on, leading to more sexual activity:

> Obviously, we got a bit turned-on and one thing leads to another. I think you know what I mean. And you know, it gets you turned-on. It perks you up. (Dominic)

> A lot of giggling and a lot of turn-on and embarrassment towards the sexual turn-on. Like we're watching it and getting turned-on and saying 'Oh my God, this is turning us on'. (Dylan)

The particular sexual pleasure being described here is, in large part, about the erosion of the gap between the producer and the consumer, or between the voyeur and the exhibitionist, the seer and the seen. There is obviously also an emotional aspect to a couple's sharing of this viewing experience. As Paul puts it:

> As well, we are really happy watching it back. Happy basically, because we are sharing something. We are sharing the passion we've got. We are really sharing a tender moment … And a turn-on. (Paul)

These emotional dimensions will be considered in more detail in a later section of this chapter.

Keeping it real: Celebrating the 'ordinary' and 'natural'

> It's better than if you watch a professional film that probably cost thousands and thousands of dollars or pounds to make and it's so staged and it's so orchestrated and it's boring. But when you do it yourself, you know what's gone into it, you know the fun you've had doing it and you really do get a lot more enjoyment and you can see and you can learn from it. Obviously you can improve your sexual technique. (Dominic)

Like several other interviewees, Dominic claims that his footage is better than that which appears in a professional porn film. As indicated earlier, Barcan (2002) argues that the growth in amateur pornography is partly related to a backlash against a culture of commercialised glamour. The 'taste for the ordinary', which she identifies, is a theme which runs through all the interviews conducted for this chapter. Like Dominic, all of the interviewees claim that their home-made porn is better because, among other things, it feels more 'real'. To illustrate the theme:

> I think if you're going to make home-porn videos then make them look amateur. It makes them more attractive and … more sexually attractive. If things go wrong, the camera goes out of focus and stuff like that, it's more fun. If you start planning it with a Spielberg

movie-production, it looks too orchestrated. Tacky little cameras, bad film sets, bad lighting and it's more fun. It's a turn-on. It's amateur and it looks it and it's such a sexual turn-on. It is. So, more real and more fun. (Dominic)

Oh certainly. I find it so much better, something about the rawness, the authenticity … the women in professional stuff, yeah they're beautiful but it's very obvious that they are airbrushed. Just not real. (Dylan)

It's definitely more real-feeling. Apart from the fact that it's you in it, there's something about just that amateurish, DIY feel that's incredibly intense. It's kind of more erotic because it feels real. (Lisa)

Virtually no preparation (in terms of equipment, props or narrative) precedes videotaping for any of these interviewees. It is either a spontaneous, 'heat of the moment idea' (Peter) or at most, something the couple has talked about very loosely and simply put into practice once sex has already begun. However, Peter says that during his first attempt, his partner wanted a bit of time to put her make-up on, while for Paul, who is a 'dominant' in a BDSM relationship (involving bondage, discipline, submission, sadism and masochism), setting up the camcorder is part of the preparation involved in his sex play. Even so, most interviewees emphasise the need for spontaneity, and the lack of planning and preparation:

You just think it up as you go along. You don't have a script. You're just coming up with all these fantasy ideas as you go along. Just put the camera directly onto the tripod, direct it at the area you're going to be filming. That's it really. Just a tripod with a light shining down and away you go. It's as simple as that … We were just kind of laughing and we kind of ran out of ideas after about twenty minutes and you make it up as you go. Just a bit of raunchy fun. (Dominic)

No preparation. I had the camcorder in my hand and we started to be intimate. Then I put it down on the bed next to us and half way through I did mount it on a tripod in the corner of the room. (Dylan)

All five respondents say that their average recording lasts 20 minutes. Apart from Dominic, all have kept their tapes, although Peter deleted his first recording in a 'moment of anger', which he now seriously regrets.

Technology and bodies

The interviews illustrate that the camcorder, far from simply being a neutral recording device functioning solely for the purposes of recording something which can be reviewed later, can have its own visceral effects *in the present*. During sex, the camera becomes 'sexy' in itself, primarily because it is given the status of a 'third eye'. The camera takes on a presence which actually contributes to (as opposed to simply recording) the intensity of the pleasure. The material presence of the camera 'affects' the moment. Dovey (2000) makes the same observation:

> The camera is actually an accepted part of the event itself. It is not outside, controlling and structuring, in the way a stills photographer might orchestrate a scene, it is inside the action, part of the flow, both provoking events and recording them.
>
> (65)

As evidence for the role of the camcorder as a 'third eye', Lisa has recordings which she has never watched. Clearly, in her case, the practice is about the camera's actual presence during the moment of sex. It is essentially a 'sex toy'; although it is also an important recording device in as much as it allows her to have a 'keepsake' of the moment.

When it comes to the enjoyment of the camera's material presence during sex, Paul is an exception here. For one thing, he says that because he works daily with technology, he doesn't really want to think about it at home. Secondly, because he is involved in a BDSM relationship where sex takes a lot of preparation, setting up the camcorder is a nuisance, what he calls a 'necessary evil' ('necessary' because he enjoys watching the material later). For him, the camcorder cannot really be considered a 'sex toy' in and of itself. As he puts it:

> It's quite different. It's got a special status because another toy is something we use on-the-spot and gives us immediate satisfaction. The camera is a toy that gives us delayed satisfaction. A satisfaction afterwards, so I wouldn't put it as a toy.

Irrespective of whether it affords immediate or deferred pleasure, all interviewees agree that owning a camcorder is an important part of their sexual practice, adding to sexual pleasure. All indicate that new easy-to-use and inexpensive technologies have made the practice of recording sex possible, and previously they would not have considered doing so – although two interviewees say that before owning camcorders, they very occasionally took still photographs during sex. Paul describes the situation very clearly:

> Basically it happened at the same time as technology. You know, 'cause before I tried to take some still pictures to be developed you know, and I got a letter from the processing company that they were not allowed to do it. And then digital cameras and digital movie cameras came along and then I was free to do whatever I wanted and that was nice.

Yet, as was outlined in Chapter 2, it would be simplistic to regard technology as the sole, determining factor of these possibilities and pleasures. Technology clearly plays a fundamental part (for example, unless he had processed them himself, Paul would not have been able to produce his erotic photographs, and Dominic would not have been able to experience the 'huge turn-on' he gets when seeing himself on video) but it does not tell the whole story. Video technology does have its own inherent possibilities and constraints, but its use within a particular social context is all important. These practices are happening within a context where sexual experimentation is positively encouraged within women's, men's and 'lifestyle' magazines, where the visual recording of the 'everyday' and the once-'private' is becoming increasingly common and where one important strand of 'post-feminist' discourse celebrates a 'sex-positivity' for women.

Men, women and camcorder sex

In September 2007, AskMen.com (a men's online magazine) ran an article entitled *Make Your Own Erotic Video,* which offers advice to men who 'want to film you and your lady doing the nasty'. The article gives a series of tips to men about how to 'make her come round' to the idea. Interestingly, all four of the men interviewed for this article said that it was they rather than their partners who wanted to video sex in the first place. Similarly, in the interview for this chapter, Peter explained that recording sex was something that he had always wanted to do. He had asked all his lovers for the past 15 years to make a sex video, but all (except one) were unwilling. Two years ago, he met a woman who was willing, but admits that it was all his idea and that she consented mainly because it was a 'treat' for him around the time of his birthday. Other interviewees paint a similar picture:

> Well, I had been thinking about it for a long time. And then, I just suggested to her once or twice and then once, in front of the camera, I suggested again, and it just went along … like most men's fantasies I guess. Just mentions of it. No more than that. (Dylan)

> Yes, my idea, virtually always. Yes, you see we've got a BDSM relationship, and I'm the dominant one and … First she cannot always take the camera, for obvious reasons – she's tied up. I mean she can sometimes suggest, 'oh it would be nice to take a picture or a movie of that', but not always, 'cause I call the shots and I just grab the camera and start shooting. (Paul)

> I dropped hints then said, 'd'you want to have a bit of fun with the video camera?' She said 'yes', so I said, 'let's make some raunchy, fun, film'. (Dominic)

Although it is difficult to generalise from such a small sample, together with the AskMen.com article, this would suggest that in some respects at least, DIY porn-making is structured in terms of the same sexual-political economy as that of the mainstream porn industry. In Dylan's terms, this is 'most men's fantasy'; and it is mainly men doing the 'persuading'.

Repeatedly, the interviewees describe the common assurances made by men to their partners, that the video will never be seen by anyone else. Trust, respect and privacy are terms to emerge repeatedly with regards to the practice. As Paul describes in relation to gaining his partner's consent:

> She trusted me. I assured her it would never go outside our relationship. And she agreed. Since then, there's been no more negotiation.

Such statements suggest an extremely traditional scenario. Men ask, persuade, reassure, and women resist, come round or give in. Significantly, Gia, the woman who finally agreed to video sex with Peter as his birthday 'treat', and then took time to apply her make-up, never once watched the footage. According to Peter, she simply had no interest, suggesting that this was purely a birthday 'treat' for him. Although there is not adequate space to engage with the arguments here, Gia's case clearly indicates one of the alarming aspects of certain contemporary modes of femininity, and the extent to which they remain constructed in terms of a distinctly male desire. With her final surrender to Peter's request and her stopping the 'action' in order to prepare her make-up for a video which she does not want to watch, Gia presents a figure reminiscent of John Berger's classic argument (1972) that traditionally, men watch women, while women watch themselves being watched, thus becoming surveyors of themselves from a male perspective. Or as Dylan puts it, 'she was turned on by the thought that it turned *me* on.'

Lisa, however, indicates another side to the situation. With her, it was a joint decision with her male partner to record their sex. Unlike Gia, Lisa clearly fits a picture developing within a variety of 'sex-positive' feminisms, which attempt to disturb the traditional associations between women, sexual passivity and victimhood. Instead, and in line with certain arguments about so-called 'post-feminism', the active, desiring, hypersexual woman is celebrated as indicative of a very positive sexual-political progression. Indeed, it is from this kind of perspective that Clarissa Smith (2007) argues that women are now the main consumers of pornography.

Memories: Recordings as 'keepsakes'

As well as having an erotic function, camcorder footage also carries certain 'emotional' properties for these interviewees. Dylan says:

> The footage is important. I keep it all. That relationship finished because I had to leave the country. It ended very well. We both have kept copies of the footage.

Peter describes regretting having erased footage of his ex-partner in 'a moment of anger', because this partner was 'really very sweet' and he would like to have kept the footage as a 'memory aid' to remember the 'good parts' of the relationship, the 'tender, loving times'. He uses the term 'collector's item' in trying to describe what this footage means to him. The footage acts for him, almost like a fetishised object, a 'condensation' or signifier of a particular time and person. Paul says something very similar with regards to the erotic still photography he engaged in before getting his camcorder:

> Before, I was taking pictures. Kind of on/off one-night-stands and stuff like that. Because it was just a one-night-stand and I would be interested in keeping just a little memory of that. Because I was afraid of forgetting about it.

Like many of the others, Paul and Lisa say that they would never delete any footage, and that the footage is very important for retaining memories of good, loving times in their lives:

> I would never delete it. I would keep it and give a copy to my partner. But I would definitely not share it with anyone else. I just want to capture some good moments basically. A bit like if I was on holiday and I would snap my holiday. Or you're going to a concert or something like that, right. Any kind of good moment that I want to remember. In the back of our minds I think we'd like to see that in ten years time and remember the good old times. (Paul)

> I like it as a reminder of the relationship. It's an important memory-cue in a way. Like hanging onto old love-letters really. I couldn't just erase it. (Lisa)

In this respect, the sex video is not so different from the home mode video or the family photograph album showing children's birthday parties or family outings: both help to bring a special person or time that has passed back into the viewing present (see Chapter 4).

Conclusion

New technologies have undoubtedly changed the ways in which sexually explicit images can be produced, distributed and consumed. Yet for many commentators, nothing less than a 'revolution' has taken place. In this rhetoric, anyone with access to a camcorder can make porn, and anyone with access to the Internet can distribute and consume it. Technological developments are seen here as inherently liberating, signaling new and progressive trends in sexual expression. Most importantly, the rhetoric signals a radical collapse of the gap between the 'professional' and the 'amateur'. This is a form of democratisation, an empowerment of 'ordinary people': no longer is the production and distribution of porn the preserve of the commercial 'Sex Industry'.

As with several of the other areas considered in this book – not least that of 'citizen journalism' (Chapter 5) – contemporary Internet porn has been seen in extremely celebratory terms. One typical example of such celebration comes in Benjamin Cool's *Sex and Camcorders: The Complete Guide to Producing Low-Cost, High-Profit Adult Videos and DVDs* (2001). Cool writes:

> Back when celluloid film was the only way to produce 'movies', adult entertainment was the domain of a very few. Adult films were

expensive to make. The process was slow. And before VHS came about, the only way to catch a flick was to go downtown and sneak in some low-rent back-alley movie house... The arrival of the internet created a new marketing system and gave adult entertainment some powerful economic steroids ... The availability and affordability of digital video has made producing low-cost, high-profit adult videos a reality that is now accessible to you.

(13–15)

For Cool, the market is now open for independent cybersex entrepreneurs to earn immense profits doing it 'for themselves'. Indeed, industry estimates indicate that DVD sales and rentals of professionally produced porn dropped by up to 20% in 2006 (Bakker and Taalas, 2007) – although this may simply have been a result of migration to subscription sites online. Some argue that the sex industry, which is often credited with being the driving force behind new technologies, is now suffering a major blow from them. As Bennett (2001) describes, in critically surveying this particular reading of Internet porn:

[I]t would appear that Walter Benjamin's vision of the democratizing potential of the daily press as a medium in which any reader might become a writer, any consumer, a producer, is being realized in the so-called 'pornutopia' of the internet where any owner of a camcorder, laptop and modem can, as Benjamin put it 'gain access to authorship' and assert 'modern man's legitimate claim to being reproduced'.

(323)

Fundamentally missing from all of this debate, however, is the camcorder user who is not interested in distributing, exchanging, selling or necessarily doing anything other than privately enjoying their footage. Very rarely, if ever, do we encounter casual producers such as Dylan, Lisa or Dominic within such commentary. Here, the practice is far more mundane, and its significance far more private. The interviews analysed in this chapter clearly demonstrate that amateur pornography is indeed being made by 'ordinary' people in the privacy of their own homes, primarily for their own personal entertainment; and none of them considers this to be unusual, harmful or deviant. Yet this practice does not appear to be as culturally or economically significant as some of the more enthusiastic commentary tends to suggest. Videoing sex at home is a relatively banal, even conservative, practice. It is practiced in a largely private context, and it functions primarily to intensify an individual couple's sexual pleasure, although it may very often involve men 'persuading' women to partake. It is relatively insignificant in terms of effecting serious structural, economic and ideological change within the mainstream porn industry. Ultimately, this situation is far better summed up by Irvine Welsh's comparison with Karaoke or eating at McDonald's than it is by overexcited ideas about a radical democratisation of sexual representation.

References

Adams, T. (2006) Everybody's doing it... *The Observer.* 26 November 2006. Available at http://www.guardian.co.uk/film/2006/nov/26/features.review (accessed 12 June 2008).

Bakker, P. and Taalas, S. (2007) The irresistible rise of porn: the untold story of a global industry. *Observatorio Journal.* 1(1): 99–118.

Barcan, R. (2002) In the raw: 'home-made' porn and reality genres. *Journal of Mundane Behavior.* Available at http://www.mundane behavior.org/issues/v3n1/barcan.htm (accessed 12 June 2008).

Bennett, D. (2001) Pornography-dot-com: eroticising privacy on the internet. *The Review of Education, Pedagogy & Cultural Studies.* 23(4): 381–91.

Berger, J. (1972) *Ways of Seeing.* Harmondsworth: Penguin.

Brooks, L. (2002) Lights, cameras. Phwoar! *The Guardian.* 29 October 2002. Available at http://www.guardian.co.uk/film/2002/oct/29/internet.technology (accessed 31 January 2006).

Campbell, K. (1994) *Video Sex: Create Erotic and Romantic Home Videos with your Camcorder.* Buffalo, New York: Amhurst Media.com.

Cool, B. (2001) *Sex and Camcorders: The Complete Guide to Producing Low-Cost, High-Profit Adult Videos and DVDs.* Plantation, Florida: Brandel Publishing.

Dovey, J. (2000) *Freakshow: First Person Media and Factual Television.* London: Pluto Press.

Galvin, N. (2003) The Porn Star next door. *FairfaxDigital*.com (10 January 2003). Available at http://www.smh.com.au/articles/2003/01/09/1041990052444.html (accessed 4 April 2008).

Keen, A. (2007) *The Cult of the Amateur.* London: Nicholas Brealey.

Leadbeater, C. and Miller, P. (2004) *The Pro-Am Revolution.* London: Demos.

O'Toole, L. (1999) *Pornocopia: Sex, Technology and Desire.* London: Serpent's Tail.

Patterson, Z. (2004) Going online: consuming pornography in the digital era. In L. Williams (ed.) *Porn Studies.* pp.103–22. Durham: Duke University Press.

Perry, T. (1991) America's raunchiest home videos from America's finest city. *The Los Angeles Times.* Metro Section, page B1. March 27, 1991.

Smith, C. (2007) *One For The Girls: The Pleasures and Practices of Reading Women's Porn.* Bristol: Intellect.

Stebbins, R. (2007) *Serious Leisure.* New Brunswick, NJ: Transaction.

Welsh, I. (2002) *Porno.* London: W.W. Norton and Co Inc.

10
The Hidden World of Organised Amateur Film-Making

Daniel Cuzner

In addition to the more informal networks of amateur video-makers we have explored in previous chapters, many local communities have well-established film- and video-making clubs. The clubs coexist with both mainstream film-making and home mode use, occasionally acting as a 'feeder' for the former and, more often, a 'next step' for those with experience of the latter. In the UK, the majority are now organised under the auspices of the IAC, formerly the Institute of Amateur Cinematographers and now renamed the Film and Video Institute. The IAC is organised regionally and is responsible for most local film-making competitions, as well as an annual national event, and participation in European and worldwide events. At the time of writing, there are around 250 IAC-affiliated film-making clubs in existence throughout the UK. Some are exclusive in their membership – for example, a few are attached to schools or colleges, and thus for students only – and others have a specific focus, for example, preferring to maintain the use of Super 8 or cine cameras when most clubs have already progressed through video and on to DV. Most clubs appear to be dominated by elderly and retired people; and, as we shall see, concern is often expressed about the need to attract younger members.

In Chapter 2, David Buckingham refers to the work of Robert Stebbins, who, in his writing on 'serious leisure', distinguishes between casual, serious and project-based types of leisure (Stebbins, 2007). These film-making clubs often have the scope to cater to those engaged in all three types of activities, but they can be best understood as a focus of serious leisure, which is undertaken within existing networks of dedicated amateurs, and involves significant commitments of time, money and identity. In other chapters of this book, we have seen people – for example, video diarists, vloggers or amateur pornographers – who use film-making technology in various ways, without necessarily seeing themselves as film-makers: in such cases, the medium involved is secondary to the process of documentation. By contrast, amateur film club members are highly likely to have adopted the identity of 'film-maker' (and, indeed, even those members who are *not* regularly involved in making films can and do claim this label). This partly ties in with a need to legitimise a leisure activity, but also reflects the way that, within clubs, *what* is filmed, or *why*, is often less important than *how*. Likewise, within the clubs, painstaking technical skills exercised through editing are often prized over artistic flair in writing or shooting.

Given their investment in developing film-making skills, one might expect these members to live up to the hype about a 'Pro-Am Revolution', outlined in Chapter 2. Like Leadbeater and Miller's Pro-Ams, many film club members are 'knowledgeable, educated, committed and networked by new technology' (2004: 12). However, the encouragement for Pro-Am practitioners to market and sell their skills would not be likely to find favour among film clubs (other than occasional dabbling in wedding and event videography). This is not only because film club members are amateurs in the traditional sense of the term, more focused on improving their film-making within the amateur film world than breaking out of it, but also because, as mostly retired people, they have already had a working life and prefer to see film-making as an enjoyable (and serious) leisure pursuit.

Neither the work of Stebbins nor *The Pro-Am Revolution* looks specifically at media-making. In this chapter, I will discuss some of the social functions that amateur film-making clubs perform, and the ways in which they operate. In the process, I will be addressing broader arguments to do with social capital and social identity, which provide different theoretical explanations of the issues at stake.

Research context

Data for this chapter come from a larger project which involves case studies of two film-making clubs (one in a market town in a county adjacent to London, the other in suburban London) and one online film-making forum. I have collected data by attending the clubs over two years, distributing questionnaires to IAC club members and forum participants, interviewing members from the two clubs and the forum, and observing the forum over 18 months.

While the two clubs I have studied might be said to hold the same values – the importance and relevance of amateur film being the obvious link – there are distinct differences between them. Harland, the market town club that I discuss in this chapter, has a regular schedule of film-making that takes place both within and outside the monthly meetings. It has strong connections with the local community and uses film-making activities to support other social and charitable organisations within the local area. By contrast, the London club, which meets weekly, bases most of the meetings on *watching* amateur films made by other clubs and individuals, and almost all film-making takes place outside the realms of the club. (Pseudonyms are used for the club names as well as for names of specific members discussed later in this chapter.) I would argue that these two approaches represent complementary flipsides of the amateur experience: while the latter club might appear to be less dedicated to the actual making of films, it nonetheless provides an important service to the amateur community, by offering a regular opportunity for the exhibition of work.

The online film-making forum shares some of the characteristics of the clubs (for example, there are clear hierarchies among members, and technical skill is prized perhaps over and above creative flair). However, the forum lacks face-to-face social contact, and this makes the possibility of group film-making difficult (at least with other forum members). My reason for examining the online group is to consider whether, if online clubs represent the future (or *a* future), they could feasibly replace current face-to-face networks. In this chapter, I focus on an analysis of the Harland club, rather than a comparison of the three settings, but return to the subject of face-to-face clubs versus online film-making communities in the conclusion.

Social capital

Robert Putnam's (2000) book *Bowling Alone: The Collapse and Revival of American Community* is largely responsible for the contemporary popularisation of the idea of social capital, although in fact the concept has a longer history, and has been used in some quite diverse ways. Putnam's primary focus is on the informal social organisations – including leisure and hobby-based clubs – that he sees as characteristic of US middle-class life. He argues that the civic values, skills and orientations (or social capital) cultivated through such organisations are essential for the health of the local community, and ultimately for democracy. These organisations can serve as a means of 'bonding' – that is, cementing relationships among members of a particular social group – and also of 'bridging' – building connections across apparently disparate groups. Putnam notes a significant decline in the membership of such organisations over the second part of the twentieth century: to use his central metaphor, while more people are going bowling, fewer people are doing so in the context of clubs or leagues. According to Putnam, this is leading to social fragmentation and individualisation, a loss of trust and confidence in the political process, and a decline in volunteering, collective action and participation in public life.

Putnam's work has been widely debated – and indeed disputed – both on the grounds of evidence and interpretation (see, for example, Baron et al., 2000; Fischer, 2005). Nevertheless, the example of amateur film-making clubs provides an interesting 'test case' for some of his arguments, as well as indicating some of the limitations of the approach. One of Putnam's weaknesses is that he sees participation as an end in itself – arguing that, with a few notable exceptions, civic participation and, by extension, social capital are inherently *good things*. In the process, he tends to neglect the ways in which the organisations themselves operate: the clubs and associations serve as a kind of 'black box', which are assessed only in terms of their determinate effects on social values or attitudes. By contrast, in this chapter I seek to explore some of the ways in which social capital is explicitly created *within* the Harland club, and the functions it serves, primarily through a discussion of what the club itself calls its 'good causes'. However, I also look at the different roles that individuals take within the club, and the ways in which power and hierarchy tend both to promote and to constrain participation. In exploring these issues in this context, I will be drawing on theories of 'situated learning' and 'communities of practice' (Lave and Wenger, 1991), briefly introduced in Chapter 2, and on theories of social identity.

Before moving on, however, it is worth noting that Putnam's essentially benign view of social capital contrasts sharply with the earlier account of Pierre Bourdieu (1986). For Bourdieu, social capital is one of three 'fundamental guises' of capital, the others being economic capital and cultural capital. These forms of capital are intrinsically and intricately connected and overlapping, but since cultural and social capital can both – in certain conditions – be convertible into economic capital, Bourdieu ultimately regards economic capital as fundamental. As he states:

Economic capital is at the root of all the other types of capital and ... these transformed, disguised forms of economic capital, never entirely reducible to that definition, produce their most specific effects only to the extent that they conceal (not least from their possessors) the fact that economic capital is at their root, in other words – but only in the last analysis – at the root of their effects.

(1986: 252)

While Bourdieu has been widely accused of a kind of economic determinism, his account does draw attention to the ways in which social capital interacts with, and can reinforce, other forms of social power – a phenomenon which seems to be largely absent in Putnam's theory. While Putnam tends to regard the development of social capital as a positive aspect of healthy social interaction, Bourdieu's approach would imply that there might be more (economic) self-interest at stake, even in apparently altruistic activities such as volunteering. Here again, Putnam's failure to explore how social capital actually operates *within* the organisations he values is critical: it ultimately results in a view of community, and of social life, as somehow inherently cosy and benevolent.

Club history

The very origins of the Harland club exemplify certain aspects of social capital. The founder, Sir Arthur Masters, had made films throughout his career (including, in the 1960s, founding a film club with fellow members of the Round Table charitable organisation), and later worked at various levels within the Lions organisation, eventually becoming national PR officer. During this time he founded a Lions film library, consisting mainly of the Super 8 films he had made to promote the activities of the Lions clubs.

Masters travelled to India in 1980, taking his silent Super 8 zoom camera, to visit four eye camps run by the Royal Commonwealth for the Blind (now Sightsavers International). He later used a poem about a young man regaining his sight after receiving aid from an eye camp to accompany his silent footage, and thus promote eye camps. The film was shown internationally within the Lions community in the following two years, and in 1983 Masters entered the film in the county film festival. Having won the award of Best in Show, Masters was 'collared' by the festival's founder. Masters described the encounter in an interview: 'He said "Where have you popped up from? We haven't got a club in [Harland], why don't you start one?" I said I'd do it when I'd retired.'

In the same interview, Masters described Harland as 'an excellent place for what we call "networking", because people know each other:'

> I put a letter in the local paper suggesting that there would be scope for a film-making club in [Harland], would anybody interested please contact me on my home phone number. The result of that was that we called a meeting of eight people who came together, and six of them said 'that's a brilliant idea, let's start a club.' So we started the Harland Video Makers [in 1985].

It is quite possible that another amateur film-maker might eventually have been persuaded or otherwise decided to found a club in Harland, but Masters' background of combining charitable work (for which he was awarded his Knighthood) with film-making has had a strong bearing on the club's philosophy. The club has been able to exploit strong ties with other organisations, whose volunteers may also be Harland members, or people who know club members. As we shall see, the benefit here is reciprocal – a club film project on behalf of a local charity or organisation will raise awareness of both institutions.

The significance of social capital in this context is partly a result of Harland's circumstances: it is a small and relatively affluent middle-class market town, in which volunteering is a commonplace and respected activity, and it has a large proportion of retired people to staff such voluntary organisations. Some of the Harland members have lived in the area for a long time, and others, like Masters, retired to the area. Those with extensive local roots naturally have a wider local social circle of friends and acquaintances, but those moving to the area bring with them their existing interests and connections.

A community of practice?

In mid-1985, six months after the Harland Video Makers Club was founded, they moved to their current location, a church hall. Early meetings had taken place at Masters' home, with an initial membership of eight cine and/or still camera users, but as the club grew, and to encourage further growth, it was felt that a more suitable location was needed. The hall is on an unmade road, on the outskirts of the town of Harland – the nearest railway station is several miles away, and the area is not well served by bus routes. Certainly the directions on the club website assume that prospective members will arrive by car, and the publicity material states that the membership 'is drawn from an area of roughly 100 square miles', although most members live in Harland itself. The remoteness of the location is a hindrance to the group, but the venue has remained in use because it is cheap to hire, is of a reasonable size, quiet and because alternatives have not proved suitable.

Meetings take place on the first Friday of the month, from 7.45 pm to approximately 10.30 pm. A monthly meeting seems relatively infrequent for such a dynamic club, but it is perhaps this infrequency that leads to relatively 'businesslike' meetings. Peter Standing, who joined the club upon retirement in 2002, felt that anything more than a monthly meeting would be overkill, and that members would 'get tired of the same old faces' and end up achieving less.

For a club with only 12 formal meetings a year, the output is impressive – in 2004/5, Harland and its members made approximately 75 films. It should be noted, however, that currently films are largely produced by individuals, rather than in club projects, or by more recognised small groups within the club. This decrease in organised, collaborative club activity is considered highly problematic, as it goes against several of the club's stated aims: not only are there fewer opportunities for learning and skill sharing but also the lack of shared projects diminishes the social opportunities within the club, and also means the club is not fostering connections with, or supporting, local organisations. This has been a concern of the club, as evidenced in the following 'President's Post' submitted by Sir Arthur Masters for the club's February 2007 newsletter:

> At our last committee meeting, concern was expressed that, in the absence of any current Club Filming Projects, such as Community Films for sundry good causes which we have undertaken in previous years, the Club is currently lacking the focus which brings members together outside of Club Nights, to enjoy working as a team. This has typically provided both a new experience for members who have perhaps only been individual film-makers, and a training opportunity for newer Club Members to take part (often in the vital role of 'gofers') and learn by watching how more experienced members go about their craft, be it Producing, Directing, Lighting, Camera, Sound, Continuity or Logging (to make the subsequent Editing task much easier). And in addition to all those serious advantages, there is also the fun and social aspect of this team work, which often involve days out together in interesting places, and many a pub meal or picnic in each other's company which might not otherwise happen.

As this account implies, the social – or sociable – functions of the club are as important as the actual film-making; and while the two can be separated to some extent, they are nevertheless mutually interdependent. We could say that the club exhibits many of the characteristics that define a 'community of practice'. In terms of Wenger's (1998) account, the club entails forms of joint enterprise understood and continually renegotiated by its members; mutual engagements that bind members together into a social entity; and a shared repertoire of communal resources that members have developed over time. In the case of club members for whom film-making is their central hobby, and for whom club meetings may constitute their primary social occasion, the strength of the club is precisely in balancing community – the opportunity for sociable interaction – with practice – that is, film-making. This aligns neatly with Wenger's description:

> Over time ... collective learning results in practices that reflect both the pursuit of our enterprises and the attendant social relations. These practices are thus the property of a kind of community created over time by the sustained pursuit of a shared enterprise. It makes sense, therefore, to call these kinds of communities 'communities of practice'.
>
> (1998: 45)

However, it would be wrong to assume that this balance is easy to achieve. As Arthur Masters' comments in the newsletter suggest, the problem currently is that much of the practice takes place outside the community per se. This has several implications. Some more experienced members, including some who are former or current professionals, feel that their role is more like that of teacher than apprentice, and might be happy enough with the opportunity to lecture, or hear other speakers at meetings and undertake their film projects at home. However, for many this will not be the case. Those members who do not own their own equipment, or prefer to work in groups (but lack the drive or confidence to initiate the process) are not adequately catered for. Furthermore, given that the majority of the membership is retired, and some members elderly and/or widowed, a diminished social network is potentially very damaging to them personally as well as to the club. The few members that one already sees as friends outside the club may remain so, but in a community of practice, the strongest bonds, friendships and mutual respect will be formed *through* that practice. It is therefore not surprising that Arthur Masters, in his role of president, should feel the need to comment on this problem, as he is in his 80s and now living in sheltered accommodation, and is perhaps the kind of member for whom an active club is *most* important.

'Good causes' and social capital

Masters said that he founded the Harland club with the explicit aim of:

> [U]sing our hobby to promote good causes, partly to create a project which members could collaborate in; partly to help the good cause; and partly just to have a good social time doing it … I looked round for causes that could actually benefit from having a film made … either recruitment of volunteers, raising of money, or promoting the charity and what it does to the possible people it could help.
>
> (Interview with the author.)

In the early days of the club, this meant identifying and making overtures to representatives of such possible 'causes', almost all of which came about through personal connections between club members and such organisations. However, as the club has developed, it is now in the position where the initial approach is as likely to be made *to* the club as it is to be raised by a member. This is illustrated by my field notes from one of the monthly meetings:

> [Sir Arthur Masters] introduces 'A Precious Moment', a 1993 documentary that he and fellow [Harland] members [John Hayes] and [John Clayton] made for a Lions Club hospice in Kent for the terminally ill, and says that the club is currently planning to approach another hospice with a view to making a similar film. He comments that if the 20 minute film were made today, it would be shorter, and offers the caveat that there's a vast difference in quality between the film – made on Hi8, and with analogue editing – and that which the club is able to produce today.
>
> (Field Notes, March 2007)

This screening of a 'good cause' film from 15 years ago serves several purposes for the club. The most obvious, as acknowledged by Masters' introduction, is to highlight the fact that technological advances mean the club's films are now of a greater technical quality than ever before – as well as showing how members' skills have improved. Members are relatively early adopters of new technology, and a film made on Hi8 is thus a kind of period piece.

The second purpose for screening such a film is the sense of nostalgia it generates, even among current members who did not belong to the club at the time. For those who were members, it provides the opportunity to recall themselves or their colleagues as they were then. This leads to comments about how young everyone looked (or rather, 'how old we look now'), and to jokes about hairstyles and clothing, or reminiscences about former members who have since died or left the club. This kind of screening thus represents a 'family gathering' for the club, a chance for some to bask in reflected glory, and serves as evidence of continuity in club activity, of a shared history. (In the case of 'A Precious Moment', club member Sarah Hayes featured prominently both in the commentary and as the interviewer of workers at the hospice. However, the screening meeting was the first time I had seen her in my year of attendance, even though her husband attends meetings regularly.)

The 'good cause' films represent only part of the club's output, but are fundamental to its identity. Screening the hospice film might partly be considered a form of brainstorming for ideas for the new film, but it also injects a seriousness and sense of purpose into the club's activity; and in this respect it was particularly timely, as in recent meetings there had been comments about a lack of whole-club film projects. In the film, a member of the Lions Club Kent says that in fundraising for the hospice, 'we're dependent on what the community does for us,' and the knowledge that the Harland club has contributed to the success of the hospice is both a source of pride and a spur for the future.

The 'Welcome to Harland Video Makers' leaflet, given to new members and used as publicity material outside the club, prominently mentions that the club is 'very proud of its record of assistance to local charities and other local organisations both in making promotional movies and in showing our movies to local groups'. Such movies include productions for the local hospital, the District Council, Meals on Wheels, the Harland and District Association for the Disabled, and a regional branch of the charity Keep Mobile. As this implies, there are clear themes with regard to the kinds of organisations that the club supports, and the causes on whose behalf it works. All the examples in the club literature relate either to services for the elderly, or those with physical disabilities. These are not the *only* 'good causes' the club has supported in its history, but it is significant that they are the ones it chooses to highlight.

On average, one of these films, major or minor, is made every nine months. There are several key reasons why they are made. Most obviously, they provide an opportunity for film-making, a project that club members can work on together, with involvement (and perhaps some input) from the other organisation. The club will approach the project in a serious manner, as Arthur Masters outlined in our interview:

> The committee wants to know that it's been properly researched and that it's actually going to be used; that we know who the audience is and who the message is and how it's going to be put over; is it going to be on the website, is it going to be part of a presentation or is it going to be sent out to thousands of people to look at at home. That obviously affects what we're going to build so we really want to be sure from the film club point of view that it's properly researched and we know what we're doing. The other thing is that they've got to promote it to the members to make sure they want to join in and do it.

Having a commission – whether unsolicited or otherwise – enables the club to see itself as something akin to a 'professional' unit, and to operate as such. One key issue here is the financial aspects of the project. An external commission is likely to require more equipment than a club film (where working within the club's means is a key element), and thus money explicitly enters the world of the amateur. The club does not accept a fee for a finished film, and although for some clients it asks for club costs to be covered, for 'good causes' the club will often actively fundraise (for example, by hiring out its equipment) so that the cause incurs no costs whatsoever. Internal fundraising is not a preferred strategy, but tends to be the fastest method, and enables non-participating club members to feel they are actively contributing to the film.

Such films also serve as a means of legitimising what might be seen as merely a leisure pursuit or hobby. Some of the Harland film-makers have been making films for much of their lives – a 40-year personal history of film-making is by no means uncommon – and some are also involved with charity work, and are thus able to combine their interests in this way. However, this need for legitimation is important for all club members. Given a widespread lack of respect for the amateur, or a culture where people are encouraged to use their skills for professional or financial gain, making films for local causes moves their activity explicitly into the field of 'serious leisure' (Stebbins, 2007). Being able to point to a shared goal and a specific end product thus acts as a form of vindication for the club – evidence, if it is needed, that their hobby has relevance and worth in the wider world.

Even so, there can be also a certain reciprocal benefit, perhaps even an unspoken kind of '*quid pro quo*' in these relationships. As Masters says, the club is 'very proud of its record of assistance to local charities and other local organisations ... *in showing our movies to local groups*' (emphasis added). For a club film-maker, opportunities to exhibit one's films to a wider audience are especially prized. This is true of links with other amateur film-making clubs, where, of course, there are opportunities for swapping films and sharing ideas; but to establish a link with a non-film-making organisation, where the flow of films is one way – and particularly to an organisation that is grateful to, and holds the Harland group in high regard – is regarded as a great opportunity, even if it is not an explicit motivating factor when deciding to undertake a project.

Beyond this, there is obviously a certain 'feelgood factor' in helping others, and particularly those 'less fortunate'. While Putnam might regard such activities as a matter of disinterested altruism, there is a kind of self-interest at stake here that might be seen to be more in line with Bourdieu's account of social capital. Although it is not necessarily true of the club as a whole, for some members (consciously or otherwise) there may be an element of *patronage* in the desire – in the name of the club – to act as benefactor for such causes. Furthermore, while many club members are affected by the physical effects of ageing – deteriorating hearing or sight, physical mobility or illness – the club has no regular members with disabilities. The work for the 'good causes' is therefore work for an 'other'; and the desire to help might be motivated in part by pity rather than empathy, celebrating 'our' relative good fortune. If the work for good causes enables the club to feel morally good about itself, it enables members to feel good about themselves *physically* as well. Indeed, the work for (rather than *with*) the cause might be said to have the ultimate result of reinforcing the boundaries between the organisations and highlighting differences while apparently bridging those boundaries – although club members themselves would strongly dispute such an interpretation.

Inside the black box

According to Putnam, although the formal ways in which people connect with their communities are important, informal connections occur more frequently (2000: 93). One could add that such connections occur not only in correspondingly informal settings, but also within formal, structured environments: the Harland club, for example, operates in both spheres. From Putnam's perspective, informal social connections are a kind of glue that holds together all kinds of social interactions – the strength of voluntary, free association is that people are more likely to 'be themselves', to trust and be trusted, particularly where there is no prospect of tangible (especially financial) personal gain. In turn, the lack of ulterior motive will enable a group, informal or otherwise, to function well and build social capital.

Even so, different people are likely to perform different roles in this context, and there are likely to be various forms of hierarchy and power in operation. For example, Putnam uses the Yiddish terms 'machers' (people who make things happen in the community) and 'schmoozers' (those who spend many hours in informal conversation and communion) to distinguish between two social types. The challenge for those keen to promote social capital would be to make schmoozing a more constructive activity (perhaps a form of 'legitimate peripheral participation', to use Lave and Wenger's (1991) terms) and to recognise it as such. Certainly it plays an important role in strengthening social bonds, although in any given social situation there are many unwritten rules regarding what may or may not be said, and by whom, so the term 'informal' should not be taken to mean unstructured.

We can turn to social identity theory to explore some of these social roles or processes in more detail. According to this theory, the formation and maintenance of social groups involves three key processes: categorisation, identification and comparison (Tajfel and Turner, 1979). From this perspective, a person is seen to have a series of 'selves' that correspond to their membership of particular groups. Although there is some reciprocal influence, social identity differs from personal identity in that while the latter is concerned with a person's individual attributes, social identity relates to self-categorisation as a group member. When we apply this to Harland – in addition to the 'situated learning' theory (Lave and Wenger, 1991), which accounts for the ways in which experienced members share their skills with newer members – a picture of roles and hierarchies, and corresponding cultural capital, becomes clear. In observing the club and through in-depth interviews with members, I have identified six primary 'types' of club members. This is not necessarily an exhaustive list, but it helps us to examine the social organisation of the club and to understand how social identities are constructed through social interaction in this kind of setting.

The Beginner – A beginner film-maker will have had to actively seek out the club, perhaps via an online search, in which case they are likely to have arrived at the club website via the main IAC website. Harland's current policy is not to solicit new members, and this was explained in terms of a feeling that the club had reached a critical mass. Members wanted to consolidate the club and move on with its work rather than to increase its numbers. While new members are welcome, the Chair's responsibilities lie with catering to the needs of all members, and so an additional factor in not seeking new members is not to have to cater to *absolute* beginners, and for the basics to be taken for granted, so that technical demonstrations can operate at a higher level. However, where the social aspects of club life are concerned, new members might be valued more, and their presence may have a rejuvenating effect on the club. In practice, however, given the lack of advertising, a large proportion of new members, beginners or otherwise, are likely to have existing personal connections to one or more club members, and may alter the social dynamic less than completely 'unknown quantities': provided they fit in, they might be expected to shore up the positions of their friends where club hierarchies are concerned.

The Lone Operator – A surprising number of members are, despite lengthy personal histories in amateur film-making, relative newcomers to the club world. They cannot have been unaware that there was a network of film clubs, with their own publications, competitions and festivals, but they chose to 'go it alone' for much of their amateur film-making career. Reasons for such a lone approach are varied, and it is unlikely that such a film-maker would not have had some sort of overlap with the organised amateur world at various points, if only through subscribing to magazines or reading the same 'how to' books as the club members. However, such people will have found themselves at a point at which their non-club film-making ceases to be wholly fulfilling. This may be due to developments in their film-making, at which point they require assistance from others – knowledge, time, equipment, ideas, other forms of participation – or, more likely, that they wish to enjoy the social side of club life. This kind of new member might initially be treated in the same way as a beginner, until their level of expertise had been established, at which point they would be regarded as having 'returned to the fold', since even the club members for whom club activities are primarily about film-making tend to value the socialising and community.

The Club Mover – One result of the inevitable folding of some film clubs is that former members are likely to seek out another club to join, and will probably have met some of the members before at regional and national IAC events. In those contexts, there can be a kind of friendly rivalry between clubs, although no club member will be pleased to learn of the dissolution of another club. A benefit to the new club is that someone who already speaks 'club language' and can be sufficiently objective will be able to provide an accurate comparison between their previous and current clubs, and to identify areas of the new club that could be improved. Someone who has served on the committee of another club would be particularly well placed to offer this kind of perspective. An alternative would be a new member whose old club has not folded, but who has chosen to move clubs, perhaps having moved areas. Again, this member will probably have previously encountered some of the members of the new club, and in addition to offering a comparison between clubs, as long as they have maintained good relations with their former club, will be able to facilitate links between the two.

The Celebrity – A variation on the club mover would be the kind of new member who is previously known to many of the club members – perhaps more by reputation than personal connection. This member is likely to have been active within the regional or national IAC organisation, and their arrival would be seen as a coup, as vindication that the club is doing well. A problem that the arrival of a 'celebrity' member might bring about is a tendency among members to defer to their experience or knowledge at every opportunity.

The Professional – In the Harland club, there are several members who worked for the BBC in their professional lives, and at least one other member who currently works as an audio-visual professional. This kind of professional/amateur crossover is not unusual. The professional is likely to receive a particularly warm welcome from the club, on the assumption that they will be willing to share their expertise – a former professional who seeks to take a backseat in club training may not be so well received. On the other hand, as with the club mover, members are likely to see the presence of this new member, the fact that the member has *chosen* the club, as a sign that the club is on the right track. Where a new member with a professional background may not receive such a warm welcome is in their interactions with other former professionals, who may not be accustomed or well disposed towards sharing their privileged status and role with another. However, if their areas of expertise complement one another, it may prove a very successful arrangement, resulting in improved training for other club members.

The Social Member – The social member is the kind of new member whose presence would have the least impact on the club's film-making, given that while they *may* be interested in learning more about film-making, their primary reason for attending club meetings is the socialising. It is likely that this kind of member will be the partner of a more active film-maker, as otherwise it is hard to see what would motivate someone to join an amateur film club. As such, the social member can perform a useful role as an objective 'outsider' who is able to comment on ideas. Furthermore, even if the member is not particularly interested in film-making, it is likely that by attending meetings over time they will become relatively knowledgeable, if only by osmosis.

As these brief profiles suggest, there may well be significant diversity in the motivations, interests and expertise that members bring to the club setting. This is partly about one's position as a beginner or a more experienced practitioner, and partly about one's orientation to the 'community' or the 'practice' (that is, the sociable or the film-making) dimensions of this particular community of practice. However, one consequence of this is that hierarchies and power relationships are bound to emerge – and while in many instances these may be accepted, and indeed institutionalised in the form of the club committee and the roles of the various 'officers' (president, secretary and so on), they can also be resented or resisted. To this extent, it would seem that membership *per se* is not a guarantee of acquiring social capital: on the contrary, there are inequalities in the ways in which social capital is developed and applied *within* the clubs themselves.

An ageing membership

Whereas most of the other film-making subcultures discussed in this book are youth orientated, amateur film-making clubs are largely the preserve of elderly people. This seems to be true of individual clubs, and is also supported by my observations at local, regional and national competitions. The fact that there are relatively few young club members is something that clubs are aware of and often self-conscious about. At the first club I visited, I was told that there had been a young member who had attended regularly because she hoped to work in television and wanted front-of-camera experience, and that occasionally, a young person would attend a meeting or two, but rarely more than that.

The underlying fear of the members seems to be twofold: firstly, that clubs will die out as their membership dwindles (and indeed both clubs that I have been studying have had members die during the period of my research) and secondly, that clubs *need* young people. Club members worry that film-making is becoming a less popular hobby (although the other chapters in this book would disprove this theory) and sometimes that young people are not 'joiners'. When I have heard laments about the lack of young people, the key question is typically 'why aren't young people joining our clubs?' rather than 'how can we adapt our clubs to attract young people?' The former question rests the blame squarely on the young, whereas the latter exhibits an understanding that there may be something about the film club world which does not make young people feel welcome or catered for. In this respect the club world is in a 'catch 22' situation: to attract young members, young members are needed. Clubs are quite genuine in their desire for young members, be it to diversify the acting roles that can be played in club productions (without roping in grandchildren or children), to create a broader social circle or to bring new ideas and skills to the club.

The issues here are partly to do with styles of learning. It may be that older members find it difficult to recognise that they may have things to learn from younger ones: while most members would be happy to see themselves in the role of teacher, some will be less willing to take on the role of student. The methods in which skills are shared in club meetings tend to be more static and lecture- or demonstration-based rather than a hands-on approach, with which younger members might be more familiar and comfortable.

While some club members might prefer a broader membership in terms of supporting and extending their video-making practice, this might not fit so well with the sociable or community-oriented aspect of the clubs: it is the relative homogeneity of club membership that enables strong bonds to be formed between members, between clubs and with other organisations. To this extent, the clubs may be very successful in terms of creating 'bonding' social capital between those with similar social backgrounds and values, but rather less successful in 'bridging' between more diverse social groups.

Ultimately, however, the fact that few young members are joining clubs may prove to be less important than club members believe. While most members are of retirement age, some have long personal histories of film-making behind them, and many did not join clubs until they themselves had retired. Rather than fundamentally altering club structures in an attempt to attract young members – which may serve to alienate existing members – it is worth recognising that recent and soon-to-be retirees represent a likely source of enthusiastic new blood for club life.

Conclusion: The future of film clubs

Early in the chapter, I introduced the two other settings for my research – the London club that mainly watches rather than makes amateur films, and the online film-making forum, in which face-to-face film-making and socialising are replaced by virtual discussion, and films are presented via the Internet. Both settings share some characteristics with the Harland club – there are clear hierarchies, and experienced or talented film-makers are deferred to (in the case of the online forum, the site moderators are the equivalent of the club committee, and constructive prolific posters possess the most cultural capital). Neither setting is as explicitly concerned with 'good causes' as Harland, but both provide an important service to their members, who may then positively promote a particular club identity. Just as club members are unlikely to belong to more than one club at a given time, online film-makers tend to focus primarily on one forum rather than contribute in equal measure to a number of sites, although the anonymity afforded by the Internet means that multiple online personae (even within the same site) are perfectly possible.

Contrary to the fears of some members, I cannot imagine that there will ever be a time when clubs have become obsolete, or are simply replaced by online activity. The sociable aspects of club life cannot be fully replicated by the Internet, and film-makers will always need to share skills and labour in ways that need face-to-face contact. It is obvious, however, that the rise of the Internet is something that clubs need to address. Many have begun to do so, for example, by using a website as a recruiting tool, while the national IAC site also represents an important resource for the amateur. However, despite the ease with which one can embed a YouTube film in a webpage, or offer a downloadable file, very few clubs use the Internet to distribute and exhibit their films, so their web presence is limited to photographs and text describing their activity. This does not present a film-making club in as dynamic a manner as is possible, but I anticipate that it will change over time, and that amateurs will come to regard the Internet as a useful tool to support their activity, rather than as a threat to their traditions or as a 'flash in the pan'. Participation in online forums and club membership need not be mutually exclusive, and online and offline dimensions of amateur film-making may ultimately come to support each other.

References

Baron, S., Field, J. and Schuller, T. (eds) (2000) *Social Capital: Critical Perspectives.* Oxford: Oxford University Press.

Bourdieu, P. (1986) The forms of capital. In J. Richardson (ed.) *The Handbook of Theory and Research for the Sociology of Education.* pp. 241–58. New York: Greenwood Press.

Fischer, C. S. (2005) Bowling alone: what's the score? *Social Networks.* 27: 155–67.

Lave, J. and Wenger, E. (1991) *Situated Learning: Legitimate Peripheral Participation.* Cambridge: Cambridge University Press.

Leadbeater, C. and Miller, P. (2004) *The Pro-Am Revolution.* London: Demos.

Putnam, R. (2000) *Bowling Alone: The Collapse and Revival of American Community.* New York: Simon & Schuster.

Stebbins, R. (2007) *Serious Leisure.* New Brunswick, NJ: Transaction.

Tajfel, H. and Turner, J. C. (1979) An integrative theory of intergroup conflict. In W. G. Austin and S. Worchel (eds) *The Social Psychology of Intergroup Relations.* pp. 33–47. Monterey, CA: Brooks-Cole.

Wenger, E. (1998) Communities of Practice: learning as a social system. Retrieved from http://www.co-i-l.com/coil/knowledge-garden/cop/lss.shtml on November 30, 2008.

11
Always on: Camera Phones, Video Production and Identity

Rebekah Willett

The mobile camera phone is arguably the most contentious of the moving image capture devices discussed in this book. As we have described in our introduction, camera phones are increasingly being used as instruments of secret surveillance. They have been used to record questionable disciplinary procedures in schools, for example, and as means of bullying and harassment. Camera phones are a key component of the 'happy slapping' phenomenon, whereby innocent strangers are recorded reacting to being randomly attacked. The increase in 'up-skirting' (using camera phones to photograph or videotape up women's skirts as they stand on crowded trains or escalators) led to the passing of the Video Voyeurism Prevention Act (2004) in the US which prohibits videotaping 'a private area of an individual without their consent' (House of Representatives, 2004). Finally, one of the most notorious secretly filmed and widely distributed camera phone videos is of Saddam Hussein's execution, which includes the sounds of people jeering as well as the execution itself.

In contrast with these sensational uses of camera phones, there are clear links between the use of camera phones for making videos and the use of camcorders, as discussed in previous chapters. The portability and constant availability of the camera phone is often cited as a key factor in the rise of 'witness journalism' (Chapter 5). With increased storage capacity, better lenses and higher quality image capturing, the camera phone is now being used to make short films, which can be entered in the growing number of mobile film competitions around the world. Video diaries in the form of moblogs (mobile weblogs) can be found on numerous websites which specialise in hosting photos and videos sent straight from a camera phone. And just as the advent of video camcorders may have led to a broader range of representations of domestic life being recorded than was the case with home movie cameras, so the camera phone is capturing more mundane, everyday images than previous forms of technology (see Chapters 2 and 4).

Although there are parallels with the use of camcorders, the camera phone is set against a different backdrop. The predominant use of mobile phones is still for communication, rather than for image capturing. Users of camera phones do not generally set out to purchase a moving image recording device, as someone purchasing a camcorder would, and camera phone users are not necessarily camcorder users. Within a household, rather than sharing a camcorder, it is possible (and increasingly likely) that there will be several individuals who own camera phones with video recording functions, making the videos more personal and private. In terms of sharing images, a video captured on a camera phone can potentially be sent directly to a website for public or private viewing, sent to friends via multimedia messaging service (MMS) or email, and saved on a personal computer where it can be edited and distributed in various forms. The camera phone can be pulled out of a pocket for on-the-spot video sharing, passing moving images around like one would a photograph from a wallet. Finally, a video on a camera phone can be viewed solely by the owner of the phone almost anytime and anywhere. In all these respects, it is important to recognise the specific technological 'affordances' (properties and possibilities) of the camera phone video. This is not necessarily to imply that it is a wholly new form of moving image capture in contrast to film or video, but rather, as Goggin (2006) suggests, that it occupies 'a dynamic and contingent niche in a rapidly changing scene of digital photography, image circulation, and visual culture' (153).

One focus of this chapter, therefore, is on the affordances of the camera phone, and their social and personal implications. Research on affordances investigates how the physical properties of a particular object or technology determine the way we interpret its use (Gibson, 1979). The focus on affordances is particularly relevant as a way of comparing moving image capture on different technologies – camcorder, still camera or camera phone. In the data collected for this chapter, participants consistently referred to the physical aspects of the camera phone which determined their use of the camera. The title of the chapter 'always on' refers to one such affordance of the camera phone. Compared with camcorders, camera phones do not use as much battery power, and are able to be left on without a constant need for recharging. Several participants commented that, unlike a camcorder, the mobile is always ready to shoot. This allows the user to capture things that happen suddenly and unexpectedly, which might be lost if the user had to remove a lens cap, flip open the viewfinder and turn the machine on, as with a camcorder. The affordances of camera phones, therefore, have implications in terms of how, when, where, what and why people are filming, as well as how the images are distributed and saved.

The analysis in this chapter shows that much of the content of camera phone videos centres on friends and family. Yet although camera phone video is fulfilling some of the same functions that Chalfen (1987) analyses in relation to home mode imagery (see Chapters 2 and 4), it may also serve different functions. In particular, the increase in the amount and accessibility of video recording raises questions about the changing representation of everyday life. Chalfen (like Bourdieu in relation to photography) argues that home movies are structured through 'selection and manipulation'. According to Chalfen, 'we find a *special* reality documented in the home movie. Commonplace behaviour, mundane activities, and everyday happenings do *not* get recorded' (1987: 69, original emphasis). While it is clear that camera phone video is capturing *more* of our lives, this chapter analyses the changing nature of the 'special reality' which is being constructed and how it may be different from that of home movies created with camcorders.

As a multimedia device, the camera phone in some ways exemplifies a form of personalised or individualised image making, both in terms of the display of the object itself and the images produced with the object. Therefore, another focus of this chapter is on the role of camera phone video in defining and performing identity. This connects with Chalfen's work on the function of home mode imagery for the construction of the self, albeit 'less perhaps of the idiosyncratic aspects of the individual, autonomous self, and more of the conforming, corporate-family self' (1987: 124). Chalfen's division here aligns neatly with Goffman's (1959) analogy between social relations and theatrical performance, and his distinction between behaviour which is more conformist and ritualistic ('front stage'), and that which is more honest and potentially contradictory in relation to front stage performance ('back stage'). In addition to Goffman's notion of the presentation of self, this chapter uses Giddens's ideas about identity as part of the reflexive 'project of the self' (1991) – the claim that individuals in 'late modern' societies are continually working on constructing biographical narratives of their lives. This relates closely to the function of home mode imagery as a means of creating what Chalfen refers to as personal visual histories.

The investigation of camera phone video in this chapter, therefore, takes account of the technological affordances of the device itself, but looks at technology from an essentially sociological perspective. While seeking to avoid a 'technological determinist' position, in which the form of a given technology determines its use, I also attempt to avoid the opposite view, which would see camera phone use purely as a reflection of predetermined needs and motivations (cf. MacKenzie and Wajcman, 1999). Rather, the analysis examines how camera phone video technology intersects with people's existing uses both of mobile technology and of still and video cameras to create changes in the social construction of moving image production.

Previous research

In the US in 2006, the Pew Internet and American Life Project found that 6% of mobile phone users were recording videos on their phones (Rainie and Keeter, 2006). The quality of camera phones is rapidly advancing, and at the time of writing, phones are available with zoom, extra lenses, 3.2 megapixels and the capacity to 'shoot up to 90 minutes of video in DVD like quality' (Nokia, 2007). Given the rapid development of camera phone video recording, very little research has looked at this area specifically. However, a growing body of research is investigating camera phone photography, which has obvious links with video.

In countries with high camera phone distribution, camera phones are replacing stand-alone still cameras, with people increasingly using their phone as their main camera (Chalfen, 2006). Where traditional cameras are used, photos are taken of special occasions, rather than the 'fleeting and unexpected moments of surprise, beauty and adoration in the everyday' which some commentators see as characteristic of camera phone images (Okabe, 2004: 16). Gye (2007) also suggests that camera phone photography is 'far more individualized, mundane and everyday than much of the personal photography that preceded it' (285). Camera phone photography, therefore, contrasts with Bourdieu's description of cameras as shared family property which are used on special occasions to construct and fix the image of the family (Rivière, 2005).

This move away from photographing particular planned events and towards more random moments is seen as part of a broader change towards image capturing as a more overtly subjective process. Okabe (2004) writes:

> The traditional camera tended to take on more of the role of a third party, photographing a group photo or a scene that is framed in a more distanced way. The camera phone tends to be used more

frequently as a kind of archive of a personal trajectory or viewpoint on the world, a collection of fragments of everyday life.

(17)

Gye (2007) also argues that camera phones are leading to the production of more intimate images than previous forms of personal photography. Meanwhile, Rivière (2005) discusses how the perception of the camera phone is bound up with that of the mobile phone rather than the traditional camera, and that this 'frees photography from conventional uses associated with aesthetic or archiving purposes' (172). Whereas traditional cameras are about recording a particular time, camera phone photography is part of instant communication. Rivière suggests that mobile photos are less distant in terms of time than traditional photographs, and therefore are more about a 'quest for self-authentication'. As Gye (2007) describes, 'the transitory nature of camera phone images means that self expression is shifting away from "this is what I saw then" to "this is what I see now"' (285). Furthermore, Gye suggests that camera phone photos are ephemeral, they hold symbolic value as a reference to a shared experience, and therefore the legibility of the images is not as important.

Further comparisons with traditional cameras show that images are shared in different ways: users frequently pass them around to view on the phone, rather than sending them or printing them out (Chalfen, 2006). Users who are sending photos via MMS are using image capturing as part of the communication component of their mobile phone. Ito (2005) discusses the exchange of personal photos among friends and couples as a way of establishing an 'intimate visual co-presence' through the 'visual sharing modality that is uniquely suited to the handheld space' (1). Here, the virtual presence of another person is always possible, and images in particular are used to exchange messages that otherwise would need to be conveyed face-to-face – asking an opinion on a new haircut, for example.

Research on young people's use of camera phones in various countries (Finland, Italy, Japan, Korea, Norway and the UK) stresses the role of mobile phones in maintaining and extending social networks (Hjorth, 2007; Kasesniemi, 2003; Kato et al., 2005; Ling, 2004; Scifo, 2005; Ito et al., 2005). In the UK, Taylor and Harper (2003) describe the exchange of text messages and photos on phones in terms of gift giving, as a 'medium through which young people can sustain and invigorate their social networks' (3). Here, photos can be seen as gifts that carry symbolic meaning through their emotional significance, as they are used to recall past thoughts and feelings. Again, this points to a shift in image production and reception, with camera phone images being used for personal communication, the expression of emotion, intimate occasions and immediate access. With camera phone video, a similar shift is happening, as will be discussed in the following sections.

Studying camera phone video production

Data for this chapter consists of interviews with ten camera phone users plus their online videos. Interviews were conducted face-to-face, or via the phone or email, and 177 videos from the ten participants were viewed. The participants' use of video varied, with one participant posting three videos to her blog and another posting 30. Most videos were under five minutes long. The interviewees ranged from approximately 18 to 40 years of age, and came from a variety of locations around the UK. This was an opportunity sample, with all of the interviewees contacted via the websites YouTube or moblog:uk, where a search was conducted specifically for people in the UK who had posted videos from their camera phones. Obviously, these participants only share a proportion of their videos online, and in the case of the moblog participants, their use of the video phone was prefaced partly by their interest in blogging (with a strong reliance on visual media). The sample, therefore, is skewed towards a particular use of camera phone video, and the data are interpreted as such.

The face-to-face and phone interviews were semi-structured, and the email interviews contained a list of open-ended questions. Interview questions drew on previous research into camera phone photography (as discussed above). They were aimed at comparing the use of other image capturing technologies (e.g. camera phone, camcorder, still camera) with camera phone video, looking at what is recorded, how videos are shared and saved (or not), and the role of mobile media devices in terms of personal identity.

Affordances of camera phone video

Many people we interviewed across the wider research project indicated that they regularly made choices about their use of image capturing technology. Many of our participants had a choice of using a still camera, camcorder or camera phone, and with each of these devices they had the possibility of shooting video or taking still photographs. Looking just at the participants who were interviewed primarily about their camera phone use, seven of the ten used video either on their camcorder or on their stills camera, as well as on their camera phone. They were clear about when they used their camera phone rather than their camcorder for videoing. One of the affordances of the camera phone is obviously the size and therefore the constant availability. One participant said: 'a mobile [camera phone] I can just fit in my pocket and take it out when ever I want. So much easier'. Another said he did not use a camcorder because he did not want to spend the time editing and setting up tripods and dollies. Another participant said that camera phones are less obtrusive than camcorders, and therefore people are more willing to be videotaped, and less likely to react to the camera (to 'act up' or be embarrassed). Several of the participants indicated that camcorders were old technology, with one person commenting that she thought of camcorders as 'passé'. However, participants typically said they would still use a camcorder for special occasions, partly because the quality is better, and also because of the affordance of the storage:

> I'd use [a camcorder] if I needed better quality say for a wedding or where I need everything all on one tape/DVD/card like a road trip/ holiday.

Storage is therefore a key affordance, which differs between these technologies. Thus, another person said that he preferred camera phone video because the images can be stored on the computer alongside photographs, and would therefore be more accessible:

> My old analogue camcorder is getting much less use nowadays. The recordings stay unwatched on dusty tapes. The future is in storing media in a single place for easy retrieval.

Two participants described camcorders as having the potential for creating more elaborate productions, whereas camera phone video was more disposable. Another said that, in contrast with camcorder video used for special occasions, camera phone video is more for passing memories:

> There isn't really any production value for mobile video ... It's a throw away memory that you can share online very quickly.

As this participant states, camera phone video can be shared quickly – and as such, the kinds of events that are being documented are 'throw away', less 'special' than a wedding or birthday party. This corresponds with findings about photography on camera phones, as indicated in the previous section. Rivière (2005) and Gye (2007) discuss the concept of recording *time* as shifting, with camera phone images being about sharing what is happening now, rather than on a particular occasion in the past. This is confirmed by the data in this study. As one participant said:

> It's not usually that I particularly don't want to put a video online, it's just that I don't necessarily think it's good enough to be on the blog. But if there's something that's immediately happened, that I quickly capture and can show to friends, going, 'Hah, look, I caught this on video.'

The ease of taking and sharing videos has made the content more transitory, as this participant explains:

> It's so throwaway, it's so instant it becomes throwaway. It's already passed once you've uploaded it. And that, again, adds to its appeal. Because it's not edifying, it's just taken, captured, gone. You know, forgotten ... Because the live value is just so compelling. And also it's like, I don't want to think about it anymore ... Do it, get it done, get it up, publish, and leave.

From these responses, we can see that the affordance of sending video straight to another phone or to a website from any location for immediate viewing is resulting in video that is less about constructing a memory of a particular occasion, as with a camcorder video of a wedding or a birthday party, and more about capturing particular moments of life as they happen, for immediate and passing viewing. This aligns with Okabe's description of camera phone photography as 'collections of fragments of everyday life' (2004: 17). The appeal of camera phone video is that it does not artificially construct an occasion – as the participant above states when he discusses the appeal of the 'live value' of camera phone video and describes this video as 'not edifying'.

There are further connections here with the research by Okabe (2004), which suggests that camera phone photography is more subjective than traditional photography. The participant just quoted above discusses this point specifically:

> You don't give a monkey's about whether it's biased or not. Because I'm not putting myself up as an authority. So I don't have to worry

about personal bias. In fact, the more biased it is, the more people like it in a lot of ways, because it's me.

We can also see here that mobile phone video is about performing and defining identity. Research on mobile phones indicates that many young people, in particular, personalise their mobile phone, using it as an expression of identity (e.g. Katz and Sugiyama, 2005). Ring tones, charms, stickers and wallpapers are all part of these displays; and having the latest phone (or intentionally 'resisting' trends and having an old 'retro' phone) is also part of the way identity is displayed. Camera phones enable users to display identities as technology-orientated, as visual ethnographers, as record keepers; and displaying and sharing videos allows viewers to see day-to-day life through the eyes of the videomaker. When asked about the relation between phones and identity, comments by the participants generally acknowledged a link, and only one person said there was no relation between her phone and her 'personality'. The following responses indicate how phones can be used as a means of displaying identity (first participant), or more as a facilitator of existing practices (second participant):

> I cannot imagine doing something without having my mobile near me ... I feel naked without it. Also other people know that I always have a different and unique mobile, so this is also how people know me.

> I wouldn't call it part of my identity but I'd say it facilitates my identity ... I wouldn't like to be considered somebody who lives for my phone but more lives through my phone. The photos and videos I take I put online and that is really facilitating what's going on.

All of the participants commented that they used their camera phone more for taking still photographs than video. On moblog:uk, many of the videos are accompanied by photographs, indicating that video is used as part of the process of documenting an event. Participants said video was used when they wanted to capture movement (pets, dancing, rain) or sound (singing, speech, engines). These rather obvious distinctions were expanded on by many of the participants to provide a more nuanced indication of the difference in uses. One described video as capturing a more 'dynamic experience' than photographs, whereas another commented that he prefers holding a photograph and seeing how a single moment has been captured. Still photography was seen by several users as an easier means of producing higher quality images, not only technically, in terms of pixels, but also in terms of artistic value, as these participants explain:

> I use photos to capture a detail of a place or event, or when I try to be artistic. I use video to show a more general scene.

> Other mobloggers spend a lot of time on composition with their pictures. I'd say on video it's harder to do. You just kind of want to get it there and then.

These responses indicate, again, that camera phone video is more disposable, and also that legibility is not as important because videos are not about capturing specific visual details. One participant specifically mentioned taking photographs, particularly 'if something is good to analyse in detail', and another said about video, 'it doesn't matter what it looks like, just get those voices, get those opinions, capture that moment. And I think you forgive a lot.' This may explain the many videos of concerts (discussed in the next section) in which neither the image nor the sound is clear. Here videos are about capturing atmosphere, as this participant explains:

> I take still photos as an instant snapshot and reminder of a moment in time, whereas I use videos more for capturing the atmosphere of the moment.

Nevertheless, one of the striking findings from the interviews is that although participants refer to their videos as low quality and as throwaway, very few of them delete any videos (apart from mistakes – videotaping one's feet or inside of a bag, for example). Maintaining a digital archive of one's life 'in a single place', including what might be seen by outsiders as ephemeral material, seemed to be a crucial imperative for several participants in sustaining what Giddens (1991) calls a 'narrative of the self'.

The practice of camera phone video seems to be more about sharing, reviewing, and having a record of one's life stored somewhere for future viewing, than about creating material that has artistic value. It is the content rather than the quality that is important. As with the home mode video described by Maria Pini (Chapter 4), these sharing and projected viewing practices are part of people's memory work, a way of narrating and remembering an event, both individually and within a group. Some participants indicated that the kinds of memories captured on camera phone videos are fleeting and likely to be forgotten, but that the technology might help them to preserve them. In line with the title of his moblog, Random Access Memories, this participant comments:

> This was the crazy stuff that we'll never remember ... It's these weird moments in life that are difficult to write about and difficult to remember.

In terms of Chalfen's (1987) analysis of the functions of home mode imagery, here the camera phone video is functioning as an aide-memoire, a means to create a visual history, and importantly, a history which is full of 'random', 'crazy' and 'weird' moments. Yet although the visual history might include more diverse images than previous home imagery, it is still a construction, a 'special reality'. As discussed in the following section, this reality excludes particular things, and functions to position producers in particular ways. And importantly, in terms of Giddens's (1991) 'project of the self', the choice of images works to construct a coherent identity, one that may include random images, but one which is nevertheless narrated in a specific way. Selecting images for display on one's moblog can also be seen as part of this reflexive project of the self. This same participant indicated that he sees the constant capturing of images of people's lives, and the sharing and viewing of these images, as part of a reaction to a society in which people feel increasingly fragmented and alienated (cf. Bauman, 2004):

> If we were to really focus on our careers, we would all stop talking to each other. And these kind of technologies bring you back ... to the personal. You know, make the personal life that much more exciting again ... You want these markers in your life. You want these reflections.

Here, as is the case with many camera phone images and moblogs, the focus on the personal offers a way of projecting and defining a unified self, as someone with a particular history.

The audience for camera phone images varies, although in the current study the majority of camera phone videos were shared privately with friends and family rather than in a more public context. The selection of images for particular audiences can be seen as a way in which the performance of identity is being carefully managed in different social settings (Dowdall, in press). Even the two participants who put most of their videos online said that they also shared their videos with family or small groups of friends, either through email or when sitting in a café, for example. In terms of affordances, the portability and ubiquity of mobiles make video sharing more accessible. Instead of having to go to someone's house, and set up a video on a TV or computer, this informal sharing can happen anytime and anywhere. Furthermore, the size of camera phone videos makes them easy to send via email or MMS (though MMS was not used very frequently because of cost and quality of video, due to reduced file size). Several participants indicated that camera phones enabled them to share their video with specific people (friends who might be interested in a particular subject) rather than with a larger audience who would not be interested. Alternatively, one participant indicated that he preferred to keep control of his videos by only sharing them on his phone or by placing them on websites with restricted access.

Participants said they shared videos as a way of showing friends and family what they had been doing as well as reminding themselves of what they had done. Sharing in a face-to-face context was also used to review and relive an action immediately, both for the video-maker as well as the subject:

> It's lovely to be able to share my children's behaviour with them as well as watching from afar. I also like being able to re-watch videos after the occasion.

Sharing also constitutes what Ito (2005) calls 'intimate virtual co-presence'. Here videos are sent to loved ones, primarily as a way of feeling as though you are together when you are apart. Three of the participants mentioned sending videos to partners when they were apart, and another said he sends videos to his sister after talking to her on the phone, as a way of illustrating his narration of events. Another participant said she sends a 'hello video' if she has not seen someone for a while, indicating that such a message is more intimate than a text message. Again, the constant availability and the personal ownership of the phone enable these particular uses.

Content and function of camera phone videos

The portability and ubiquity of the camera phone means that many people are using video more frequently than would have been the case with a camcorder, sometimes under circumstances which would tend to preclude using a larger video recorder (for example, gigs, nights out and casual socialising). When asked generally what sorts of things they recorded with their camera phones, participants listed 'day-to-day things', special occasions, children, pets, sports competitions, concerts, nights out, short spoofs, people doing 'stupid' things, events, interviews and nature. The 177 videos from the ten participants, which were viewed as part of this study, largely conform to these categories. The majority fall under three broad categories based on content: *personal documentary* (family, friends and pets); *non-personal documentary* (documenting something other than family, friends or pets); or *public performances* such as concerts (see Table 11.1). These are rudimentary categories based on easily identifiable content. All three fit within familiar home mode categories (as analysed by Chalfen, 1987) and all relate to personal experiences. Approximately 10% of the videos do not fall into these categories, and include interviews with strangers, shorts (e.g. animations) or videos for purposes other than documenting a personal experience (e.g. for use as a ringtone, profile picture or MySpace video).

Table 11.1   Camera Phone Video Content

Personal documentary (36%)	Non-personal documentary (27%)	Public performance (27%)	Other (10%)
- Dancing - Drinking - Singing - Shared jokes - Birthday parties - Unusual actions (cartwheels, trampoline tricks, dares, flipping pancakes) - acting up to the camera (faces, voices, gestures) - video diary or demonstration by the video-maker - pets playing - everyday actions (children playing or saying something typical)	- rain through the window - scenery - flooding - wildlife - scenes at festivals - technology - cars - parades - items in shops	- street juggler - bands/gigs - buskers - sports competition	- interviews - stop frame animation - shorts - use as a ring tone, MySpace video, profile picture

To what extent do such videos merely document 'mundane occasions', in line with Gye's (2007) account of the characteristics of camera phone photography, or are they closer to the 'fleeting and unexpected moments of surprise, beauty and adoration in the everyday' that Okabe describes (2004: 16)? While a video of a wet dog shaking or chewing on a stick might seem mundane to me (as someone who is around dogs regularly), the video-maker clearly wanted to capture these actions in order to document the experience of being with that pet or the nature of the pet. All the pet videos in this sample featured action, so perhaps a video of a sleeping dog might be considered more 'mundane'. The definition of what is mundane, therefore, shifts not only according to the relationship of the video-maker with the subject but also in relation to what is *not* recorded. In Chalfen's data, where the focus was on special occasions such as family celebrations, videos of pets' rather ordinary actions were excluded, and seen as mundane in comparison with the special occasion. Yet as technology becomes more ubiquitous, and as more video is recorded and circulated, what might be considered mundane is bound to shift.

Looking at the *personal documentary* videos, which account for more than one-third of the sample, some do include special occasions such as birthday parties. However, most seem to be about capturing a particular momentary personal performance (e.g. singing, making faces, children saying something cute, doing cartwheels). Chalfen (1987) analyses the documentary functions of video as including creating a personal visual history, as well as validation of an experience, one's social self and one's personal relationships. This is evident in many of the videos in the *personal documentary* group from the current sample. For example, one of the videos was of the video-maker's grandparents sitting side by side in armchairs, with the grandfather singing a Christmas carol along with a broadcast of a choir (possibly on television, as both grandparents are fixing their gaze in the same direction). The video-maker's comment indicates that she wanted to document her grandfather in a particular way: 'grandad singing along to Christmas carols is quite infectious. Unfortunately this doesn't do him justice ... he had a jolly good sing.' Here, the video and the text surrounding the video seem to fulfil the documentary function of creating a visual history and a validation of one's personal relationships (documenting a typical family Christmas event and the character of the grandfather). The video also fulfils Chalfen's third function, cultural membership. It is in this category that Chalfen develops ideas about representation, particularly the notion that home video 'promotes the visual display of proper and expected behavior, of participation in socially approved activities, according to culturally approved value schemes' (139). In the Christmas sing-along video, Christian celebrations are foregrounded, and cultural value is placed on family, with elders being respected and placed centrally.

Many of the other videos in the *personal documentary* category seem to be fulfilling the cultural membership function in some way. Documents of children's 'cute' activities present happy family interactions, for example, rather than times when children are misbehaving or parents are at the end of their tether. Although there may be more family video documents being produced than ten or twenty years ago, the broad functions seem to be remaining constant. However, one shift in the documentary category is a greater inclusion of wider social networks. For example, the video of the grandfather above is the only family member represented on the 19 videos from this video-maker, who says she puts a majority of her videos online. With the portability, ubiquity and personalised nature of camera phones, video taken on phones is going well beyond the home: many of the personal documentary videos focus on friends rather than family, and the other categories (two-thirds of the sample) included no videos of family members.

Participants indicated that videos of particular spontaneous performances are shared with people who were not there at the time or viewed back immediately to add to the occasion. Videos discussed here, for example, feature people making jokes or faces, doing silly actions, dancing and singing, as well as friends larking about, having drinking competitions or doing silly gestures. Such material acts as a form of visual history: as discussed in the previous section, people rarely delete these videos, saving them on their computer hard drives for future viewing. More to the point is the way they function to document social relations, affirming one's relationship with friends and family and one's social identity. They also serve as an aide-memoire; some participants said that remembering through video was useful if the night involved heavy drinking. The silly actions, jokes and larking about all correspond with Chalfen's memory function of videos, particularly the hedonistic function of particular kinds of videos: 'Not only should one have a good time making the movies, but viewers should be able to repeat and reexperience these pleasurable times' (138–9). And finally, in terms of cultural membership, the videos function to demonstrate participation in the approved value schemes of local (age-related) cultures: so, for example, in particular youth cultures, one is expected to go drinking and perform in an uninhibited fashion.

In the *non-personal documentary* category (just over one-quarter of the sample), the videos are personal in the sense that they have personal meaning, but non-personal in the sense that no friends, relatives or family pets are featured in them. These videos document the look or sound of something, with many possible intentions including sharing with others, adding to the memory of a particular event or even sending to a news organisation (e.g. images of floods). Many of these videos seem to be saying 'I was there' or 'here's what I saw', such as pans of camping tents at Glastonbury music festival or videos of parades. Again, such material serves to create a personal visual history and acts as an aide-memoire. Another group of videos in this category features images of cars or technology. Here the videos capture speed (a car with a turbo engine racing down a road videoed from the passenger seat), sound (a speaker system with extra subwoofers) or a demonstration of a particular computer programme. The function here seems more closely related with cultural membership and performance of a particular identity. For example, masculine interest in technology and fast cars is being performed, and taste in particular kinds of cars, music and even computer operating systems is expressed. Through careful creation and selection of videos for posting online, the participants are both defining and performing their identities.

Public performance videos (just over one-quarter of the sample) consist mainly of clips of concerts. These videos occasionally include close shots of the performers with a fairly steady camera and clear audio. More often, however, the videos are of a faraway stage with shaky camera footage and lots of background sound, sometimes including pans of the audience. Occasionally gig videos are accompanied by written comments online in which the video-maker evaluates the performance. The purpose of gig videos seems to vary, with some capturing part of a performance to share the look and sound (the clearer images and sound) and others documenting attendance at a performance ('I was there'). When asked 'do you ever send video just to show where you are?' one participant specifically mentioned sending videos from a music festival 'to make people jealous'. Other videos in this category such as street performers also document attendance (they are often accompanied by tags identifying the location), as well as capturing an unusual performance and perhaps the atmosphere of a particular day or night out. Again the functions are partly about documenting presence at a particular event or a particular sight, thus providing proof that one was there and acting as a visual history and aide-memoire. And they also express cultural membership, particularly gig videos which are sometimes posted on the way home from a show, demonstrating keen membership of a particular fan culture.

A majority of the interviewees indicated that only a small proportion of their videos went online. Only two people indicated that most of their videos were shared with a wider audience online, and in both cases they were selective with their recording, only capturing things that they knew other people would be interested in (concerts) or that could not be captured with a photograph. The other eight participants said that less than 25% of their videos would be put online for a wide audience. Again, this is related to content – most participants indicated that a majority of the videos they record are personal and are shared in more intimate circles (sharing an inside joke between friends, for example). Several participants said they mainly post videos that other people might be interested in, or at least avoid 'boring personal' videos such as 'the family eating dinner'. One participant, for example, when asked what sorts of videos were posted said: '"newsworthy" things – for example, I went to the Chelsea FC celebration procession in 2006 and used my mobile phone to capture some of the images and sounds that were around me.' However, this does not necessarily mean that personal videos are not posted: the same participant says she also posts videos of her children playing.

The display of videos online could be analysed in terms of Goffman's ideas about 'front stage' and 'back stage' performance. Analysing social interaction as a kind of theatrical performance, Goffman (1959) discusses how people seek to create and manage impressions of themselves through the 'presentation of self'. He distinguishes between behaviour which he calls 'front stage' (which is typically conformist and ritualistic) and 'back stage' (which is more honest, but potentially contradicts front stage performance). Some have argued that mobile media are blurring this distinction, disrupting front stage facades and impacting on back stage interactions through the interruptions which occur as a result of the use of mobile devices (for example, intimate conversations on trains or business conversations during family gatherings) (Ling, 2004). However, through the careful selection of images on individuals' web pages, one could argue that front stage performance is being enacted and clearly delineated from back stage performance. This is evident in several interviews in the current study, particularly with participants who have accounts on moblog:uk. One interviewee said he posts particular kinds of images on YouTube (embarrassing videos, for example), rather than on his moblog site. Another interviewee commented on wanting to focus his efforts on his moblog site:

> I find putting things on YouTube and so on just dilutes what I'm trying to get out of it. I focus. All of my online contributions are on moblog because otherwise things just do get kind of diluted, really.

Both these individuals seem to be framing their participation on moblog: uk as a self-conscious performance of identity, and both express a need to maintain a particular focused front stage identity on their moblog sites. It could be argued that focusing efforts on front stage performance in the form of a website represents another attempt to construct a coherent identity or a 'narrative of the self' in a manner that Giddens and others see as characteristic of the 'late modern' world.

Conclusion

The evidence presented here clearly shows that mobile camera phones have specific affordances, and that these do have implications in terms of how they can be used and the roles they can play in social life. Compared with older technologies, camera phones are enabling different kinds of practices, both in terms of the capture or recording of moving images and in terms of distribution and sharing. The frequency of video-making is increasing, with camera phones being taken to places camcorders normally do not go, as well as being always available in a pocket or bag, ready to capture unexpected moments (ranging from floods and disasters, to children doing something silly). In the process, the camcorder is coming to be seen as something that will be used more for special occasions. In such contexts, video-making may be more likely to take an objective stance, with higher quality and longer footage than on occasions recorded with camera phones. Such videos are more likely to be stored on a tape, and watched only occasionally in particular settings. By contrast, camera phone videos at present have lower quality and are used for recording fleeting moments, as is evidenced by the short length of the videos I surveyed. Here the symbolic value that is communicated is more important than the legibility. The purpose of the videos is to capture particular moments and feelings, to give a flavour of the dynamic or the sense of an occasion, rather than to keep a full or accurate record of the occasion itself. These videos are shared more frequently and in less formal settings than camcorder video, with video sharing becoming an everyday social interaction, via MMS, the Internet or face to face. However, although the moments captured on camera phones may be less legible and more fleeting, they still hold a great amount of value for the video-makers, as is evidenced by the fact that they are rarely deleted. No less than more traditional forms of image making, these practices are equally part of building a sense of personal history and identity, of documenting everyday life, of having a container (this time on the computer) to hold memories, and of facilitating social interactions and relationships. As such, camera phones need to be seen not just as handy pieces of technology, but as resources that are increasingly important in the conduct of contemporary social and cultural life.

References

Bauman, Z. (2004) *Identity*. Cambridge: Polity.

Chalfen, R. (1987) *Snapshot Versions of Life*. Bowling Green, Ohio: Bowling Green State University Popular Press.

Chalfen, R. (2006) Can you see me now? Urban camera-phone use. Paper presented at the Conference of the International Visual Sociology Association 2006 in Urbino, Italy. http://www.visualsociology.org/proceedings_ 2006/ Chalfen_see_me_now.doc accessed 28 September 2007.

Dowdall, C. (2009) The texts of me and the texts of us: improvisation and polished performance in social networking sites. In R. Willett, M. Robinson and J. Marsh (eds) *Play, Creativity and Digital Cultures*. London: Routledge.

Gibson, J. J. (1979) *The Ecological Approach to Visual Perception*. Hillsdale, Boston: Houghton Mifflin.

Giddens, A. (1991) *Modernity and Self-Identity*. Cambridge: Polity.

Goffman, E. (1959) *The Presentation of Self in Everyday Life*. New York: Anchor Books.

Goggin, G. (2006) *Cell Phone Culture: Mobile Technology in Everyday Life*. London: Routledge.

Gye, L. (2007) Picture this: the impact of mobile camera phones on personal photographic practices. *Journal of Media and Cultural Studies*. 21(2): 279–88.

Hjorth, L. (2007) Snapshots of *almost* contact: the rise of camera phone practices and a case study in Seoul, Korea. *Journal of Media and Cultural Studies*. 21 (2): 227–38.

House of Representatives (2004) Video Voyeurism Prevention Act. Retrieved from http://bulk.resource.org/gpo.gov/reports/108/hr504.108.txt on 8 May 2008.

Ito, M. (2005) Intimate visual co-presence. http://www.itofisher.com/mito/ archives/ito.ubicomp05.pdf accessed 28 September 2007.

Ito, M., Okabe, D. and Matusuda, M. (eds) (2005) *Personal, Portable, Pedestrian: Mobile Phones in Japanese Life*. London: MIT Press.

Kasesniemi, E.-L. (2003) *Mobile Messages: Young People and a New Communication Culture*. Tampere: Tampere University Press.

Kato, F., Okabe, D., Ito, M. and Uemoto, R. (2005) Uses and possibilities of the *Keitai* camera. In M. Ito, D. Okabe and M. Matusuda (eds) *Personal, Portable, Pedestrain: Mobile Phones in Japanese Life.* pp. 300–10. London: MIT Press.

Katz, J. and Sugiyama, S. (2005) Mobile phones as fashion statements: the co-creation of mobile communication's public meaning. In R. Ling and P. Pedersen (eds) *Mobile Communications: Re-negotiating the Social Sphere.* pp. 63–82. London: Springer.

Ling, R. (2004) *The Mobile Connection: The Cell Phone's Impact on Society.* San Francisco: Morgan Kaufmann.

MacKenzie, D. and Wajcman, J. (eds) (1999) *The Social Shaping of Technology.* 2nd edition. Buckingham, UK: Open University Press.

Nokia (2007) Nokia N931. http://europe.nokia.com/A4305052 accessed 28 September 2007.

Okabe, D. (2004) Emergent social practices, situations and relations through everyday camera phone use. Paper presented at Mobile communication and Social Change, the 2004 International Conference on Mobile Communication in Seoul, Korea, October 18–19, 2004. http://www.itofisher.com/mito/archives/okabe_seoul.pdf accessed 28 September 2007.

Rainie, L. and Keeter, S. (2006) Technology and media use: how Americans use their cell phones. http://www.pewinternet.org/pdfs/PIP_Cell_phone_study.pdf accessed 28 September 2007.

Rivière, C. (2005) 'Mobile camera phones: a new form of "being together" in daily interpersonal communication'. In R. Ling and P. Pedersen (eds) *Mobile Communications: Re-negotiating the Social Sphere.* pp. 167–86. London: Springer.

Scifo, B. (2005) The domestication of the camera phone and MMS communications: the experience of young Italians. In K. Nyiri (ed.) *A Sense of Place: The Global and the Local in Mobile Communication.* pp. 363–73. Vienna: Passagen Verlag.

Taylor, A. S. and Harper, R. (2003) The gift of the gab?: a design oriented sociology of young people's use of mobiles. *Journal of Computer Supported Cooperative Work (CSCW).* 12(3): 267–96.

12
Power to the People? The Past and Future of Amateur Video

David Buckingham

Change and continuity

The research reported in this book was conducted between 2005 and 2008 – a period that might in retrospect come to be seen as a point of transition in the evolution of contemporary media. When we first planned the research, YouTube did not exist. As we write, in late 2008, the number of videos on the site is rapidly approaching 100 million.

As we have seen, the advent of 'Web 2.0' and other 'user-generated' services has led to considerable excitement about an impending media revolution. Power, it is argued, is no longer in the hands of elites and multinational corporations, but is steadily passing to ordinary people. Technology is enabling 'the people formerly known as the audience' (as Gillmor (2006) calls them) to take charge of the means of production, to create their own media and to have their voices heard. The gap between producers and consumers is converging, resulting in the appearance of a new breed of 'prosumers'; and we are seeing new forms of cultural expression and exchange that are organised democratically and collectively, rather than from the top down. Some have seen this as part of a broader 'pro-am revolution', in which traditional hierarchies of expertise and authority are being challenged, and new forms of creativity are emerging (see Chapters 2 and 5).

There has been a long history of such claims about the democratising potential of new media. For example, one can look back to the arguments being made about cable TV in the 1970s (Streeter, 1987), or indeed to the popular claims that accompanied the advent of domestic camcorders in the early 1980s (see Chapter 3). Many new media technologies have been greeted by inflated claims about their inherently radical or democratic potential, as well as by exaggerated fears about their harmful impact (see Marvin, 1988). This was certainly true in the case of television and radio, as well as the printing press: all of these technologies were apparently going to bring power to the people, to undermine the control of knowledge by elites and to enable ordinary people to express themselves. Of course, the fact that such promises have been made in the past does not necessarily mean they are going to be disappointed again this time around – nor indeed that we have seen it all before. However, it does mean that we need to pay attention to the continuities and convergences between old and new, as well as what seem to be dramatic new departures.

To some extent, our research has led us to puncture some of the hype that surrounds these developments. We have challenged the claim that armies of fearless 'citizen journalists' would somehow bring global news organisations to their knees, or – in a very different domain – that amateur pornographers would effectively ensure the demise of the mainstream porn industry (see Chapters 5 and 9). Our analyses of both the citizen journalists and the Video Nation contributors (Chapter 8) suggest that 'Big Media' are likely to be very effective in recuperating any potential challenge represented by amateur producers, and indeed in employing 'user-generated content' to their own advantage.

We would also suggest that there is a considerable amount of continuity in amateur video-making practices that belies the rhetoric of revolutionary change. This is most apparent in the case of the 'home mode' producers, whose broad aims and methods are very similar to those of the home movie-makers of the 1970s studied by Richard Chalfen (1987), or indeed those of the early twentieth century studied by historians such as Patricia Zimmerman (1995) and Heather Norris Nicholson (1997) (see Chapter 2). Such continuity is also evident in the case of the film- and video-making clubs described in Chapter 10: while such clubs may be largely the preserve of elderly people, they fulfil important social functions that are not necessarily going to be met by online forums. Indeed, there are some interesting similarities between the social interactions within the clubs and those of the much younger participants who are producing spoofs and skateboarding videos (Chapters 6 and 7).

Even when we look at the latter cases, there is a continuity that long pre-dates the advent of digital technology, let alone the Internet. Skateboarding, for example, has a long-standing tradition of visual recording and expression (see Chapter 7), while the present author is certainly old enough to remember helping young people to use Super 8 film to make their own spoof horror movies almost 30 years ago.

Such activities are certainly more widely available, and more socially organised – as well as more commercially profitable for the makers of equipment and ancillary merchandise – than they were in earlier decades; but they are by no means new.

Yet while we would resist the technological determinism that often accompanies such claims, there clearly has been an important shift in access to technology in recent years. As we saw in Chapter 1, video equipment has steadily fallen in price and gained in sophistication since the first camcorders were launched on the market a quarter of a century ago. Recent developments in editing technology – the 'bundling' of simple digital editing packages with standard home computer purchases – and in image capture devices – particularly mobile video-phones – have made production (and 'post-production') opportunities much more accessible and ubiquitous. As we have seen in the case of mobile devices (Chapter 11), such developments do have implications in terms of the 'when, where and how' of video-making – the occasions, settings and processes in and through which it occurs.

Even so, such changes are not simply a result of the 'affordances' of the technology: they also need to be seen in the context of broader changes in contemporary social life, for example, increasing mobility and urbanisation, changing lifestyles and the fragmentation of families and communities. Indeed, the desire to represent and document one's life – which is apparent not only in the growth of video-making, but in a wide range of other forms of contemporary cultural expression – could be seen as a symptom of the individualisation that characterises 'late modernity' (as defined by social theorists such as Giddens (1991) and Beck (1992)). From this perspective, video-making might be seen to serve important functions in terms of the construction and performance of identity: it offers a means of creating an archive or a narrative of the self that will offer a sense of coherence and continuity that is perhaps increasingly difficult to achieve. This may be particularly true of the most widely denigrated form of 'home mode' or family video (see Chapter 4 and Buckingham et al., in press).

However, I would argue that the most significant developments in recent years have been to do with technologies of *distribution* rather than of *production* – in the ease with which people can share and distribute video to audiences both known and hitherto unknown. The impact of this change is apparent throughout the very different cultural groups considered in this book. It is most obvious in cases like the spoof-makers, the skateboarders and the mobile video artists, for whom the Internet offers significantly enhanced opportunities to share and discuss their work (Chapters 6, 7 and 11). It is more problematic in the case of the 'citizen journalists' and the Video Nation contributors (Chapters 5 and 8): here, the involvement with mainstream media companies offers benefits in terms of enhanced visibility and prestige, but it also involves compromises. Yet even with the more private, or seemingly more traditional, practices of the home video-makers, the porn producers and the film-making clubs, it is clear that the possibility of online sharing and (in some cases) wider distribution is beginning to impact on their activities, making it possible for them to circulate material and build networks in ways that were more difficult (although of course far from impossible) in earlier times.

However, this too should be seen as an incremental process rather than a step change; and we should be wary of assuming that it is now universal. Access to media production technologies, and the skills that are needed to use them, are still unequally distributed among different social groups. It seems likely that the new opportunities provided by online distribution will be taken up most enthusiastically by those who already have a well-established interest, and the cultural and economic capital that is required for participation. Survey research is now beginning to show that such activities are largely dominated by the 'usual suspects', leading some to identify a new 'participation divide' (e.g. Hargittai and Walejko, 2008; Jenkins et al., 2006).

Persistent themes

These continuities also imply that some of the long-standing themes that applied to earlier forms of amateur media production may well continue to apply – albeit perhaps in different ways – in the new media environment. Several of these issues were discussed in general terms in Chapter 2, and have threaded through our specific case studies.

Public and private – For example, the ambivalent status of video production as a private and public practice was a key theme in the chapters on home video production, pornography, mobile phone video and Video Nation. In the case of 'home mode' production, we found that video not only functions partly as a way of generating and displaying a sense of family 'belongingness' or identity but also as a means of dealing with private feelings of nostalgia, loss and desire. There are many similarities here with the production of amateur pornography: what might be seen merely as a form of exhibitionism also has important emotional functions for the participants, with tapes serving as private 'keepsakes' of former relationships. In the case of the mobile phone videos, the circulation of images from everyday encounters serves many of the familiar functions of home mode imagery, albeit more within the peer group than the family; but such material also feeds into individuals' ongoing public 'archiving' of their everyday lives. Some of the tensions between the public and the private arose most acutely in the case of the Video Nation contributors, where the institutional constraints appear to promote particular public representations of individuality or private identity, and to discourage others.

Social relationships – The social (and sociable) dimensions of video production are apparent in all our case studies, but they arose particularly in our analyses of the clubs, the spoof-makers and the mobile phone video-makers. In each case, the making of video serves as a focus for – and a means of mediating – relationships within peer groups and communities. In the case of the spoof-makers, this centres on the performance of particular kinds of masculine identity, while for the mobile video-makers, the exchange and circulation of short videos is a way of building and consolidating relationships among friends. In the more organised (and indeed hierarchical) context of the clubs, the social identities performed through video-making interface with other forms of identity developed within the local community, and serve as a means of building particular forms of 'social capital' among participants.

Amateurs and professionals – The shifting boundaries between amateurs and professionals was a key theme in the chapters on skateboarding, pornography, citizen journalism and Video Nation. In the case of the skateboarders, amateur video-making is seen by some as a 'career' that offers the possibility of moving across into professional production. For the porn-makers, amateur production is implicitly seen as more authentic than professional porn, but there is little sense – at least among the producers whom we interviewed – of wanting to move into, or challenge, the mainstream industry. In the case of the citizen journalists, there is a more developed attempt to offer alternatives to dominant media, albeit of quite different kinds; but in Video Nation, such alternative forms of production are only possible within generic constraints and relationships that are quite tightly controlled by the BBC.

Creativity – Issues relating to creativity surfaced particularly in our discussions of the spoof-makers, the skateboarders and the citizen journalists. In each case, the participants are working within, but also themselves helping to create and extend, a particular video genre, with its own codes and conventions. In the case of the spoof-makers and some of the citizen journalists, their reference points are primarily drawn from mainstream media. While the citizen journalists are attempting to broaden the conventions and the subject matter of mainstream news, the spoof-makers' relationship with the objects of their parody is much more playful and ambivalent. Meanwhile, the skateboarders are seeking to imprint a personal creative touch on a genre that is in many respects highly constrained, not only in its content but also in its aesthetic form. In different ways, each of these studies suggests that creativity is not simply a matter of spontaneous 'self-expression' but something that occurs within – and indeed depends upon – particular social contexts and cultural conventions.

Learning – Finally, questions relating to learning threaded through our discussions of the clubs, the spoof-makers and the skateboarders. In each case, learning involves a combination of individual dedication and collaboration with others. It entails not only sustained purposive work but also participation in a 'community of practice', which may offer opportunities for forms of 'apprenticeship' (as in the case of the skateboarders) as well as peer-to-peer interaction. In the case of the clubs, in particular, this is a context in which particular roles are clearly demarcated, and distinctions between 'newbies' and 'old timers' need to be sustained.

New questions

These quick thematic 'slices' across our case studies by no means exhaust the possibilities; but we hope they point to a broad agenda of issues that will be helpful in guiding future research in this area. When we take these themes and questions forward to analyse the impact of online distribution, several new questions arise. For example, the Internet is an ambiguous technology in terms of the distinction between public and private – as studies of young people's uses of social networking sites are increasingly suggesting (Willett, 2009). As more and more people upload videos, both to generic sharing sites such as YouTube and to their social networking profiles, what are the implications of this in terms of the public performance of 'private' identities? Is video production creating new opportunities for identity play (and display), or is it becoming the ultimate technology of self-surveillance?

Online distribution potentially creates new relationships between video-makers and their audiences. The possibility of obtaining feedback (not least in the form of video responses, or even re-edited 'mashups' of one's own work) may mean that video production is no longer simply a matter of creating a finished 'text' which is then transmitted to an 'audience'. This has potentially very significant implications in terms of how we think about mediated communication. In the world of online video sharing, are the boundaries between 'producers' and 'consumers' – or between mass communication and interpersonal communication – becoming increasingly blurred? And are we seeing the emergence of new forms of 'multimodal' public communication, in which different communicative modes interact in new ways?

Meanwhile, the Internet has been seen to promote a broader reformulation of the relationships between amateurs and professionals – and indeed, as being culpable for the damaging consequences of this move (see Chapter 2). It is also believed to create new possibilities in terms of networked communication and social interaction, and hence for learning. So is online sharing of video likely to result in a broader reformulation of the relationships between amateurs and professionals, or will this be confined only to quite specific practices? Will the 'horizontal' virtual networks of online communication come to replace face-to-face interaction of the kind made possible by amateur video-making clubs, or merely supplement it? Does the Internet offer genuinely new styles of learning, as its advocates suggest, or is it much more limited in its ability to promote sustained collaboration?

Enthusiasts for YouTube and similar developments seem to have already decided the answers to these (and indeed many other) questions. Yet these technologies and services are still rapidly evolving. At the time of writing (late 2008), for example, it appears that YouTube has yet to turn a profit; and it is currently in negotiation with major 'old media' companies like MGM and CBS with a view to hosting full-length films and TV shows, accompanied by advertising. In the present situation, we would prefer to be more cautious about the apparently revolutionary possibilities of these technologies, and to await the results of further empirical research.

With a few exceptions, our focus in this book has largely been on the 'serious amateurs' – groups and individuals for whom video production is a significant and often time-consuming leisure pursuit. This is entirely appropriate, but we should beware of assuming that such people are necessarily representative. As we have noted, Cultural Studies researchers – in this as in many other areas – are often keen to fix on areas of cultural activity that appear somehow subversive, radical or challenging. Henry Jenkins' (2006) work on 'convergence culture', for example, focuses largely on highly dedicated groups of media fans, who are busily appropriating and reworking existing media texts through their own creative media productions. As Jean Burgess (2006) argues, this may lead us to neglect the more banal, everyday ways in which people use media – which in the case of video-making are typically much less cool and glamorous. Just as enthusiastic fans cannot stand in for media users in general, the dedicated amateurs we have explored here do not represent 'ordinary' people's use of video. We have taken this challenge forward in another book resulting from our research, which looks very closely at 'home mode' video-making among a group of inner London households (Buckingham et al., in press).

Indeed, one inevitable consequence of the growing accessibility of video technology (as described in our first chapter) is that video is rapidly becoming a mundane, even banal medium. As video camera phones become as ubiquitous as snapshot cameras, and as video is routinely distributed online, the sense of video-making and appearing on video as special experiences – even as in some way glamorous or empowering – is bound to disappear. In the process, the boundaries between 'film-making' as a controlled and deliberate creative practice and the more routine uses of video in the form of webcams or short clips transmitted via mobile phones, and even closed circuit surveillance cameras, may begin to blur. As the cultural 'aura' of video dispels, it may come to be seen less as a distinct *medium* and more as a routine form of communication like speech or writing. The implications of these developments are hard to foresee, but they are certainly worthy of further research.

Despite the long history of amateur media production, and the increasing accessibility of video production technology, there has been surprisingly little research into what happens when ordinary people take charge of 'the means of media production'. As Media and Cultural Studies scholars, we already know that popular representation – and indeed self-representation – is a complex and sometimes paradoxical practice. Amateur video-making is a form of popular representation that is worthy of much more serious and sustained attention. We hope that this book has at least made an engaging start in this process.

References

Beck, U. (1992) *Risk Society: Towards a New Modernity*. London: Sage.

Buckingham, D., Willett, R. and Pini, M. (in press) *Home Truths? Video Production and Domestic Life*. Ann Arbor, MI: University of Michigan Press.

Burgess, J. (2006) 'Hearing ordinary voices: Cultural Studies, vernacular creativity and digital storytelling'. *Continuum: Journal of Media and Culture Studies*. 20(2): 201–14.

Chalfen, R. (1987) *Snapshot Versions of Life*. Bowling Green, Ohio: Bowling Green State University Popular Press.

Giddens, A. (1991) *Modernity and Self-Identity*. Cambridge: Polity.

Gillmor, D. (2006) *We the Media: Grassroots Journalism By the People For the People*. Sebastopol, CA: O'Reilly.

Hargittai, E. and Walejko, G. (2008) 'The participation divide: content creation and sharing and the digital age'. *Information, Communication and Society*. 11(2): 239–56.

Jenkins, H. (2006) *Convergence Culture: Where Old and New Media Collide*. New York: New York University Press.

Jenkins, H. with Clinton, K., Purushotma, R., Robison, A. J. and Weigel, M. (2006) *Confronting the Challenges of Participatory Culture: Media Education for the 21st Century*. Chicago: MacArthur Foundation.

Marvin, C. (1988) *When Old Technologies Were New*. New York: Oxford University Press.

Norris Nicholson, H. (1997) 'In amateur hands: framing time and space in home-movies'. *History Workshop Journal*. 43: 198–213.

Streeter, T. (1987) 'The cable fable revisited: discourse, policy, and the making of cable television'. *Critical Studies in Mass Communication*. 4(2): 174–200.

Willett, R. (2009) Media technologies, identity and social networking sites. Keynote presentation for ESRC seminar series 'The educational and social impact of new technologies on young people in Britain'. 2 March 2009, London School of Economics.

Zimmerman, P. (1995) *Reel Families: A Social History of Amateur Film*. Indianapolis: Indiana University Press.

Index